Growing Pains

A Planet in Distress

Valorie M. Allen

iUniverse, Inc.
New York Bloomington

Growing Pains
A Planet in Distress

iUniverse books may be ordered through booksellers or by contacting:

iUniverse
1663 Liberty Drive
Bloomington, IN 47403
www.iuniverse.com
1-800-Authors (1-800-288-4677)

ISBN: 978-1-4502-0427-9 (pbk)
ISBN: 978-1-4502-0429-3 (cloth)
ISBN: 978-1-4502-0428-6 (ebook)

Library of Congress Control Number: 2010900333

Printed in the United States of America

iUniverse rev. date: 3/17/10

This book is dedicated to three special people who all left this crowded planet behind in 2007–2008. Before they left, each one in his or her own way encouraged me to write this book and share my story with the world …

To my partner, Blaine

To my mother, Doris

To my dear friend, Marvis

> "I think of death as some delightful journey that I shall take when my tasks are done."
>
> Ella Wheeler Wilcox, 1850–1919
> American writer and poet

These three special people urged me to write a book that would appeal to the average person, not just to scientists and academics. So I have tried to create a book that includes opinions from people of all walks of life, a variety of races and ages, and a wide range of views. Although there are a lot of statistics, I have endeavored to write a book that most people can easily read and understand. After all, when it comes to the population crisis, it is imperative that every human being be part of the solution.

CONTENTS

ACKNOWLEDGMENTS

> The power of accurate vision is commonly called cynicism by those who do not have it.
>
> G. B. Shaw

Since writing a book is a collaborative endeavor, I would like to thank all those who shared my vision and helped me express it in an accurate and enthusiastic way—hopefully with a tolerable dose of cynicism. Thanks also to all those groups, institutions, and individuals whose quotes I have borrowed. I hope that I have accredited them properly, as they have greatly contributed to the credibility of this book.

A special thanks to the distinguished individuals who agreed to proofread, edit, and comment on my book. Without your help I never would have been able to accomplish this goal: Dr. Bonnie Bukwa for her close scrutiny and encouraging banter, Dr. Brian Horejsi for his detailed commentary, Madeline Weld for her expert population facts, Brishen Hoff for his helpful and constructive comments, Rick Taggart for his insight and encouragement, and Prof. Al Bartlett for sharing his extensive knowledge and good judgment. You are all an integral part of this book.

I would also like to extend a special and heartfelt thank you to those respected experts who have read and endorsed my book: Dr. Madeline Weld who wrote the foreword, Professor Al Bartlett, Dr. Brian Horejsi, author Edward C. Hartman, and author Ben Gadd.

When writing this book, perhaps my biggest obstacle was my weak computer skills, along with owning a finicky computer and printer. So I would like to thank Alexander Parkinson, Jason Cummer, and Kelly Wood for all their computer help, as they were truly lifesavers when I was about to throw all my equipment out the window.

And of course, I am most thankful to my sisters and dear friends for their support and encouragement throughout this endeavor. My publishing crew at iUniverse deserves special mention for their professional and friendly assistance throughout the publishing process. Also, the World Society for the Protection of Animals kindly allowed me use of their wolf photo—thanks! If I have neglected to mention anyone, please forgive me.

This book is a POPULATION IN SYNC project. The goal of Population in Sync is to bring the human population back into harmony with the natural world.

www.populationinsync.net

FOREWORD

Val Allen has written a very readable book on a very serious subject—Earth's human population in overshoot. Her book provides plenty of facts and data, but it does much more than that. It also reaches us at an emotional level and invites us to consider what we are destroying and to mourn the loss we are inflicting upon ourselves even as we decimate other life-forms. For those who will consider it and connect a very few dots, the evidence of what we are doing has become incontrovertible. And yet, as stated in *Growing Pains*, "Never before on this planet have so many inhabitants been so misinformed about something that is so important and urgent, as with the population issue." Allen illustrates with examples how, at many levels, political priorities are misguided, to say the least. She also describes the futility of so many of the "solutions" to our environmental, social, and economic problems, because they ignore the Real problem—that infinite growth of population and consumption on a finite planet is impossible.

Humankind's most noble objectives, such as human rights for all as endorsed in the Universal Declaration of Human Rights in 1948, will not be attainable in a world in which overpopulation is unraveling the web of life. Allen offers some rays of hope. She uses citations from and describes the efforts of many population activists and scientists. A quote from Victor Hugo reads, "Nothing is as powerful as an idea whose time has come." Perhaps the increased reporting on population that is now starting to occur reflects the slowly dawning awareness among a critical mass of people that we humans are biological organisms that can and indeed have exceeded the carrying capacity of our environment. Val Allen's straightforward book is a great tool to help spread this idea whose time has most certainly come.

Dr. Madeline Weld

President, Population Institute of Canada

INTRODUCTION

It was 1966. *Dr. Zhivago* was playing in local movie theaters, and we were listening to the hits of the Supremes and Simon and Garfunkel on our record players.

It was a calm spring afternoon when I looked out the window and was amazed by what I saw in the garden, sniffing through the vegetable scraps we had thrown out that morning. Its luxuriant, reddish-gold coat shimmered in the sunlight, and its bushy tail swept the ground like a feather duster.

My mother said that it was a red fox, seldom seen in town. This was my first sighting of such a magnificent wild creature close up. My heart was pounding like a tribal drum, and so began my lifelong love affair with wildlife and the places they call home. Soon pictures of foxes and wolves started to appear on my bedroom wall alongside posters of the Beatles and the Bee Gees. Even at the tender age of twelve, I instinctively knew that there was something special about the kinship between man and beast. It was a symbiotic relationship as ancient as mankind and as compelling as our fascination with fire.

When I turned fourteen, I got my first camera, an inexpensive Kodak that captured my cat's many antics and many a luring rainbow. Later I would use it to record the black bears eating garbage at our town dump and the beautiful butterflies that dropped in to visit our garden.

That was also the year that I met my high school sweetheart, and together we explored the many special places in the backcountry. At that time wildlife was still comparatively abundant in our area, and frogs and salamanders could still be found in nearby ponds. We were young and carefree and had no inkling that this would all be changing soon.

In the spring of 1971 I was busy sewing my graduation dress and pondering life after high school. The music of the Beach Boys and the Mamas and Papas lulled me into a romantic reverie of the California lifestyle and a longing to travel. I vowed to visit those sandy beaches some day. Later I would travel and witness firsthand some of the destruction our species was causing on this planet.

Then one day in class we were studying world affairs, and the topic of overpopulation came up. This was a "light bulb moment" for me, as in the blink of an eye many of the world's problems suddenly made perfect sense to me. That very day I decided not to have children, as I wanted to become part of the solution rather than part of the problem. Little did I know that three decades later "Childfree" groups would be starting up all over the world.

I also felt very fortunate that I had the freedom and opportunity to choose to not have children, since I had read that millions of women around the world had no access to family planning programs. They often had no choice but to have one child after another, only to watch them slowly starve to death. I couldn't even imagine how heartbreaking that would be.

At that time the primary industry in my small community of the Crowsnest Pass (Alberta, Canada) was coal mining. Recently, the mining companies had brought in hundreds of immigrants to work in the underground mines. It struck me then that multinational companies relied heavily on overpopulated countries for their cheap labor. These companies, often more powerful than empires or countries, would not look favorably on any attempts to reduce their cheap labor force. I realized then that there would be a great deal of resistance to any attempts to curb the excessive population growth.

Thus began a thirty-year quest to find ways to help stop the insanity of overpopulation and its resulting environmental destruction, which has brought me to this point. The crafting of this book is a global citizen's passionate appeal to humanity to change our destiny for the sake of future generations and the other critters with which we share this planet. It may very well take a *global revolution* to convince our masses to make a U-turn at this dead-end impasse we are now facing.

> The rich require an abundant supply of the poor.
>
> Voltaire

> Things will be better after the revolution.
>
> Marjorie Taggart,
> Wildlife Activist, 2007

> The future of everything we have accomplished since our intelligence evolved will depend on the wisdom of our actions over the next few years. Like all creatures, humans have made their way in the world so far by trial and error: unlike other creatures, we have a presence so colossal that error is a luxury we can no longer afford. The world has grown too small to forgive us any big mistakes.
>
> Ronald Wright
> *A Short History of Progress*

It can be said with a great degree of certainty that it would be a serious mistake to continue to ignore the population crisis that is swallowing up and fouling our natural ecosystems. Unfortunately, human population size and growth remains a taboo topic in the media and even in the environmental community. It is not "politically correct" to voice our concerns about the role of population pressure in causing, exacerbating, and multiplying many of the troubles of mankind.

In his recent book *The Treason of the BBC*, Jack Parsons describes how in forty years of correspondence with the BBC, he failed to get it to include a mention or discussion of the probable role of overpopulation in exacerbating many of the political, economic, social, and environmental troubles it was vividly portraying in its documentary programs. Similar attempts have been made by myself and others to get the CBC to include a meaningful discussion on population, with no success.

Of course, there have been many brave souls over the years who have defied the powers that be and tackled this seemingly overwhelming issue. I would like to start by expressing my humble thanks and gratitude to these pioneers of the population movement for their foresight and wisdom.

As an advocate and activist for the environment, I think we need to decide what kind of world we want for our children and grandchildren. Do we want a balanced healthy society, living in harmony with the natural world? Do we want sustainable economies and communities?

In order to achieve sustainable lifestyles, it is essential to develop a strategy to achieve sustainable population and consumption rates. While the global warming issue and the human footprint concept have triggered an attempt to reduce our consumption rates, population rarely gets a mention—as if the staggering number of people consuming our resources had no relevance to how great our footprint is on this planet.

In this book I will demystify, with brutal honesty, the causes and consequences of our disturbing population dilemma. I will explore the solutions, some surprisingly simple and practical, that everyone can begin implementing right now. If we fail to recognize the important role overpopulation is playing in our ecological, social, and financial predicament, we may soon find that the destruction is irreversible.

Note: Many of the quotes I have used come from a variety of quote sites that give only the name of the author, since they are considered to be well-known to most readers. Also, I have quoted some groups that have changed their names, so I have used the name given at the time the quote was made. For example, Zero Population Growth changed their name to Population Connection, and I have used both names often throughout this book.

GROWING PAINS

I chose the title *Growing Pains* for this book because in a sense the malady affecting this planet is not so different from the malady that affects many of our children as they are growing, often causing them great pain. Growing pains have been described as a medical condition where the bones are growing faster than the muscles and connective tissues around the bones. As this support system struggles to keep up with the bones, it often goes through a painful stage of adjustment.

This reminded me of our situation on earth at the present, where the human population is growing too fast for our life-support system to keep up. This is causing tremendous growing pains, at both a population and personal level, as all life-forms are trying frantically to adjust. Unfortunately, many species have already been destroyed in this difficult struggle.

The only sure way to alleviate growing pains is to stop growing. Just as the human body cannot continue growing indefinitely, neither can the human population.

But the problem is actually two-fold. First, there is this physical, or biological, growing that is taking place far too rapidly. On the other hand, in an intellectual and personal sense we are not developing nearly as quickly as our situation demands. We are at a point in our evolution where, as individuals, we need to take a little time out for some soul-searching and decide what is really of value in our lives. Are material things and large families truly making us happy, or do we really find our greatest comfort in the natural world that is so quickly disappearing?

Tanis Helliwell, founder of the International Institute for Transformation, uses the butterfly as a symbol of transformation in our path to consciousness. She explains, "The four stages that the butterfly undergoes in its transformation are ones that we also undergo in our journey from unconsciousness (dominated by personality) to consciousness (partnered by the soul)."

These are similar to the stages of human involvement/awareness that have been identified by sociologists and psychologists as well. Helliwell outlines the four stages:

1. Individuals in the *egg* stage of transformation are unconscious. Never questioning the rules, they're at the mercy of their environment. Because they are passive, others control them, and their careers are usually unplanned.

2. The second stage is that of the *caterpillar*, and these people are further along the path because they do make choices. Our world and organizations have been run by caterpillars with an insatiable appetite who have destroyed their environment.

3. The third stage, *cocooning*, is an inner time, often a time of rest and seclusion when people reflect on their life's purpose.

4. In their fourth stage *butterflies*, feeding on nectar and water, are creatures of beauty who destroy nothing in their path. Formerly, these men and women were often found on the fringes of society living alternative lifestyles. Often they were the craftspeople, artists, writers, environmentalists, social activists, healers, and teachers who brought beauty, love, and wisdom into the world.

Helliwell believes that at this time in our evolution, many individuals are going through the cocoon stage, and that the number of butterflies is increasing. They are creative people, who act as catalysts for new personal growth. As we enter the fourth cycle of human evolution, these individuals are the forerunners and the way-showers of the principles of interconnectedness and sustainability.

It seems to me that this symbolic transformation in our personal growth is exactly what is needed at this time. It is this soul-searching exercise that will lead to a clearer understanding of our situation and a vision of what is needed to rectify it. As this new awareness reaches the critical mass, we will intuitively know that we must deal with the population crisis that is facing our planet. An understanding of our place in the scheme of things is imperative if we are to create a meaningful partnership with the earth.

A CHILD'S LEGACY

> There is no human circumstance more tragic than the persisting existence of a harmful condition for which a remedy is readily available. Family planning, to relate population to world resources, is possible, practical and necessary. Unlike plagues of the dark ages or contemporary diseases we do not yet understand, the modern plague of overpopulation is soluble by means we have discovered and with resources we possess. What is lacking is not sufficient knowledge of the solution but universal consciousness of the gravity of the problem and education of billions who are its victims.
>
> Rev. Martin Luther King Jr. (May 1966)

We may find that we are leaving our children and grandchildren a planet greatly diminished in resources, beauty, and social benefits. Will the growing concern for children's well-being lead to a global movement to stabilize population and improve the quality of life for the world's children?

In 1993 Zero Population Growth released the Children's Stress Index, the most comprehensive study ever made of children's well-being in the United States. More than 800 metropolitan areas, counties, and cities were evaluated using seventy population-related indicators that affect the lives of children. Data was gathered and analyzed in ten categories: population change and crowding, family economics, maternal and child health, education, crime, air quality, water resources, toxic releases and sewage, and energy and transportation.

Their conclusion? Bigger is clearly not always better. ZPG found a strong correlation between the size of a community and the level of "children's stress." Communities across the country are increasingly plagued by population-related problems from pollution to overcrowding to crime. And unfortunately, this has become a worldwide epidemic.

The world's youngest citizens suffer disproportionately from poverty, malnutrition, and disease. Also, their young, growing bodies are most vulnerable to widespread environmental hazards, such as air, soil, and water pollution.

In its 1994 report, The State of the World's Children, the United Nation's Children's Fund (UNICEF) emphasized that population stabilization is a prerequisite to ensuring the health and well-being of children everywhere, noting, "There is an obvious and profound connection between the mental and physical development of children and the social and economic development of their societies."

> As children are better spaced through family planning, it has a tremendous impact on the health, the education and the general well-being of children. And as child health and education—particularly of girls—improves markedly, more families actively seek family planning and have smaller families.
>
> James P. Grant
> Executive Director of UNICEF

Of course, in 1994 the world was already beyond a sustainable threshold, so population sustainability, versus reduction, was even then no longer an option. One would hope that improving children's living conditions would be the powerful motivator needed to convince authorities that population is an urgent issue that needs immediate attention.

ZPG's Children's Report clearly indicated at that time, and that was fifteen years ago now, that it was essential to achieve population stabilization sooner rather than later. Yet, since then funding to many of these family planning programs has been cut rather than increased. The only encouraging action has been Obama's recent executive order reversing the Bush administration's restriction on funding family planning programs.

That restriction was a travesty, since concern for the world's children goes beyond the realm of compassion or economic and political decisions. True concern for the world's children incorporates a vision of a "quality future" based on a clear understanding of population impacts. These children, by default, are depending on us to create that quality future

Carl Jung, one of the fathers of psychology, famously remarked, "People cannot stand too much reality." Perhaps that explains why warnings about overpopulation from many of our most respected authorities are being ignored. To find the real reasons, the operational reasons, you must look to the power of religion and corporate economists and their "growth at any cost" ideology. Let's consider a few of the warnings:

- "There is no single thing more significant for the future of the world than the fact of human population growth … There will not be an environment left to worry about unless we get the population crisis under control."

John Adams,
Executive Director of the Natural Resources Defense Council, 1997

- "Population growth is the primary source of environmental damage."

Jacques Cousteau

- "Achieving and maintaining a sustainable relationship between human populations and the natural resource base of the earth is the single most critical long-term issue facing the peoples of the world and this issue will increasingly be the focus of international affairs for the foreseeable future."

Russel E. Train, World Wildlife Fund

So how did we get to this desperate state of global destruction that is now threatening our planet? After all, the human species is the most advanced, intelligent, reasonable species on earth, right? Then how is it that we have allowed ourselves to spread over our planet like a plague, causing tragic human misery, wiping out other species, and destroying habitat without even a second thought?

It seems to me that this is a situation that desperately needs a hero. We need a champion for the planet who will lead a movement to defend our homeland against this senseless human onslaught. And we need an army of defenders, a billion strong, to rally behind this movement if we are to save what remains of our life-support systems for our benefit and that of future generations.

In 1968, Stanford University biologist Paul Ehrlich warned about runaway population growth in his thought-provoking book, *The Population Bomb*. Unfortunately, his warnings went unheeded, and since then global population has grown by over 2.5 billion. At the time, some thought that he was merely an alarmist, but his predictions have proven to be quite accurate. Of course, little did he know that science and technology would be willing to break all boundaries in order to accommodate and facilitate the growing numbers.

Our governments, corporate leaders, and economists have continued to push for growth at any expense. As President Eisenhower stated after WWII, **"We have to make consumption a way of life, and convince Americans that buying things makes them happy."**

We have submitted to the growth lobby's powerful influence, many of us very willingly, allowing our food and water to be contaminated with pesticides, fertilizers, antibiotics, and growth hormones. We have allowed smog and indoor pollution to sicken us with asthma, cancer, and lung disease. We have knowingly stood by and watched as one species after another has been decimated, and people in poverty have perished.

Yes, we are a very accommodating species, very good at adapting to almost any situation. The example of our ability to adapt that Al

Gore used in his documentary, *The Inconvenient Truth*, would be very appropriate here. He pointed out that a frog that jumped into a pail of boiling water would quickly jump back out. However, if the frog jumped into a pail of warm water that was gradually heated to boiling, the frog would stay in the water until it died. I think it is safe to say that the population crisis is getting pretty heated at this point.

It is clear that the time has come for a new consciousness, a global revolution of sorts!

Although this is not a new idea, this is the first time in our evolution that the stakes have been so high and the folly of our ways has been so evident. We are at the point of no return, and if we don't take action now there will be no hope for future generations.

Mark Hume outlined the problem quite well in the 1994 *Vancouver Sun*,

> In laboratory experiments with Norway rats, behavioral scientists have observed a disturbing phenomenon. Allowed to breed at will, the rats multiply until they reach a point where they just can't stand it any more. **When the overcrowding becomes too great, they stop breeding and start killing each other.**

Aprodicio Laquian is the scientist who conducted this study. As he ponders the behavior of the rats and the alarming rate at which the human population is growing, he can't help but wonder if the rats are warning us about our future. "What happens with the rats is not too far-fetched a scenario for humans. We are just biological creatures, after all," he says.

In fact, isn't this already occurring, especially in our overcrowded cities? A person can be killed for his fifty-dollar sneakers, gangs are fighting for their turf, and road rage has become a common occurrence. Governments perpetuate wars all over the world to gain power over land, water, or natural resources. Millions of women are raped or killed by their partners or stalkers every year in a struggle for power and dominance. We are a species at war with each other and the planet, yet the critical role that population undoubtedly plays is rarely mentioned.

This all must sound very grim, but the good news is that it doesn't have to be this way. We possess the means and ability to turn things around, as I will outline in Part 4.

Comic used with permission from Mike Keefe

PART 1:
THE DILEMMA

A PLANET IN DENIAL

> Imagine taking a journey into uncharted territory without a compass or a guide and with no idea whether you have enough provisions for everyone who is going with you. Crazy, right? But that's exactly what our country is doing—lumbering into the future, poorly prepared, with the sketchiest of plans and perhaps not even headed in the right direction.
>
> Zero Population Growth
> (Renamed Population Connection), 1993

The dilemma is that humanity's self-proclaimed dominance over the earth is really a 10,000-year experiment we have unleashed that is now threatening to destroy our planet We are muddling our way through history in trial-and-error mode with little more understanding of the big picture than we had in the Stone Age. What is desperately needed at this time is a plan of action that acknowledges the folly of our ways and the urgency of changing our course.

For most of history human population had little impact on our planet. In fact, for most of the 2 million years of human history, human population was less than a quarter million. When Columbus came to America 500 years ago, global population was still only 425 million. If it had remained at that level, we would not be facing the high level of species extinction, global warming, or water shortages that are so worrisome today.

It wasn't until 1800 that the planet was host to 1 billion people. Since then, growth has greatly accelerated, and humans quadrupled in the twentieth century. Although this is an average growth rate of just 1.39 percent per year, this innocent-sounding growth rate produced this enormous quadrupling in just a century.

That rate of growth is referred to as "plague phase" by biologists. If any other species had begun to multiply at this rate, governments would have instructed biologists to take drastic measures to bring them under control. Carrying capacity would have been calculated, and limits determined to bring the species into balance with its environment. I wonder, is it possible that these same limits could also apply to the human species, known scientifically as the "wise hominids"?

Instead, ANTHROPOCENTRISM has guided our stewardship of the planet. The *Oxford English Dictionary* defines anthropocentrism as "regarding humans as the central element of the universe, and interpreting reality exclusively in terms of human values and experience." We have chosen to deny our natural place in the scheme of things, or our role in mismanaging the world's resources.

At one time humans actually thought that the earth was the center of the universe. It wasn't until 1543 that Copernicus disproved this theory, causing quite a stir. This revolutionary new thinking caused a reemergence of atheism that lasted for almost two centuries. So the idea that man is not intended to be the central element of our planet, but rather an integral part of an ecocentric (ecology-centered) life system, is equally incredible today.

The earth-centered solar system is like the human-centered ecology system that persists because of strong religious dogma. We need to make the transition to the Copernican system in which we throw off the dogma and look at the facts. We are part of the environment, not independent of it.

We have also chosen to deny that overpopulation is the missing link in achieving sustainable lifestyles and bringing humanity back into harmony with our environment. Yet, television brings us graphic scenes of human suffering and landscapes being savaged by the effects of ever-growing numbers of people every day. As populations in these poor countries become unmanageable, the countries export their overpopulation problems to developed countries, where the immigrants often adopt our high-consumption lifestyles, causing even greater strains on the world's resources. It is hard for them to resist, with their higher wages, greater variety of products available, and tremendous advertising and societal pressures.

Usually this is a situation of people from tropical climates migrating to countries with colder climates, where they will require far more resources just to survive. The basic necessities of food, clothing, and shelter needed to survive varying and often extreme seasonal temperatures are far greater. That is why there are greater numbers of wildlife and species found near the equator, and much smaller numbers found near the poles. For example, the Brazil rain forest is teeming with life, while diversity of wildlife in the Arctic is greatly reduced.

In addition, when the growing number of immigrants is exposed to the "American Dream" mentality, it is a temptation few can resist. In many ways, the 1.5 billion people in developed countries are doing more damage than the 5 billion in developing countries. However, as incomes and technologies in the Third World continue to improve, the gap between consumption rates is rapidly decreasing.

If we want people in developing countries to have the basic necessities they require for a humane existence, their standard of living will have to improve dramatically. This, of course, will increase their consumption rate and eventually bring it almost up to par with developed countries, factoring in their climate requirements. The best scenario would be to help people live a humane existence in their own country, rather than taking them away from their families and homeland in order to help them.

Valorie M. Allen

How Many Is Enough?

Why is it that our numbers
Tend to double and to triple?
Like a pebble in the pond
The waves just want to ripple

Who will ask the question
How many is enough?
How many can earth handle?
Aren't times already tough?

To make more room for humans
We've cut down most our trees
And wiped out many species
That once were wild and free

We've polluted all our waters
And fouled our soil and air
We've encroached upon our critters
But no one seems to care

We've fished out most our rivers
Our oceans and our seas
And we've done it in a lifetime
Please tell me, can that be?

If our numbers keep on growing
What will there soon remain
But a planet full of people
On a barren, empty plain?

By Val Allen, 1994
Sketch courtesy of Gerri Elder, 2009

HOW MANY IS ENOUGH?

Human beings are composed of recycled atoms from other life-forms that have previously decomposed. The reality is that humans, like every other species, are a vast collection of atoms arranged in distinctive ways. The arrangement varies from species to species, but the basic building blocks, the atoms, stay the same. The amount of matter on our planet is finite and does not change. What changes is how it is organized.

In a human being, the calcium in a thigh bone may contain atoms that, 70 million years ago, may have been part of a dinosaur. Carbon atoms in a nose may have come from grass eaten twenty years ago by a steer. Therefore, all life on earth implies kinship and sharing.

This reminds me of a statement Dr. Bonnie Bukwa made at a Sustainable Population Workshop in 1993. She said,

> As a scientist what I'm recalling here is the first law of thermodynamics, which says that matter and energy can be neither created or destroyed, which sometimes is cynically paraphrased as: You can't win—more for us, less for them.

Dr. Bukwa further explained:

> If we regard us as the center upon which everything else is measured, then what about the animals and plants that we somewhat arrogantly feel we are stewards over? What happens is that we squeeze them out, and there will have to be less of them and more of us. What we've done, in a sense, is elevated ourselves up to infinity in terms of value, and they are reduced down to nil.
>
> I think we have a tendency to see this planet and its resources from that pedestal we've put ourselves on. I think we need some humility here, and we need to

> leave some space for the other critters, and we are just awful stingy about doing that.

So, it seems to me that however you look at it, if our human population increases by another 4-5 billion by midcentury, our plant and animal populations will have to decrease by a similarly large amount. Our drain on the biological resources will drastically reduce populations and diversity in native wildlife. Is that really what we want?

The dynamic atoms are not the only time-travelers here, having witnessed man's first encounter with fire, the rise and fall of the Roman Empire, and the killing of the last carrier pigeon. Our most primal thoughts and instincts have also traveled through time to influence us today. Our fight-or-flight response still guides us in times of stress or danger, often causing our adrenal glands to work overtime to cope with our fast-paced society. Our feelings toward nature compel us to surround ourselves with nature's bounty.

We have windows in our homes to bring the sun into our private world, and we often surround ourselves with houseplants. Many of us bring cats and dogs into our environment and place bird feeders in our backyards. Those who can afford it have a pool on their property, and living near a park is considered an asset. If we can't be a part of nature, we try to capture a piece of it to be part of us. Deep down, we know that there is something special about this relationship. If at all possible, we try to create our own little rain forests in our concrete jungles.

Yet, overpopulation threatens this very nature that we crave and value as part of our lifestyles. It's a paradox that so many people think of population growth as non-threatening and inevitable—even desirable—in a world in which our very success as a species threatens our present-day and future survival.

Each day we share the earth and its resources with a quarter million more people than the day before. With 300,000 people being born each day, and 50,000 dying, that leaves us with an additional 250,000 bodies to feed, clothe, and shelter every day. Our population is increasing by three people per second, with a growth rate of over 80 million each year. Today's grand total is about 6.5 billion and is expected to reach between 8 and 11 billion by 2050 if it continues at the present rate.

Our phenomenal growth has prompted the National Academy of Science and Royal Society of London to release a first-ever joint "Warning to Humanity" in 1993. It warned that if population continues to grow as predicted, science and technology cannot be expected to rescue the environment or society at large.

People are slow to recognize how much population stresses affect each one of us individually, socially, and environmentally. This growth is taking its toll as natural habitats are being paved over, polluted, logged, developed, and mined—all to "benefit" encroaching human civilization.

Of the many environmental issues, population is the one most neglected, yet the most crucial for the well-being of future generations. At the Rio Earth Summit, Secretary General Maurice Strong put it this way, "Population must be stabilized, and rapidly. If we do not do it, Nature will, and much more brutally."

There are hundreds of books on the market now discussing the impact humans are having on the environment. However, few dare to mention the "taboo" population factor, or consider that it may be the missing link in achieving sustainable societies. They give simple, and fundamentally trivial, solutions like changing a light bulb or turning down the heat. I have written many articles recommending these actions myself. In fact, in 1994, I was presented with the Canadian Volunteer Award for my work on recycling.

However, just compare this to the impact having one child has. Imagine the amount of energy and resources each person consumes in a lifetime. Merely providing the simple necessities of life (food, clothing, and shelter) for an average life-span of sixty years demands a great deal from the earth. Then imagine the amount of garbage, carbon dioxide, and human waste produced by one person over an average lifetime. Now multiply this by 10 billion, and you are looking not just at the future we will be leaving the next generation, but what is playing out in ever-expanding parts of the world now. In fact, the economist Kenneth Boulding once suggested that couples get an environmental impact statement before having a child.

So, are we really making this planet a better place to live? Indeed, there are a lot of us who are working very hard to improve our quality of life and save what remains of our wildlife and special places. We certainly wouldn't want to think that it's all been in vain.

Unfortunately, this may very well be the case, for our growing numbers are quickly undermining any progress we do make. That is why, despite our best intentions, all indicators show that global degradation continues to increase. The problems of widespread deforestation, disappearing species, sprawling cities, escalating crime rates, third world poverty, pollution, environmental health problems, erosion, and wars over natural resources continue to escalate.

> "If steps are not taken soon to stabilize population growth, all our efforts in conservation will have little or no impact."
>
> Russell A. Mittermeier, Conservation International

In fact, at this point we don't want to stabilize population growth. It's now around 1 percent per year. This is the last thing we want to stabilize. We want to stop population growth and stabilize or decrease the size of the population.

ECOLOGICAL OVERSHOOT

A study reported in the *Globe and Mail* (25 June 2002) by reporter Alanna Mitchell warns that earth is facing a supply crisis. The first comprehensive, science-based estimate of human demands on the biological functions of the Earth revealed some sobering facts about a phenomenon the authors of the study are calling "ecological overshoot."

The report was written by an international who's who of ecologists and economists, including conservationists Edward Wilson of Harvard University and Norman Myers of Oxford University, and reported in the National Academy of Sciences.

They have calculated that humans started taking more from the living planet every year than the planet could replenish in the 1980s. That means that humans have been borrowing for two decades against the ecological production of future years. In 1961 humans were using 70 percent of the planet's yearly potential for biological productivity, but by 1999 it was 120 percent.

"We are preparing for ecological bankruptcy," said one of the study's authors, Mathis Wackernagel of the Oakland-based ecological think tank Redefining Progress.

One of the reasons they give for things getting so much worse so quickly is that the biological capacity of the planet is diminishing as some land becomes too damaged to grow crops. Even worse, they point out, the demands on that biological capacity are increasing as the world population grows.

Also, this study does not factor in any land being set aside for animal habitat. Many scientists have calculated that 12 percent of the planet's land and water ecosystems should be protected as parks and reserves for species that are not human. Doing so would set back human overshoot to the 1970s.

If fact, Wildlife Conservation Scientist Brian Horejsi believes this notion of 12 percent ecologically functional land is a serious miscalculation and that it continues to have damaging political and industrialization repercussions. He adds, "For grizzly bears, for example, at least 50 percent of the land base must be roadless, and protected as such, and that land base must be large enough to contain 2000 bears in a population to assure genetic viability [could be four areas of 500 bears each, as long as there is exchange between] to increase even to a hundred year horizon, the probability of survival at a level of even 50 percent."

According to David Delaney in his essay, "Overshoot in a Nutshell,"

> A species may greatly overshoot the long term carrying capacity of its environment (its population may become greatly larger than its environment can sustain). Overshoot becomes possible when a species encounters a rich and previously unexploited stock of resources that promote its reproduction.

A huge stock of resources may be available for millions of years before it encounters a species that can exploit it easily. After such an encounter, only predation and disease limit reproduction of the species. Without these two limiting factors, the population of a species can grow to a size hundreds of times that which can be supported at long-term viability levels by the resources.

Delaney notes that eventually individuals begin to compete desperately for the remaining resources. To exist, they resort to alternative resources of lower and lower quality. This destroys the ability of their environment to restore its resources or produce alternative resources. Eventually, most of the population dies. Ecologists call this a crash or die-off, and it results in the carrying capacity for the overshot species being reduced to below original levels.

The question that many are asking is, "How much longer can we continue in this overshoot situation?" It is all up to the one species among the 25 million that inhabit this planet, the one species that is causing this overshoot dilemma: humans!

SETTING THE LIMITS

So what is the magic number? Unless we make an effort to determine optimum population numbers, we will have no compass to tell us what direction to take. With an optimum population estimate to guide us, we will have a benchmark against which we can measure success.

The Union of Concerned Scientists has sounded the alarm with their "World Scientists' Warning to Humanity" (1993):

> Human beings and the natural world are on a collision course. Human activities inflict harsh and often irreversible damage on the environment and on critical resources. If not checked, many of our current practices put at serious risk the future that we wish for human society and the plant and animal kingdoms, and may so alter the living world that it will be unable to sustain life in the manner that we know. Fundamental changes are urgent if we are to avoid the collision our present course will bring about.
>
> We must stabilize population. This will be possible only if all nations recognize that it requires improved social and economic conditions, and the adoption of effective, voluntary family planning.

Any cause is a lost cause without a reduction in population.

Negative Population Growth

This US population group, founded in 1972, states, "World population is now 6.6 billion, and continues to grow rapidly by about 75 million a year. It is expected to reach 9.2 billion by midcentury even though it already far exceeds the long-range carrying capacity of our planet's resources and environment. That growth is not inevitable and we must do everything within our power to prevent it. Beyond any doubt, the most vitally important issue facing us is to decide at what level to stabilize the size of our population."

2 or 3 Billion?

The World Wildlife Fund, in their publication Living Planet,has this to say: "The world's optimum population is between 2 and 3 billion—less than a third of its forecast midcentury peak."

The human population has become a force at the planetary scale. Collectively, our exploitation of the world's resources has already reached a level that, according to the World Wildlife Fund, could only be sustained on a planet 25 percent larger than our own.

1 Billion?

Dr. Bonnie Bukwa, Chemistry Instructor at the College of the Rockies, passionately makes this comment, "With almost 6 billion people, we probably have about six times as many as this planet can sustain in any sort of a humane way to human beings, and leave room for free roaming elephants, caribou, wolves, grizzly bears, and tall timber." (1993)

2–3 Billion?

> "Very few writers seem to recognize that growth cannot continue forever in a limited space, and that mathematical truism applies to the real world, today. Dr. Smail is one of those few who do. Moreover, he suggests that human numbers have already passed the long term capacity of the Earth to sustain us and that an optimum world population lies perhaps in the range of 2–3 billion. So short is memory that the proposal sounds revolutionary—almost blasphemous—to most ears. Humans' ability to accommodate to change is both our strength and our peril. People have learned to consider 6 billion "normal," and presumably they will try to adjust to 10 or 12 billion, desperate as their situation may be by that time."
>
> Lindsey Grant,
> from his essay, "In Support of a Revolution," 1997
> Former National Security Council member

1 Billion or Less?

> "Ecocentric ethics that value earth and its evolved systems over species, condemns the social acceptance of unlimited human fecundity. Present need to

reduce numbers is greatest in wealthy countries where per capita use of energy and earth materials is highest. A reasonable objective is the reduction to population levels as they were before the widespread use of fossil fuels, that is, to one billion or less. This will be accomplished either by intelligent policies or inevitably by plague, famine, and warfare."

Ted Mosquin and Stan Rowe
"A Manifesto for Earth"

2.5 Million

Unless earth is hit by a massive meteor, we will be vastly overpopulated for well over forty years even if everyone is immediately sterilized. This means we will experience a die-off and more species extinction. I suggest that earth's sustainable population is only 2,500,000.

Yes, that's million, not billion. If you think that is extremely low, think again. That is over seven times the current population of all great apes (chimpanzees, bonobos, gorillas, and orangutans) combined! That is ten times earth's population that persisted for the majority of our 2 million year human history! Perhaps if you think 2.5 million is too low for a global sustainable human population you are underestimating:

- the scale to which we convert land into food using non-renewable fossil fuels
- how much we've already permanently degraded earth's carrying capacity
- how unsustainable our current "6th Mass Extinction" is

Brishen Hoff
Biodiversity First (2009)

TRANSITION TO AN OPTIMUM POPULATION

The College of Agriculture and Life Sciences at Cornell University has been giving population limits a great deal of thought and in 1999 produced a paper entitled "Will Limits of the Earth's Resources Control Human Numbers?" This is the number that they came up with:

> The human population has enormous momentum for rapid growth because of the young age distribution both in the U.S. population and in the world population. If the whole world agreed on and adopted a policy so that only 2.1 children were born per couple, more than sixty years would pass before the world population finally stabilized at approximately 12 billion (Weeks, 1986). On the other hand, a population policy ensuring that each couple produces an average of only 1.5 children would be necessary to achieve the goal of reducing the world population from the current 6 billion to an **optimal population of approximately 2 billion.**
>
> If this policy were implemented, more than one hundred years would be required to make the adjustment to 2 billion people. Again, the prime difficulty in making the adjustment is the young age distribution and growth momentum in the world population (PRB, 1996; Bartlett and Lytwak, 1995; Bartlett, 1997–1998).

Another supporter of the 2 billion optimum population comes from the Sustainable Scale Project. The advisory panel for this project consists of Brian Czech (B.S. in wildlife ecology), David Batker (directs the APEX Center for Applied Ecological Economics), Dr. Herman Daly (professor at University of Maryland), and Dr. Joshua Farley (degree in biology from Grinnel College).

Their vision is for a socially just and ecologically sustainable world. They warn that current global consumption is unsustainable, since it exceeds by about 20 percent our planet's ability to regenerate itself. The amount of bioproductive land and sea available to supply human needs is limited to 11-plus billion acres of productive earth; divided by 6.3 billion people, this results in an average of about 1.8 hectares per person as the "equal earth share" available. Collectively we are currently using approximately 2.2 hectares per person, or over 20 percent more than replacement levels.

Since current population policies encourage increasing consumption in countries dealing with poverty, this will increase the "equal earth share." On the other hand, many developed countries have set goals to decrease their "equal earth share." So, for purposes of discussion, a balanced consumption rate of six hectares per person is used.

So, what would the population have to be to allow the "equal earth share" to be six hectares per capita? Divide the 11-plus billion Bioproductive hectares by six hectares per person to get a total population of 1,830,000, which is close to 1930 population levels. The Sustainable Scale Project estimates that this would be achievable by around the year 2100 if we implemented a 1.5 child per family policy now.

They warn that the alternative would be to leave billions of people currently alive in misery and chaos and to continue to degrade ecosystems for all future generations.

Regardless of whether the optimum population is 1 billion or 3 billion, I think it is safe to say that at 6.5 billion we are at least double a sustainable level and accelerating. Would it not be logical, then, to assume that we need to address this crisis as soon as possible? Or, will we continue to debate the numbers until, as we did with global warming, the problem is irreversible?

It is this generation that has a responsibility to tell our political leaders that we no longer want growth, and that we must first stabilize the population in all countries, so that we can begin to reduce it to a sustainable level. Otherwise, what will we tell our children? That we knowingly chose to continue to rob future generations of their rightful resources, healthy environment, and diversity of nature? That we were so preoccupied with our self-interests that we ignored the warnings of disaster?

Most of the world's policy makers have backgrounds in law, business, or economics—very few have backgrounds in biology or ecology. We cannot expect them to make the right decisions for us. We must let them know that there is a quality of life that cannot be measured in economic terms, and that we want this lifestyle to be available to our children and grandchildren.

The grim predictions of population impacts do not make for comforting news. In fact many people find it so overwhelming and depressing that they are paralyzed by it. The apathy and complacency that plague our society are symptoms of a society in denial. However, the wisdom is now emerging that we can no longer afford to be compliant bystanders. There is a new consensus toward the population crisis based, not only on the science and math, but on our primal connection to nature and sacred places.

> Poverty is the worst form of violence.
>
> Gandhi

> The population problem concerns us, but it will concern our children and grandchildren even more. How we respond to the population threat may do more to shape the world in which they will live than anything else we do.
>
> Lester Brown,
> Worldwatch Institute

THE SILENT LIE

The following passage comes from the Negative Population Growth Internet Forum:

> American author Mark Twain wrote, "If one has information that would be helpful to others, but does not share that information, then one is telling a Silent Lie." Quotes from American literature often prove very useful in describing current events. In a very thought-provoking review of the September 2006 issue of *Scientific American*, Albert A. Bartlett, Professor Emeritus of Physics, University of Colorado at Boulder, uses Twain's words in a most poignant way, and we feel it is important for our readers to appreciate his reference.
>
> This particular issue of *Scientific American* features nine articles on global warming, each focusing on a particular cause. What do all of the articles have in common? Sadly they all fail to mention the central cause of ALL environmental problems—population size and growth. And, as Professor Bartlett so directly states in his review (which appeared in "The Physics Teacher," December 2006, Vol 44, Pgs 623–624), "The editors and writers at *Scientific America*[n] know that population growth is the underlying source of the problems, but it is politically incorrect to state this obvious fact. Because it does not address population size and growth as the main underlying cause of global warming, this issue of *Scientific America*[n] is a serious'silent lie.'"

It is not only the media, but also our world leaders, who have proven to be irresponsible and blind to our actual situation.

Like a teenager discovering the joys of a credit card for the first time, they consider themselves unique, and they smugly scoff at suggestions of self-imposed restraint. They have spent far too much and are now in great debt, having dipped into the resources of future generations. And like a teenager who has first been made aware of his limitations, dependencies, and responsibilities, our leaders have shown reactions characteristic of a temper tantrum. This refusal to face reality, and insistence on hiding behind the silent lie is unacceptable, and we must tell them so.

Dealing with the consequences of overpopulation and the nasty little disasters Mother Nature keeps throwing at us is keeping us busy just putting out fires. We are too preoccupied to even give any meaningful thought to healing our planet or our societies. We need to take a TIME OUT! The continuous growth experiment we are presently conducting is now conclusive—it is not working. Every indicator will confirm this. A discussion of the indicators can be found in Part 2.

> Smart growth destroys the environment. Dumb growth destroys the environment. Smart growth just destroys the environment with good taste.
>
> Al Bartlett,
> Professor Emeritus of Physics
> at University of Colorado

> In the long run the problem of overpopulation of the countries of the south can be fully resolved only through their development. But action to contain the rise of population cannot be postponed.
>
> Julius Nyerere,
> President of Tanzania
> and Chair of the South Commission, 1990

Nobel Peace Prize winner in 1985 for the prevention of nuclear war Eric Chivian and Evangelical minister Richard Cizik are working on a project to bring science and faith together for the sake of the environment. Their goal is

> To really make the point that there is no such choice about whether we protect people or we protect the environment. It is not a choice, because if we don't protect the environment, we are not going to protect ourselves.
>
> Eric Chivian,
> Director of Harvard Medical School's Center for Health and the Global Environment, From Oprah's Website

> Overpopulation of the earth is a danger to the planet's life-support system and to the people themselves.
>
> David Brown,
> Earth Island Institute

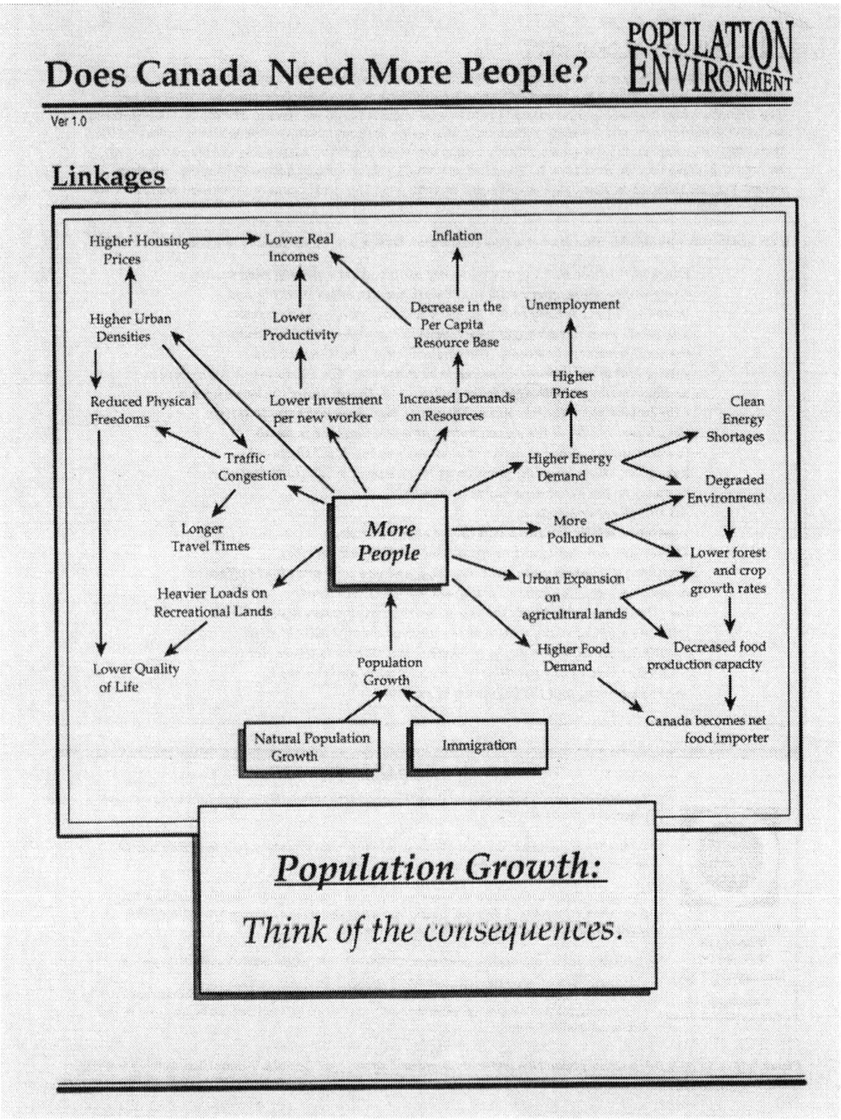

Does Canada Need More People?

POPULATION ENVIRONMENT

Ver 1.0

Linkages

Higher Housing Prices
Lower Real Incomes
Inflation
Higher Urban Densities
Lower Productivity
Decrease in the Per Capita Resource Base
Unemployment
Reduced Physical Freedoms
Lower Investment per new worker
Increased Demands on Resources
Higher Prices
Clean Energy Shortages
Traffic Congestion
Higher Energy Demand
Degraded Environment
Longer Travel Times
More People
More Pollution
Lower forest and crop growth rates
Heavier Loads on Recreational Lands
Urban Expansion on agricultural lands
Lower Quality of Life
Population Growth
Higher Food Demand
Decreased food production capacity
Canada becomes net food importer
Natural Population Growth
Immigration

Population Growth:

Think of the consequences.

Population Growth—Consequences Flow Chart
With permission from Zero Population Growth Canada

THE GREAT DEBATE: CONSUMPTION OR POPULATION

> Can you think of any problem in any area of human endeavor on any scale, from microscopic to global, whose LONG-TERM solution is in any DEMONSTRABLE way aided, assisted, or advanced by further increases in population, locally, nationally, or globally?
>
> A. A. BARTLETT, 8 January 1996
> Professor Emeritus of Physics,
> University of Colorado in Boulder

Herein lies one of the greatest obstacles in tackling the overpopulation issue. Those who feel that we have something to gain by continued growth would have us believe that this is an EITHER - Or debate between population versus consumption, when common sense would dictate that we need to work on both issues simultaneously.

Of course, there is no question that developed countries need to reduce consumption, and I don't believe anyone would dispute that fact. That doesn't mean that overpopulation isn't of equal importance. In fact, many would argue that it is the underlying cause of all human suffering. They make the point that even considering the basic necessities of life—food, clothing, and shelter—more people still equals more consumption. If you want the majority of world citizens to be provided with medical care, education, and social services, this basic consumption will likely double. Many varying formulas have been used to find a balance, but I like to start with this basic equation:

> SUSTAINABLE POPULATION x SUSTAINABLE CONSUMPTION = SUSTAINABLE SOCIETIES

This one seems to me fairly easy for anyone to wrap his or her mind around, as it is the one we all use to plan supper every evening. We need to know how many family members will be home for supper and estimate how much they will each eat to plan how much food to cook to make everyone happy. If someone decides to bring home a surprise guest for supper, it may be a little inconvenient but not a real problem. However, if another whole family drops in unexpectedly, it could cause chaos.

Many would say that our planet is already in a state of chaos. The Population Institute of Canada, in their proposal, "Population, Sustainable Development and Security," raises a very valid question: "Given the huge benefits that would result from population reduction, one wonders why the issue has not been dealt with more effectively." Their proposal accepts the following premises:

- Overpopulation is the chief cause of ongoing ecological damage
- Overpopulation is the fundamental cause of growing insecurity
- Overpopulation is the prime reason that sustainable development remains beyond reach

They suggest that if we humans reduce the global population to a fraction of its present level, to, for example, one billion or the equivalent of the population of the earth in 1850, it would provide extraordinary benefits. The quality of life of all people would soar. We would have all the advantages of modern technology but little, if any, environmental deterioration.

Our escalating population is also having a negative affect on world poverty. The World Health Organization reports that more than 3 billion people are malnourished, and per capita grain availability has been declining since the eighties. According to a UK parliamentary group, the UN's Millennium Development Goals (MDGs) are "difficult or impossible to meet" without curbing population growth.

"No country has ever raised itself out of poverty without stabilizing population," said the group's vice-chairman, Richard Ottaway MP, at a seminar on population issues.

The United Nation Millennium Development Goals:

1. Eradicate extreme poverty and hunger
2. Achieve universal primary education
3. Promote gender equality and empower women
4. Reduce child mortality
5. Improve maternal health
6. Combat HIV/AIDS, malaria, and other diseases
7. Ensure environmental sustainability
8. Develop a global partnership for development

It is estimated that at present about three hundred million women globally would like to limit the size of their families but do not have access to family planning assistance. We must ask why stopping population growth isn't the number one goal! It is the link to achieving all of the other goals.

TABOOS AND MYTHS

So who benefits from promoting the many taboos and myths surrounding the population issue? Some have dared to suggest that it is those who refuse to recognize the relationship between humans and Nature. Ecocentrism is a time-tested standard of thought, which shifts our focus from a human-centered value system back to an *earth*-centered reality. Returning to this ecocentric philosophy, which allowed humans to live in harmony with the planet for most of our history, would require a new code of conduct toward the planet.

Most taboo issues, such as population, family planning, and ecological economics, are taboo because of myths. So, perhaps by dispelling these myths we can remove the taboo aura from these issues and finally begin addressing them.

The Population Institute of Canada has given many of these myths consideration in their publication of "Confronting the Population Crisis" and encourages people to borrow from it for discussion purposes. The authors, Madeline Weld and Whitman Wright, have made a very convincing argument for addressing this urgent issue. Some points from their arguments have been included here, with their permission.

> The concept of sustainability is essential to our survival and should be viewed as the intent and central operating principle of planning … If we are to achieve sustainable development, we will have to go beyond the notion that land is a mere commodity. Land is one of the fundamental components required for the continuation of human life. We should now recognize the rights of the ecosystem and the species, as well as the rights of individuals. Clearly, this principle holds numerous significant implications for planners and land use planning.
>
> Canadian Institute of Planners, 1990

Myths

1. *Feeding people should be a priority over saving nature*

There are many who believe that when we must choose between feeding the hungry and conserving nature, people must come first. After all, we wouldn't sacrifice starving African children in order to save the threatened black rhino, would we?

Well, it isn't all that simple. Here again, this should not be polarized into an either/or solution. Logically, we should be doing both. There are many different opinions as to where we should be spending our money and energy for the betterment of the common good. Governments and people around the world feel it is important to spend billions of dollars on art, music, and entertainment to improve our quality of life. This money could, in fact, be going to save those in poverty. Why not consider nature as important a commodity?

In his article, "Feeding People versus Saving Nature?" Holmes Rolston III has this to say about it:

> Humans win? Nature loses? After analysis, sometimes it turns out that humans are not really winning, if they are sacrificing the nature that is their life-support system. Humans win by conserving nature—and these winners include the poor and the hungry. After all, food has to be produced by growing it in some reasonably healthy natural system, and the clean water that the poor need is also good for fauna and flora.

Natural ecosystems provide humans with food, water, shelter, air, clothing, fuel, and medicine. We depend on insects to pollinate crops and on forests to regulate climates, recycle carbon dioxide, slow erosion, and prevent floods. So, not only feeding people but all other life necessities ultimately depend on nature. Like putting on your own oxygen mask first before you try to save others, we need to protect nature first so that it can sustain us.

All countries face the global problems of poverty, unemployment, and crime. Yet, their economic interests and spending cover a diverse range of programs, recognizing that a humane and healthy lifestyle requires more than just food and clothing. The World Bank has acknowledged that poverty is not simply a lack of income but a lack of access to food, clean water, education, and other services that have a marked impact on opportunities for the poor. Having a rich diversity of resources and interests gives societies a safety net in times of unexpected hardship or disaster.

A Cornell University study of population trends, climate change, increasing pollution, and emerging diseases concludes that "life on earth is killing us." An article published in the journal *BioScience* reported that an estimated 40 percent of deaths around the world can now be attributed to various environmental factors, especially chemical pollutants.

Our choices will become even more difficult as the population continues to grow and our resources continue to dwindle. As it is, mankind is already taking far more than our fair share, robbing not only other species, but future human generations as well.

As *Scientific American* warned in 2007, humans are now consuming 23.8 percent of all the world's energy produced by plants, energy that would normally fuel native ecosystems.

> Every first-world city has within it a third-world city of malnutrition, infant mortality, homelessness and unemployment. Every third-world city has within it a first-world city of high tech, high fashion, and high finance. Seeing the cities of the world as a global laboratory breaks down the stereotype North/South technology transfer, and opens up the rich possibilities of South/North and South/South exchange, vastly increasing the number of potential solutions.
>
> Perlman, 1990

> The opposite of wealth is not poverty but sufficiency. This is critical. Sufficiency is not a matter of sacrifice and deprivation. It is a means of working out different ways of achieving satisfaction in our own lives.
>
> Porritt, 1989

OVERPOPULATION—THE ELEPHANT IN THE CHINA STORE!

2. *We need population growth to stimulate the economy.*

> The expanding global economy is outgrowing Earth's ecosystems. As the Dow Jones goes up, the Earth's health goes down … Failure to reverse environmental trends will lead to reversals in economic progress … If we have learned anything over the past year, it is that accounting systems that do not tell the truth can be costly … China is now at war. It is not invading armies that are claiming its territory, but expanding deserts. Old deserts are advancing and new ones are forming, like guerrilla forces striking unexpectedly, forcing Beijing to fight on several fronts. And China is losing the war. The deserts are claiming an ever larger piece of territory each year.
>
> Lester R. Brown,
> Worldwatch Institute, 2000

> Sustainable economies should be designed to recognize the needs of future generations, to ensure that all costs of products and services are reflected in their value, and to sustain the ecosystems of the planet on which all life depends. Our current economic system recognizes only short term costs and benefits, and has no way of considering our grandchildren's needs when decisions are made.
>
> East Kootenay Environmental Society
> (now known as Wildsight)

Money is a form of energy. It is a human invention that represents the energy we expend through work, investments, or various other means. Like any other form of energy or human behavior, it can be used to improve the earth situation or degrade it. The use of money to form our modern economic system is fairly recent, replacing the barter system that prevailed for much of human history.

Throughout the years many items have been used to pay for food, including items such as feathers, shells, beads, cattle, and tools. This all depended on where and when one lived. In the South Pacific, at one time one paid for food with dog's teeth. In ancient Rome soldiers were paid with lumps of salt. That is where the word "salary" came from.

This "salary" has become part of the present-day economy, based on supply and demand. The problem with this system is captured in the phrase: supply is limited, demand is not. When you have a variable like demand that knows no limits, the outcome is somewhat unpredictable. Also, this basic formula fails to take into consideration the value of our life-support system.

Economists measure the success of an economy by tracking the Gross National Product (GNP), a measure of the total value of goods and services produced by a country. An increase in the GNP is seen as a good thing. Unfortunately, as the East Kootenay Environmental Society points out, fighting epidemics, cleaning up oil tanker disasters, and cutting down old growth forests all help increase the GNP. However, few of us would argue for more disease, bigger oil spills, or the elimination of ancient forests.

When calculating the GNP, economists measure only those activities that enter the monetary economy. They put a value on the timber from a logged forest, but no value on the forest that is destroyed. So, this system puts very little value on the resource base. It isn't until the resource base starts to run out, as with oil, that the market starts to reflect its scarcity. Then the market goes looking for an alternative commodity.

However, this doesn't work with water. When water is scarce, unlike with oil, there is no replacement. Water is the one resource that every life-form depends on, and as our population increases it becomes increasingly valuable. In the future, it will be the most highly prized commodity that wars will be waged over. As many rivers and aquifers are already running dry, millions of people are migrating toward abundant water supplies.

> Americans lose $68 billion a year from immigration.
>
> David Weinstein and Donald Davis,
> Columbia University, 2005

Immigration, as a form of population growth, often allows us to track the impacts of increased population on a country more easily than a country's own population growth. This study conducted at Columbia University used a new approach to measure the economic losses from immigration to the United States. This new model is not just based on supply and demand, but also takes into account globalization, technology, and standard of living. Some of the report findings:

- In 2002, the net loss to US natives from immigration was $68 billion.
- This $68 billion annual loss represents a $14 billion increase just since 1998. As the size of the immigrant population has continued to increase, so has the loss.
- While natives lost from immigration, the findings show that immigrants themselves benefit substantially by coming to America

Harvard economist George Borjas, who is generally recognized as the nation's leading immigration economist, stated:

> Weinstein and Davis' work represents an important new approach for calculating the net benefits accruing to the United States from immigration. As in earlier calculations, immigration does not create substantial net economic benefits for native-born Americans. In fact, Weinstein and Davis conclude that the effect on natives may be both large and negative.

Although immigrants benefit greatly financially, it is a difficult transition for these desperate people, and most of them would prefer to remain in their homeland if their living conditions were improved. Many of them only stay in North America until they have saved enough money to return to their home and live in comfort, or until the war, drought, or other disaster is no longer a threat. So, would it not be of more benefit to use this $68 billion each year to improve conditions and family planning programs in the developing countries, so that people can remain in their homeland with their families and familiar customs?

> Refugees are often forced to flee their homes due to war, natural disasters, and environmental catastrophes. In fact, many events that are labeled as natural disasters or wars—e.g. floods, droughts, battles for water, land or oil, etc.—are actually a result of overpopulation, but this misconception is rarely challenged.

~

> The accusation that a stand to reduce immigration is racist is music to the ears to those who profit from the cheap labor of immigrants. They are the same people who love to see environmentalists make fools of themselves. And there is no environmentalist more foolish than one who refuses to confront the fact that uncontrolled human population growth is the no. 1 cause of the world's increasing environmental problems.
>
> Captain Paul Watson,
> Founder of Sea Shepherd Conservation Society

The impact is that each additional person on this planet is now putting a greater demand on our ecosystem than ever before, as our numbers escalate. The total impact of our population, and its resulting consumption, is increasing exponentially. That means that a person born to this planet today, even existing at the standard of living of Gandhi, Mother Theresa, or Saint Francis, has a far greater impact than someone born fifty years ago. Food, shelter, and other resources are far more difficult to find and produce today than they were in the past.

Similarly, each birth in 2025 will increasingly be recognized for the tremendous burden it is placing on our already overtaxed ecosystem. There will come a day in the near future when the birth of a child might not be seen as such a cause for celebration as it is today.

As our resources decrease, the energy required to find substitutes increases. The technology and chemical farming practices become more destructive, and we claim more and more of the wildlife's domain for our own. Of course, this situation can only worsen as our numbers increase, since we have passed the "tipping point" and failed to act.

This population growth is a basic economic force that puts unsustainable pressure on the environment. The economic consequences of this pressure are dwindling resources, higher costs, lower incomes, higher unemployment, and increasing poverty. By casting every problem in an economic light at the expense of the environment, we are ignoring strategies that could help us stabilize or reduce our human population.

Increasing population may make the growth lobby (cheap labor businesses, media industry, land developers, economists, energy sectors, and governments) happy, but it is creating unprecedented human misery and ecological suicide for future generations. We need to restructure our economic system to recognize full-cost accounting, based on sustainability not growth. We need to make prices reflect reality, and consumers need to use their spending power to reflect the value they place on a healthy and sustainable environment.

> If we are to support the population of the world at a level of nutrition and living standards enjoyed by Canadians, we would need the resources of two

> and a half more planet Earths. These extra two and a half planet Earths needed to give all people the standard of living projected for them in 1987 by the Brundtland Commission, (whose report made "sustainable development" the oxymoron of the twentieth century), are nowhere to be seen.
>
> Any country aiming for environmental and economic sustainability must have a population policy which is based on the human-carrying capacity of its land and its natural resources. There are already sinister indications that Canada is exceeding its carrying capacity in areas like marine fisheries and prairie topsoils, both of which are severely depleted.
>
> Vivian Pharis
> Alberta Wilderness Association, 1994

So, what is at the root of this myth that we need continuous economic growth spurred on by a constantly growing population? Are our politicians and business leaders so stuck in this mindset that there is no hope for the future? Perhaps President Eisenhower's message after WWII will shed some light on our present situation.

> He said, **"We have to make consumption a way of life, and convince Americans that buying things makes them happy."**

He was very successful in accomplishing this goal, but if we were as motivated today by our world leaders to reverse this global trend toward growth, we could be just as successful. We have a better-educated global population now that could respond by their votes and demands to a vital message to protect our home planet. Don't you think it's worth a try?

3. *Early warnings of environmental damage and mass starvation by such scientists as Ehrlich and Malthus were false alarms.*

Thomas Robert Malthus, 1766–1834, famously observed that human population, if unchecked, would grow faster than its food supply. He argued that education in "moral restraint" might prevent starvation from being the operative check on population growth. His warning went unheeded.

Of course, Malthus was right, as we can see from the big die-off scenario happening in Africa and many other countries. In today's terms the message of Malthus would be that populations have the potential to grow more rapidly than we can grow any of the support systems we need for populations.

> Malthus was rash enough to predict that the crash would come by the second half of the nineteenth century. Because it didn't, economists in general tend to believe that he was wrong. If he was wrong, then Ron Brooks is wrong. More importantly, Brooks' guru Charles Darwin, is wrong. All in all, it seems much more likely that Malthus was simply premature. The fact remains that Malthus, for all his shortcomings as a social theorist, formulated a principle of population growth that no one has been able to falsify and that forms a foundation stone of the theory of evolution by natural selection.
>
> Ward Chesworth,
> Michael R. Moss, Vernon G. Thomas
> *Malthus and The Third Millennium,* 2000 Series

"It is a wonder that anyone still listens to American 'population biologist' Paul Ehrlich, whose 1968 book *The Population Bomb* was so spectacularly wrong about the threat of world overpopulation," says Lorne Gunter, a journalist for the *Edmonton Journal*

> in 1995. He adds, "We should laugh after 'bomb' explodes in Ehrlich's face."

Well, I don't think too many people are laughing now. According to a report in the April 2005 *New Scientist*, the Millennium Ecosystem Assessment (MA) report indicates that we have every right to be alarmed about overpopulation, and millions of people are in fact starving as Ehrlich predicted. This $24-million report took more than 1,300 experts in ninety-five countries four years to put together. It confirms earlier reports that humans have far exceeded the earth's carrying capacity and population limits.

The following statistics are clear indicators of these findings:

- Three billion humans are malnourished worldwide
- Water demands already far exceed supplies in nearly eighty nations of the world
- Food production per capita started declining in 1980, and continues to decline
- Grain production per capita started declining in 1984 and continues
- Forests have been almost completely eradicated in twenty-five countries; in another twenty-nine the area covered by forest has fallen by more than 90 percent
- Crop fertilization has doubled the availability of nitrogen worldwide since the mid-nineteenth century and tripled the availability of phosphorus since 1960. This leads to eutrophication of lakes and rivers and creates dead zones on the ocean floor due to oxygen depletion
- Over 16,100 species of wildlife are threatened with extinction, but this may be a gross underestimate because fewer than 3 percent of the world's 1.9 million described species have been assessed by the Red List

- 99 percent of threatened species are at risk from human activities. Humans are the main cause of extinction and the principle threat to species at risk of extinction (Tropical Conservancy, 2006)

Never in our history have there been so many people malnourished. The World Health Organization warns that malnutrition is a serious disease because it increases susceptibility to other diseases like malaria and AIDS. In addition, it reduces the quality of life and often takes these people out of the work force.

Never in our history have there been so many species threatened with extinction, over-exploitation, habitat loss, pollution, and invasive alien species as a result of human activity. Habitat loss and degradation are the leading threats. They affect 86 percent of all threatened birds, 86 percent of the threatened mammals assessed, and 88 percent of the threatened amphibians.

> The first rule of intelligent tinkering is to save all the parts.
>
> Aldo Leopold, *Sand County Almanac*

> I wish I could have a free lunch for every time I've heard someone declare, "Malthus was wrong." ...
>
> With the world population growth outpacing food supply, say goodbye to the era of unlimited improvement ... Some people worry about peak oil—when we reach the peak of petroleum production. I worry about peak grain. World per capita cereal production has already passed its peak—in the mid-1980s—not least because of collapsing production in the former Soviet Union and sub-Saharan Africa. Meanwhile, rising incomes in Asia are causing a worldwide surge in food demand.

> Already, the symptoms of the coming food shortage are detectable. The International Monetary Fund recorded a 23 percent rise in world food prices during the last eighteen months. Of course, we're not supposed to notice that prices are going up. In the U.S., the monetary authorities insist that we should focus on the "core" consumer price index, which excludes the cost of food and fuel, and has the annual U.S. inflation rate at just 2.2%. But food inflation is roughly double that.
>
> Niall Ferguson,
> "The Population Bubble"
> *Los Angeles Times*, 30 July 2007

Ferguson points out that Malthus was twenty-three years old the last time a British summer was this rain-soaked, which was in 1789. The consequences of excessive rainfall in the late eighteenth century were predictable. Crops would fail, the harvest would be dismal, food prices would rise, and some people would starve. It was no coincidence that the French Revolution broke out the same year. Malthus concluded that there must be "a strong and constantly operating check on population." This would take two forms: "misery" and "vice," by which he meant not only alcohol abuse but also contraception and abortion (he was, after all, an Anglican minister).

> The human family has suffered sickness, but rare is the plague that can kill a third of a nation's adults—as AIDS may well do in Botswana over the next decade .... Our planet has regularly seen species die-offs, but only five times in 4 billion years has it experienced anything like today's mass extinction ... Nations have long grappled with inequality. But how often have the assets of just three individuals matched the combined national economies of the poorest forty-eight countries, as happened in 1997? ... Are

> tragedies of this magnitude needed to steer the world toward a new model of development?
>
> Gary Gardner
> *State of the World,* 2002

4. *The rate of population growth is decreasing, so it is no longer a problem.*

Yes, it is true that the annual *rate* of population growth in most countries has decreased, but the *growth* in actual numbers continues to increase. This is similar to taking your foot off the accelerator when driving down the highway. The car continues to go forward for some time, just due to momentum.

For example, according to Chris Rapley in the *Independent* (27 June 2007), population growth hit a peak of about 2 percent in the late 1960s, and has fallen to 1.3 percent in 2007. This decline is mainly a result of increased use of birth control since the 1960s. Population growth is calculated by subtracting the number of deaths from the number of births per year.

However, world population continues to increase by over 80 million people each year. So, while the rate of increase is slowing, in absolute numbers world population growth continues to be substantial. The population of this planet is expected to surpass 8 billion before mid-century, so the problem is clearly not solving itself.

For example, according to the, *UN Wire* (8 June 1999, *www.unfoundation.org*) Mexicans are moving away from traditionally large families and choosing to have fewer children. This is resulting in a tremendous reduction in the fertility rate—from seven children per family in 1965 to 2.5 children in 1999. However, experts predict that even with these slowing fertility rates, Mexico's population will continue to increase until 2045. This is called a "population momentum" or "lag time."

To reach a *zero* level population *growth rate*, a family would have to limit the number of children to replacement level, which would be a *fertility rate* of two children. So, the growth rate means the number of children over the replacement level. If you factor in the "births minus deaths" calculation, this number could be a fraction higher than two if births are higher than deaths.

The growth of human population has been, is now, and in the future will be almost entirely determined in the world's less developed countries. According to the US Department of Commerce, Bureau of the Census, 99 percent of global natural increase now occurs in the developing regions of Africa, Asia, and Latin America.

However, this by no means should lead those in developed countries to conclude that we are not part of the problem, as our high consumption rates more than make up for it. This is due partly to our climate, and partly to our greed and wasteful habits. Consequently, developed countries should be making every effort to achieve a declining population rate as well.

The number of both births and deaths continue to decline in most world regions, yet both have reached levels unprecedented in human history.

5. *It is a woman's right to have as many children as she likes, and we should not interfere.*

This argument is based on the assumption that women in developing countries choose to have large families, when in fact hundreds of millions of women around the world do not have access to any sort of family planning. It is estimated that at present about three hundred million women globally would like to limit the size of their families but cannot obtain access to family planning assistance.

As the Population Institute of Canada points out, even in areas where some form of family planning is available, most women have at best some input into deciding the size of their families. A woman's husband, or even her in-laws, are likely to have more say in the matter than she does. In many parts of the world, there is strong social and religious pressure on women to have more children than they personally would choose, and the pressure to produce a "sufficient" number of sons is often enormous.

Many, if not most, births are unplanned or unwanted, and I will be exploring this issue in detail in Part 3 of this book.

However, along with human rights comes a human's responsibilities to this planet and other living beings. People do not have the absolute right to implement personal decisions that affect others' lives without considering the common good. Parents do not pay all the costs of bringing up children—society as a whole picks up the rest. Overpopulation affects us all, and it threatens the life-support system that sustains us all. We are all forced to deal with its consequences.

If we do not deal with overpopulation now, through education and family planning, we may not be able to avoid more coercive methods down the road. The other option is to allow Mother Nature to deal with it through starvation, disease, increased human suffering, and loss of biodiversity. However, when making this decision, the public should be informed of the options, and everyone should be allowed to be involved in a fair and meaningful public consultation process.

John Guillebaud, co-chairman of Optimum Population and emeritus professor of family planning at University College in London, put it this way: "The effect on the planet of having one child less is an order of magnitude greater than all these other things we might do, such as switching off lights. An extra child is the equivalent of a lot of flights across the planet."

Guillebaud added, "The greatest thing anyone in Britain could do to help the future of the planet would be to have one less child. When couples are planning a family they should think about the environmental consequences. As a general guideline, couples should produce no more than two offspring." (*London Times* 2007)

Since many now see it as an "environmental misdemeanor" to have a big family, we must make family planning services available to all couples who would like to access these programs.

6. *Technology can solve all our overpopulation problems.*

> What about technology? Some economists imagine that computer chips or nanotechnology will save us from the laws of nature, but every technical efficiency in history has resulted in more consumption of energy and resources, not less. Remember when computers were going to save paper? That never happened. Computers increased paper consumption from about 50 million tons annually in 1950 to 250 million tons today. Meanwhile, we lost 600 million hectares of forest.
>
> Rex Weyler,
> *Biophysical Economics,* 2009

The more desperate the overpopulation problem becomes, the more people are looking to technology to bail us out. Yet, as technology flourishes and we continue to make spectacular breakthroughs, the number of people living in absolute poverty continues to increase. At the present time there are about 2 billion people living at a decent standard of living, and about 4.5 billion living in poverty.

So what would make us think that technology could solve the problems of the future, when it falls so far short of dealing with the problems of the present?

The Union of Concerned Scientists has warned that human beings and the natural world are on a collision course, and we cannot expect technology to save us from the problems caused by overpopulation.

Technical experts have come up with a number of schemes, from launching the world's excess population into space to colonize other planets, to replacing natural systems with man-made ones to increase output. However, many of the world's leading scientists believe that these schemes would only cause other, possibly more destructive and unpredictable, problems.

There is no magic bullet that is going to make this problem disappear, so we should stop fooling ourselves and get down to the business of solving it ourselves. We already know what measures are needed, and we have the resources available to begin the process of stabilizing the population. Then we can focus on reducing it to a sustainable level of approximately 2 billion.

> Intensification of production to feed an increased population leads to a still greater increase in population.
>
> Peter Farb, 1978

7. *Large numbers of children are desirable because they provide labor and old-age security for their parents.*

> "Is slave labor acceptable just because you create the slaves yourself?" asks the Population Institute of Canada.

It is the children that are the losers in this scenario, for not only are more and more children being born into poverty, but they are being born into a world greatly diminished in resources, opportunities, and environmental integrity. This mentality is very self-centered on the part of the parents and very cruel to the millions of children who are starving to death and living in misery.

Not only that, but this thinking is extremely flawed. Having large numbers of children now will only cause more hardship for everyone, including seniors, in the future. Besides, these additional children will also grow old, resulting in still more children being needed, who will in turn also grow old, etc. The incentive programs tax-payers are funding now, such as family allowance, child tax reduction, child tax credits, baby bonuses, and day care services, are also putting a heavy burden on our societies. Instead, we could be putting this money toward senior programs and universal family planning programs. Those presently employed in caring for our children could be caring for our elderly, if we reduced our growth rate.

Countries with decreasing population growth are finding that there are alternative ways of dealing with a reduced work force. Perhaps we should be looking to them for advice regarding pension plans, home care, raising the retirement age, etc.

In countries with increasing population, foreign aid could more effectively be focused on dealing with poverty and family planning if there were far fewer children to support. Tragically, many of these children are starving to death before they are old enough to enter the work force, so this argument holds little merit where there is such a high mortality rate.

I suppose this issue comes down to the question of quality of life over quantity. Millions of children today work long hours, are malnourished, and receive little or no education or medical attention. They provide a cheap, easily exploitable source of labor for parents and industry and have a very grim future to look forward to.

"EVERY 14 SECONDS A CHILD IS ORPHANED"

World Vision, 2008

> The human race's prospects of survival were far better when we were defenseless against tigers than they are today when we have become defenseless against ourselves.
>
> A. Toynbee

8. *It is racist and coercive to put pressure on people to limit family size.*

> If you can't answer a man's arguments, all is not lost; you can still call him vile names.
>
> Elbert Hubbard,
> American journalist

Those who bring up the argument of racism make use of two important facts:

1. There are genuine racists.
2. Most (about 95 percent) of global population growth occurs in the developing world among non-white people.

Therefore, according to the non-logic of population deniers, people who raise thoughtful concerns about global population and resource issues must be motivated by racist fears. In reality, racists rarely speak thoughtfully about declining fish stocks, erosion, loss of species, water shortages, and the increasing inability of agricultural technology to keep up with population growth. Scientists and other concerned people do. Yet the fear of being labeled racist no doubt keeps many people from voicing the concerns they feel about global population and resource issues. The accusation of racism is a form of intellectual terrorism.

Actually, most people who want to remedy the population problem at the same time desperately want to help the women and children in the poor countries. This is especially true since most women in the developing world do not choose to have large families but are given little other option.

Having fewer children has many benefits for these women. It enhances their health, and their ability to participate in the labor force enhances their social status and allows them to be more independent. The money they earn can go toward further education, improving their diets, and better health care for themselves and their children.

As the Population Institute of Canada points out, those concerned with population growth in developing countries are very likely to believe that the industrialized nations are overpopulated as well—as also evidenced by groups such as Negative Population Growth in the United States. However, birth rates in most industrialized nations have already dropped close to or even below the replacement level of 2.1 children per woman.

In industrialized nations, population growth is due to growth momentum (a large percent of women entering their childbearing years) and to immigration. But to advocate a limit to immigration also leaves one open to charges of racism, as most of the immigrants to developed countries are not white. So, in order to avoid being labeled as racist, most industrialized countries have high immigration rates, and are giving up their innate sense of nationalism to foreign takeover.

> All countries with nationwide unconstrained access to fertility regulation have a TFR (fertility rate) of 2.0 or less, and all countries that have not achieved replacement-level fertility have constrained access to fertility regulation methods. **There are no exceptions**.
>
> Malcolm Potts,
> "Sex and the Birth Rate,"
> *Population and Development Review*,
> Vol. 23, No.1, March 1997

9. *Continued population growth is inevitable—there is nothing we can do to stop it.*

Martin Luther King addressed this issue on 5 May 1966 in the speech he gave when he received the Planned Parenthood Federation of America/Margaret Sanger Award. He assured Americans that family planning was possible, practical, and necessary. He pointed out that we possess sufficient resources, means, and knowledge to address the modern plague of population, and he urged American citizens to take action on this issue.

There has been a lot of hand-wringing going on about the perils of overpopulation, and for anyone with a sense of humanity, this is an agonizing time in our history. However, mankind has evolved to the point where we can modify our environment and our thinking. We can construct mental models of the world we inhabit and choose what kind of future we want to create. We do have the ability to understand and rectify the overpopulation crisis.

Eventually, human population will be controlled. It is up to us whether this is accomplished through the undesirable means of famine, disease, and war—or the more humane means of family planning and sustainable lifestyles.

Part 4 of this book is dedicated to solutions at the government level, as well as things all global citizens can do to reach an optimal population level.

> It happened that a fire broke out backstage in a theater.
>
> The clown came out to inform the public.
>
> They thought it was just a jest and applauded.
>
> He repeated his warning, but they shouted even louder.
>
> So I think the world will come to an end
>
> amid general applause from all the wits,
>
> who believe it is a joke.
>
> Soren Kierkegaard
> from *Provocations*

10. Promoting family planning means promoting abortions and coercion.

In fact, the contrary is quite true. *Promoting family planning prevents abortions and coercion*! The word *planning* is defined as "a way of doing something that has been worked out beforehand." So it is unlikely that a woman would intentionally plan beforehand to have an unwanted pregnancy, which she would have previously planned to abort. Why would any woman plan to have an unwanted baby, or to have an abortion that could put her health at risk?

The whole idea of planning your family size is meant to prevent unwanted pregnancies, abortions, or coercion of any kind. If this planning is done responsibly, it will take into consideration a number of factors:

1. Does the woman actually want children, or is she being coerced into having the children?

2. How many children would a family willingly choose to have, considering their ability to support them?

3. What effect do you think each additional person has on the environment?

4. What kind of burden will each family's size place on society and our social and environmental systems?

5. What kind of birth control program will it require to meet the desired family size?

By considering these factors when doing a "family planning" exercise, we can prevent the vast majority of abortions and coercive programs that have caused so much concern. According to a report released by the Population Reference Bureau in Washington, 5 February 1997, "Family planning is a lifesaver for millions of women and children in developing countries. It permits the healthy spacing of births, prevents the spread of sexually transmitted diseases like AIDS, reduces the number of low birth-weight babies, allows for longer breast feeding, prevents unsafe abortions, and averts death from childbirth."

The report stated that an estimated 20 million unsafe abortions take place each year in places where access to safe abortion is limited. Unsafe abortions result in at least 76,000 deaths every year, mostly in developing countries.

On the other hand, most methods of family planning have a low rate of failure if used correctly and are completely safe for the majority of users. So, family planning is a low-cost way to prevent many needless maternal and child deaths, as well as reducing population growth. The number of unwanted pregnancies each year could be greatly reduced by providing increased access to family planning programs.

> In general, we would choose a population size that maximizes very broad environmental and social options for individuals.

G. Daily, A. Ehrlich, and P. Ehrlich, 1994

11. Developed countries still have plenty of land available to accommodate more people.

> In my view every place in the world, including Canada, is overcrowded.
>
> Robert Bateman

Population Growth is Making it Impossible for Canada to Achieve Environmental Balance

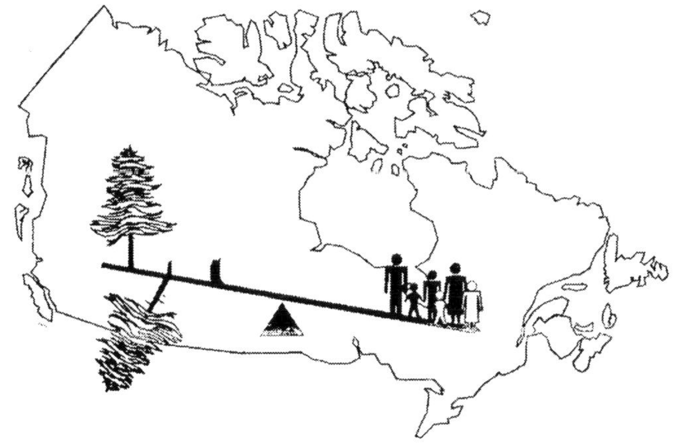

Map used with permission from ZPG Canada

Much of the land in developed countries, such as Canada for instance, is unsuitable for settlement and already contributes to the economy as farming and pastureland, forest resources, and mining sites. There is a huge movement toward urbanization, with large cities totally dependent on produce, water, and resources from rural land. These lands are also needed to provide resources to export to undeveloped countries.

According to the Sustainable Population Society (Edmonton, 1997, "Know the Facts"), space is less a limiting factor than water, resources, and good arable land. Less than 5 percent of Canada is usable arable land, and between 1966 and 1986, the growth of cities claimed 175,000 hectares of the best of it. Presumably, at least as much has been lost in the ensuing decades.

The days of the wild west when there were vast unsettled lands and plentiful resources and nature was yet unspoiled are long gone. Many of our resources, such as our fisheries and forests, are greatly depleted. Much of our water and soil is contaminated, and many species of wildlife are threatened with extinction under the pressures of the population we presently have.

This reminds me of the "lifeboat" scenario. How many more people will we be able to take on before our lifeboat sinks? Colder climates were never meant to support the kinds of numbers that can be sustained in warmer climates. Our growing season is much shorter, warmer clothes and houses are required, and our resource base is less dependable. For example, boreal forests take twice as long to grow as tropical forests.

Rather than encouraging immigration, we should be increasing foreign aid to third world countries, especially for family planning programs.

> Overpopulation is perhaps the biggest problem facing us, and immigration is part of that problem. It has to be addressed.
>
> David Brower
> Former Executive Director of the Sierra Club

12. The solution to the global population problem is to raise the third world's standard of living.

While raising the standard of living in the third world may alleviate some of the starvation and human suffering, this by itself is unlikely to decrease their population. It is only by providing access to safe and effective family planning programs, which many third world women desperately want, that we can reduce fertility rates.

As Dr. Andrew Macpherson, Past Regional Director General of Environment Canada (*Environment Network News*, September 1992) pointed out:

> Many of us, apparently including most of our political leaders, live in a state of denial. We have fabricated a web of self-delusion, which obscures the reality. We go along with the demographic myth that poor societies with high birth rates will reduce them if they are made richer.

It is not wealth, but access to family planning programs, that has caused the decrease in fertility rates in developed countries. Just imagine, for example, what Canada would be like today if Canadian women had never had access to birth control. I shudder to think of what my life would have been like if I had been forced to have seven to ten children, as many women in third world countries are.

Despite what the Pope and former President Bush are preaching, abstinence is not a viable form of birth control. It never has been and never will be. So Canadian women, if not allowed any form of family planning, would have likely had the same number of children that African women are having today, a fertility rate of at least six children. Rape is slightly less acceptable in Canada than in some third world countries, but our health care system would keep more children alive, so these two factors would balance each other out. So, in this scenario, Canada's population would be more than double what it is today. Yet, the Population Institute of Canada, and many others, are saying that Canada is already overpopulated.

Education is not really a factor here, since it is common sense and access to birth control that actually limit family size in most cases, not education. The issue is not that women have to be educated about contraception. It is that the millions of women who are desperately wanting contraception need to be given access to it. Perhaps it is the men who are making the decisions about providing family planning programs that need to be educated.

If it were true that raising living standards would solve the population problem, then all wealthy countries would have population growth rates of less than two. Yet according to the *Pherologist*, August 1999, annual population growth rates in some of the oil-rich nations in the Middle East in 1999 were 6 percent in Kuwait, 6.5 percent in Qatar, and 7.3 percent in the United Arab Emirates. So, although these countries are wealthy, their growth rates remain very high due to lack of family planning programs.

A staff reporter for the *Wall Street Journal*, Pascal Zachary, in "An Unconventional Academic Sounds the Population Alarm," 31 July 1998, asks, "Could the population bomb do in the human race, after all?" He adds that most population projections today assume that global fertility rates will decrease as women become more affluent and better educated. As they pursue schooling and careers and learn about contraception, the idea goes, they will delay having children and have fewer of them. This explanation, known as the "demographic transition" theory, is so universally held that many experts feel only a crackpot would challenge it. Yet Ms. Abernethy, who is sixty-three years old, is doing just that.

Virginia Deane Abernethy, Ph.D., Professor Emeritus of Psychiatry, Anthropology (Vanderbilt University, 1999) said,

> I am sorry to have to explode the comforting myth that declining fertility is the byproduct of doing "good" in the conventional sense of international transfers of wealth.

She pointed out that it is not growing prosperity, education, and health that have led to the fertility decline observed nearly worldwide today. It is exactly opposite conditions that prove to people that large family size is not affordable. In fact, it is clear that the promises of the 1960s and 1970s cannot be kept, so family size must be sharply curtailed.

For instance, she notes that prosperous nations such as Japan, France, and Italy have seen their birthrates drop in recent years because people in these countries have a growing perception of scarcity and more limited economic opportunity than in the past. These examples have put professional demographers on the defensive.

Ms. Abernethy's argument, which she calls the "fertility-opportunity hypothesis," explains some striking facts that the mainstream view doesn't account for. In the United States, for instance, relative affluence has always positively influenced birthrates. Births fell sharply during the Depression and then soared after World War II when the economic good times sparked a baby boom. She concludes that both those trying to escape abject poverty and those hoping to cling to a middle-class existence now believe that small families are an essential component of survival.

I am quite a fan of the fertility-opportunity hypothesis, so I find it very troubling that critics openly sneer at her:

"She's a nut," says Lant Pritchett, an economist at the World Bank in Washington. Adds John Bongaarts, research director at the Population Council in New York, "Her ideas are ignored by the demographic community. I'd say that's justified."

I would have to concur with Dr. Andrew McPherson here, in his observation that many of our economists and political leaders have fabricated a web of self-delusion that obscures the reality. The missing component of most of our foreign aid programs is family planning, and I find it quite incredible that program directors have failed to recognize this obvious fact.

Despite billions of dollars being pumped into countries in Africa to help alleviate the poverty, disease, and human suffering so prevalent there, we have made little progress. This is because our efforts are being undermined by the growing population, which continues to escalate. The people in Africa cannot escape their poverty if they are given no means of controlling their population.

> What becomes of the surplus of human life? It is either,

> 1. destroyed by infanticide, as among the Chinese and Lacedemonians:
> 2. it is stifled or starved, as among other nations whose population is commensurate to its food;
> 3. it is consumed by wars and endemic diseases; or
> 4. it overflows, by emigration, to places where a surplus of food is attainable.
>
> James Madison, 1791

13. No one ever dies of overpopulation.

Just as we refuse to acknowledge that anyone ever dies of overeating, we also refuse to acknowledge that anyone ever dies of overpopulation. When an obese person dies, the medical examiner declares the cause of death as heart failure, diabetes, stroke, cancer, or some other ailment that has been brought on by overeating. If the true number of deaths due to obesity were known, the medical profession, the food industry, and the media would be forced to finally take some responsibility and change the way they do business.

Similarly, when overpopulation brings about a person's death, it is always declared as malnutrition, flooding, drought, or one of the numerous calamities caused by people being forced to live in an undesirable location or under adverse conditions as a result of overpopulation.

Garrett Hardin from the University of California discussed this issue in the February 1971 issue of *Science* magazine in "Nobody Ever Dies of Overpopulation". He pointed out:

> Those of us who are deeply concerned about population and the environment—"econuts" we're called—are accused of seeing herbicides in trees, pollution in running brooks, radiation in rocks, and overpopulation everywhere. There is merit in the accusation.

> I was in Calcutta when the cyclone struck East Bengal in November 1970. Early dispatches spoke of 15,000 dead, but the estimates rapidly escalated to 2,000,000 and then dropped back to 500,000. A nice round number: it will do as well as any, for we will never know. The nameless ones who died, "unimportant" people far beyond the fringes of the social power structure, left no trace of their existence. Pakistani parents repaired the population loss in just 40 days, and the world turned its attention to other matters.
>
> What killed those unfortunate people? The cyclone, newspapers said. But one can just as logically say that overpopulation killed them. The Gangetic delta is barely above sea level. Every year several thousand people are killed in quite ordinary storms. If Pakistan were not overcrowded, no sane man would bring his family to such a place. Ecologically speaking, a delta belongs to the river and the sea; man obtrudes there at his peril.

Hardin explains that in the web of life every event has many antecedents, and that only by an arbitrary decision can we designate a single antecedent as "cause." Our choice is biased—biased to protect our egos against the onslaught of unwelcome truths.

> Were we to identify overpopulation as the cause of a half-million deaths, we would threaten ourselves with a question to which we do not know the answer: *How can we control population without recourse to repugnant measures*? Fearfully we close our minds to an inventory of possibilities. Instead, we say that a cyclone caused the deaths, thus relieving ourselves of responsibility for this and future catastrophes. "Fate" is *so* comforting.

We routinely blame AIDS, tuberculosis, leprosy, and malaria as the cause of death of millions of people each year. Yet, it is common knowledge that malnutrition is an important antecedent of death in all these cases. However, few people make the obvious connection between malnutrition and overpopulation.

Zero Population Growth (Population Connection) explains it this way:

> As the population grows, it expands onto productive agricultural land permanently destroying it. Therefore, the larger population must be fed from a smaller land area or more marginal land. Greater stress on the existing land through pollution and more intensive use reduces the fertility of the soil and forces the use of more fertilizers and pesticides. The result is greater pollution and stress on the environment as a whole.
>
> The productivity of the land gradually declines and real food costs increase reducing living standards. This cost squeeze makes it increasingly more painful for society to undertake the necessary but expensive conservation measures required to stop the decline of our agricultural resources.

Degradation of global agricultural land is continuing unabated, and food production per capita is now decreasing. The demand for more food to sustain a growing population has led to over-fertilization of the land, leading to eutrophication of our water sources. This in turn has led to lessened fish production. Nine of the world's seventeen major fisheries have collapsed or are in decline. Yet, we cannot bear to admit that any of this is caused by overpopulation. Garrett Hardin asks:

> What will we say when the power shuts down some fine summer on our eastern seaboard and several thousand people die of heat prostration? Will we blame the weather? Or the power companies for not building enough generators? Or the eco-nuts for insisting on pollution controls?

> One thing is certain: we won't blame the deaths on overpopulation. No one ever dies of overpopulation. It is unthinkable.

These are only a few of the common myths, and you can find others on the Population Institute of Canada website, as well as most other population group sites.

PART 2: WHO CARES? —LET'S GET A SECOND OPINION

At the present time, there is a great deal of confusion about the population issue. Unlike the open and honest dialogue taking place in the 1970s, population has become a taboo topic that is not considered politically correct to bring up. What has changed? Who are the powerful influences that have forced this discussion underground? What role do government, media, industry, religion, science, and environment play in this complex tapestry? Is it possible that myths have clouded the issue to the point that discussion is at a standstill? These are many of the questions that I will address in Part 2 of this book.

> "It is vitally important to recognize that some of the major participants in the population debate have no interest in rationally solving our problems, but are using this issue to advance their own agendas."
>
> Madeline Weld
> Population Institute of Canada, 1995

FACING A TITANIC CATASTROPHE

Do you remember the part in the movie *Titanic* where a few of the crewmembers realized that they were heading directly for an iceberg, and sure disaster, and gave the order to reverse the engines? Of course, at this point they had waited too long, causing great chaos and enormous loss of life. Those that the passengers had entrusted to take care and look out for them had failed miserably. The captain and those that influenced him had other priorities and goals in mind in their race to reach their destination.

Similarly, are we heading recklessly for disaster as well? Should we not be reversing the engines? Every indicator is pointing toward population growth as the engine propelling our planet to destruction. The leaders and decision makers we entrust to steer us in the right direction are sadly failing us. As on the *Titanic*, the wealthy first class passengers may survive, as we sacrifice the poor people in steerage to ensure the safety of the rich. Wildlife and the poor will be allowed to perish, as they are seen as expendable.

However, what do you think would have happened if the commanding officers had not believed or listened to the lookouts who alerted them of oncoming danger? Would every one of the passengers have died in those cold, dark waters? You can be sure of it. So what will happen if our world leaders continue to ignore the warnings of our greatest danger ahead—the danger of continued population growth? What will happen if we don't reverse the engines immediately?

INDICATORS

We are currently experiencing increases in the following conditions that are unlikely to improve without a decrease in global population levels. Every one of these indicators would be positively impacted, either directly or indirectly, by decreasing our population.

- Poverty
- Water shortage and pollution of both fresh and ocean water
- Urban expansion
- Displacement of people due to disasters
- Animal abuse

- Suicide rates
- Loss of biodiversity
- Air pollution and climate change
- Childhood diseases
- Waste production
- Habitat loss
- Loss of old-growth forests
- Soil erosion and depletion
- Collapsed fisheries
- Food contamination
- Abandoned and unwanted children
- Lack of access to family planning programs
- Energy demands
- Traffic congestion
- High housing costs
- Loss of quality of life
- Reduced ability to interact with nature
- Food shortages
- Destruction from motorized recreation
- Dust storms and super-storms
- Environmental refugees
- Trade in illegal animal parts
- Noise pollution

- Overcrowded schools, hospitals, and prisons
- High transportation costs
- Deteriorating health care systems
- Child prostitution and sexual violence
- Dead zones in our oceans

Here I would like to give a few examples of the above indicators, and how some experts believe population is connected:

WATER POVERTY

> The water problem is "chilling" and getting worse as Earth's population grows.
>
> Richard Daley
> Canadian Professor
> at United Nations University in
> Tokyo, Japan, 1999

How would you feel if you woke up one day and there were a quarter of a million more people around you than the day before? What if this happened the next day too, and the next? Would you start to panic just a little?

Well, this is exactly what is happening. Every day the world's population increases by a quarter million people. That is three people per second or 10,000 per hour more inhabitants to feed, clothe, and shelter. This certainly has me concerned.

It also has Lester Brown at the Worldwatch Institute concerned, for he warns that population growth is sentencing millions of people to water poverty. In August 2000 he addressed the Water Symposium in Sweden to draw attention to this desperate issue. He stated, "We live in a water-challenged world, one that is becoming more so each year as 80 million additional people stake their claims to the Earth's water resources. Unfortunately, nearly all the projected

3 billion people to be added over the next half century will be born in countries that are already experiencing water shortages. Even now many in these countries lack enough water to drink, to satisfy hygienic needs, and to produce food."

Despite numerous conferences around the world, experts still don't know how to solve global water shortages that are killing millions of people and causing conflict. Some experts point out that when the demand exceeds the supply, the problem can't be solved. The demand for water has tripled since 1950 and is continuing to rise as we add over 80 million people each year. Even with today's 6.7 billion people, the world has a huge water deficit. Water tables are now falling on every continent. Even more disturbing, the population is expected to rise to 9 billion by 2050 because our leaders are refusing to deal with the population problem in any meaningful way.

Many countries lack enough water to drink, satisfy hygienic needs, and produce food. So, in many cases, water shortages are becoming food shortages. With a lack of sufficient water to produce grain, many countries, such as China and Egypt, are importing record amounts of grain. It is now believed that future wars will be more likely to be fought over water than oil.

Aquifer depletion is a relatively new problem that has emerged in the last half century. The Punjab aquifer in India is falling by half a meter per year, and the aquifer under the North China plain is falling by 1.5 meters per year. Closer to home it is estimated that within twenty-five years the Ogallala aquifer, extending under eight US states, will be pumped dry to the point where it can no longer supply any serious quantity of water.

Even more alarming, many of the world's major rivers fail to make it to the sea or have very little water left when they do. The Colorado River in the United States rarely reaches the Gulf of Mexico. The Nile has little water left when it reaches the Mediterranean, and the Ganges in India is almost dry when it reaches the Bay of Bengal. China's Yellow River runs dry for part of each year, and in 1997 it ran dry for more than half the year.

Because water has traditionally been an abundant resource, and essentially free, we have been taking it for granted. However, it is now increasingly clear that with population increasing at an alarming rate, Earth's fresh water supplies are becoming a scarce resource. The Worldwatch Institute recommends that the time has come when we need to begin thinking about trying to stabilize or reduce population everywhere, limiting families to two children.

"Nearly 47 per cent of the land area of the world has international water basins that are shared by two or more countries. When levels get low, conflict can be expected," said Ralph Daley, of the International Network of Water, Environment, and Health, McMaster University in Hamilton, 1999. Lester Brown had this comment:

> It is now often said that future wars in the region will more likely be fought over water than oil. Perhaps, but given the difficulty in winning a water war, the competition for water seems more likely to take place in world grain markets. The countries that will win in this competition will be those that are financially strongest, not those that are militarily strongest.

George Monbiot in the 10 October 2006 *Guardian* stated,

> Even this account—of rising demand and falling supply—does not tell the whole grim story.
>
> Roughly half the world's population lives within 60 kilometers of the coast. Eight of the 10 largest cities on earth have been built beside the sea. Many of them rely on underground lenses of fresh water, effectively floating, within the porous rocks, on salt water which has soaked into the land from the sea. As the fresh water is sucked out, the salt water rises and can start to contaminate the aquifer. This is already happening in hundreds of places. The worst case is the Gaza Strip, which relies entirely on

> underground water that is now almost undrinkable. As the sea level rises as a result of climate change, salt pollution in coastal regions is likely to accelerate.
>
> As these two effects of climate change—global drying and rising salt pollution—run up against the growing demand for water, and as irrigation systems run dry or become contaminated, the possibility arises of a permanent global food deficit. Even with a net food surplus, 800 million people are malnourished. Nothing I could write would begin to describe what a world in deficit—carrying 9 billion people—would look like.

A 2006 United Nations report warned that the world's oceans had two hundred "dead zones" —places where pollution threatens fish, other marine life, and the people who depend on them. This showed a 34 percent jump in the number of such zones from just two years earlier. The United Nations marine experts said the number and size of oxygen-deprived zones has grown each decade since the 1970s. Not all the dead zones persist year-round, as some return seasonally, depending on winds that bring nutrient-rich water to the surface.

UN officials stated,

> The low levels of oxygen in the water make it difficult for fish, oysters and other marine creatures to survive as well as important habitats such as sea grass beds. These (low oxygen) areas are fast becoming major threats to fish stocks and thus to the people who depend upon fisheries for food and livelihoods.

So, both our oceans and rivers are being threatened by our growing population. Although our fresh water supplies are renewable through the water cycle, these supplies are also finite. That means that as our population increases, the amount of fresh water per person decreases. This is a problem that we cannot expect technology to remedy. In fact, the apparent onset of global warming has additional implications for future water supplies, and increasing our population can only worsen the situation.

Then there is the "Great Pacific Garbage Patch," which is twice the size of France. There are now 46,000 pieces of plastic per square kilometer of the world's oceans, killing a million sea birds and 100,000 marine mammals each year.

> The most significant characteristic of modern civilization is the sacrifice of the future for the present, and all the power of science has been prostituted to this purpose.
>
> William James

NOISE POLLUTION

As the population increases, it becomes more and more difficult to find peace and quiet. Most people, especially those living in cities, are bombarded daily with a barrage of noise. Traffic, sirens, and electronic gadgets are part of our everyday life. Even out in the "wilderness" it is rare to find a place to recreate without the roar of snowmobiles, quads, or dirt bikes disrupting our activities.

According to George Monbiot in *Bring on the Recession*, in 2007 the World Health Organization (WHO) warned that two in every one hundred deaths from heart disease may be caused by stress related to long-term exposure to noise. Our constant exposure to noise also contributes to strokes, high blood pressure, tinnitus, broken sleep, and other stress-related illnesses.

The racket that surrounds us creates chronic stress that keeps our bodies in a state of constant alert, even while we sleep. The WHO conducted a study that suggests that thousands of people may be dying from a lack of peace and quiet. They have yet to finalize what levels of exposure cause problems, but the threshold for cardiovascular troubles is above fifty decibels at night or sixty during the day. This is equivalent to the noise of a dishwasher.

As a study of children living close to airports in Germany suggests, it also damages long-term memory, reading , and speech perception. All over the world, complaints about noise are rising.

However, it isn't only humans that are being negatively affected by noise pollution. Studies have shown that many animals are being negatively impacted by the tremendous noise caused by off-road vehicles (ORVs) in the backcountry. These ORVs include such vehicles as quads, dirt bikes, 4x4 trucks, dune buggies, and snowmobiles.

According to the Alberta Wilderness Association, ORV use causes extreme noise pollution. Some wildlife species are adversely affected by noise in four ways:

1. hearing loss—resulting from noise levels of eighty-five decibels (dB) or greater
2. masking—the inability to hear important environmental cues and animal signals
3. non-auditory physiological effects—including anxiety, increased heart rate and respiration, and general stress reaction
4. behavioral effects—vary greatly between species and noise characteristics and can result in the abandonment of territory and lost reproduction. Long-term exposure to noise can cause excessive stimulation to the nervous system and chronic stress that is harmful to the health of wildlife species and their reproductive fitness.

The Castle Crown Wilderness Coalition in Alberta warns that Off Road Vehicles affect the behavior of many wildlife species, causing them to avoid areas used by these motorized vehicles. Of the species that have been studied, bears, wolves, and elk show the greatest negative response, with resulting large losses of habitat, as well as increased mortality.

Wolves and bears especially prefer areas away from roads and noise. In a study of grizzly bears in Yellowstone National Park, Mattson (1987) determined that collared bears tended to avoid habitats within 500 meters of roads in spring and summer, and within three kilometers of roads in the fall. Studies have also shown that songbirds avoid habitats in areas where off-road vehicle use occurs, even when the vegetation is still intact. This avoidance is believed to be due to the noise factor.

Impacts of ORVs on other recreationists can be just as disturbing. Surveys and studies show that traditional, non-motorized recreationists felt that their solitude and tranquility were compromised by the presence of ORVs, due to the extremely high levels of noise and air pollution. In 2002, the US government had to provide park service employees with respirators and earplugs to mitigate the pollution and noise of the snowmobiles in Yellowstone National Park.

The US Occupational Safety and Health Administration, the federal government agency charged with safeguarding the health of American workers, found that Yellowstone employees were being exposed to dangerous levels of noise, carbon monoxide, and benzene. Yet, the Bush administration preferred to cater to the ORV industry, despite an overwhelming public outcry.

DUST STORMS

Besides their significant noise and air pollution, the increasing numbers of off-road drivers are also being blamed for increased dust storms. In the 20 August 2004 *Ottawa Citizen*, Gillian Harris warns that desert driving is the leading cause of decay of desert ecosystems and higher air pollution. The use of off-road vehicles in deserts has contributed to a tenfold increase in dust storms around the globe and is damaging the environment and human health.

Harris notes that off-road driving in the Middle East and the southwestern United States is being blamed for destroying the deserts' fragile crust and allowing clouds of fine dust particles, smaller than a grain of sand, to be swept away.

Scientists estimate there are now three billion tons of dust being whipped thousands of kilometers around the world, generating storms across Africa, China, the Middle East, and the United States. They say Europe has yet to suffer dust storms, which can be 120 kilometers wide and last more than six hours, but Saharan dust has reached Britain, where it falls as "blood rain"—red dust particles that are borne on wind from Africa and fall in Britain as rain.

Andrew Goudie, professor of Geography at Oxford University said,

> There are a huge number of these vehicles driving across deserts now. It is quite extraordinary that, in the Middle East, nomads who used to ride camels now tend their flocks in 4x4 vehicles ... In the U.S., it is staggering how many people ride around in dune buggies, which is fun, but is also a significant cause of dust storms and pollution.

Addressing the thirtieth congress of the International Geographical Union in Glasgow in 2004, Mr. Goudie said that, in addition to creating storms that can reduce visibility to less than a kilometer, increased dust production had serious consequences for human health. He added:

> Dust storms pump herbicides and pesticides out of agricultural soil and dried-up lakebeds and send them out into the atmosphere. They carry allergens which affect people's health. In the U.S. a disease called valley fever is a big problem because it causes the nasal passages and skin to puff up ... The cross-boundary nature of dust makes it a truly global issue and one that is not receiving the attention it deserves.

Environmentalists who have monitored dust-storm data from 1947 to the late 1990s say drought, wind, overgrazing, and deforestation have led to increased dust production in areas such as the Bodele

Depression in Chad—the world's biggest source of dust—and the Taklamakan Desert in central China. They are warning that dust storms could jeopardize the future of African rural areas in the same way that the Dust Bowl of the 1930s destroyed the prairie lands of the American west, forcing the populations of states such as Oklahoma and Nebraska to migrate.

On 23 April 2009 Juliet Eilperin, *Washington Post* staff writer, had this to say about dust storms in the Colorado Rockies:

> The dust storms are a harbinger of a broader phenomenon, researchers say, as global warming translates into less precipitation and a population boom intensifies the activities that are disturbing the dust in the first place. Jayne Belnap, a research ecologist at the U.S. Geological Survey who has studied the issue, predicts that by midcentury, the fragility of the region's soil "will be equal to that of the Dust Bowl days."
>
> "We're headed for this massive soil movement, these massive dust storms on a frequency we're not used to, and it's going to have enormous ecosystem impacts," Belnap said. "No one has an appreciation for the scope of the calamitous impacts."
>
> Dust storms are not new in the West, but the fact that so much dust is on the move reflects that across vast areas, soil is being loosened by off-road vehicles, livestock grazing, and road development for oil and gas production, much of it on public land. A *Washington Post* analysis of federal data from areas managed by the Bureau of Land Management found that between 2004 and 2008, off-road vehicle use rose 19 percent, the number of oil and gas wells increased 24 percent and grazing acreage climbed 7 percent.
>
> Lawrence Odle, director of the Maricopa County Air Quality Department, said officials have little choice.

"We have vehicles that just tear across the desert," he said, adding that the county stands to lose $7 billion in federal transportation funds if it does not improve its air quality. "Do you allow for recreational activity, or do you try to get into compliance with federal health standards?"

But the Bureau of Land Management says it sees no reason to change its rules for issuing permits for dust-generating activities on the land it controls.

Wolf photo courtesy of World Society for the Protection of Animals (WSPA)

BIODIVERSITY

The loss of genetic and species diversity is the folly our descendants are least likely to forgive us.

Edward O. Wilson,
Professor at Harvard University

If trends continue, our grandchildren may live on a planet inhabited by less than half the species of plants and animals populating ours. Some people argue that extinction is a natural process, that species have always come and gone. But the National Audubon Society warns that species are vanishing from the Earth at a rate of one a day, surpassing even the mass extinctions 65 million years ago when the dinosaurs perished. And there is a major difference: today's extinctions are being caused by humans. The Audubon Society asks:

> Do we have the right to destroy a quarter or more of the Earth's species and consequently shift the course of evolution forever? And what price will we pay?

They remind us that our lives depend in myriad ways on the Earth's great diversity of species, subspecies, and ecosystems. Collapsing biological diversity threatens our food supplies, medical advances, the development of new industrial products, and many other practical needs. Even greater is the price of losing all the indirect values of rich, diverse ecosystems—including water and soil protection, climate regulation, and pest control, as well as such intangibles as recreational, scientific, and spiritual values.

> The greatness of a nation and its moral progress can be judged by the way its animals are treated … I hold that, the more helpless a creature, the more entitled it is to protection by man from the cruelty of man.
>
> Mahatma Gandhi

> What do the snow leopard, giant panda, whooping crane, green pitcher plant, noonday snail and the Queen Alexandria birdwing butterfly have in common? They are all endangered species.
>
> But not only do these, and thousands of other plants and animals share their threat of extinction, they also share a common enemy—the human species. The phenomenal growth in human population is

taking its toll as natural habitats are paved over, built on, polluted, lumbered and mined—all to "benefit" encroaching civilization ... The clash between humans and wildlife is evident in virtually every part of the country

Zero Population Growth
(now known as Population Connection),
1990

Two hundred fifty million years ago, a monumental catastrophe devastated life on Earth. We don't know the cause—perhaps glaciers, volcanoes, or even the impact of a giant meteorite—but whatever happened drove more than 90 percent of the planet's species to extinction. After the Great Dying, as the end-Permian extinction is called, Earth's biodiversity—its panoply of species—didn't bounce back for more than ten million years.

Aside from the Great Dying, there have been four other mass extinctions, all of which severely pruned life's diversity. Scientists agree that we're now in the midst of a sixth such episode. This new one, however, is different—and, in many ways, much worse. For, unlike earlier extinctions, this one results from the work of a single species, *Homo sapiens.* We are relentlessly taking over the planet, laying it to waste and eliminating most of our fellow species. Moreover, we're doing it much faster than the mass extinctions that came before. Every year, up to 30,000 species disappear due to human activity alone. At this rate, we could lose half of Earth's species in this century. And, unlike with previous extinctions, there's no hope that biodiversity will ever recover, since the cause of the decimation—us—is here to stay. On the other hand, some experts believe that we will also become extinct due to unlimited population growth.

To scientists, this is an unparalleled calamity, far more severe than global warming, which is, after all, only one of many threats to biodiversity. Yet global warming gets far more press. Why? One reason is that, while the increase in temperature is easy to document, the decrease of species is not. Biologists don't know, for example, exactly how many species exist on Earth.

Estimates range widely, from three million to more than 50 million, and that doesn't count microbes, critical (albeit invisible) components of ecosystems. We're not certain about the rate of extinction, either: how could we be, since the vast majority of species have yet to be described? We're even less sure how the loss of some species will affect the ecosystems in which they're embedded, since the intricate connection between organisms means that the loss of a single species can ramify unpredictably.

But we do know some things. Tropical rainforests are disappearing at a rate of 2 percent per year. Populations of most large fish are down to only 10 percent of what they were in 1950. Many primates, and all the great apes—our closest relatives—are nearly gone from the wild.

Jerry Coyne and Hopi Hoekstra,
"A Fate Worse Than Global Warming"
The New Republic, 24 September 2007

There are more human babies born each day—about 250,000—than there are individuals left in all the great ape species combined, including gorillas, chimpanzees, bonobo and orangutans like this one.

Richard Cincotta,
ecologist,
Population Action International

Ohio State University anthropologist Jeffrey McKee and his colleagues have been seeking a direct correlation between population growth and the number of threatened species. In a 2003 model of the impact human population growth alone has on biological diversity, they focused on mammals and birds as a kind of "canary in a coal mine" phenomenon. They concluded that if the world's human population continues to rise at its current rate, the planet will increase the numbers of threatened species at least 7 percent worldwide in the next twenty years and twice that many by the year 2050. They warn:

> If other species follow the same pattern as the mammals and birds in our study, then we are facing a serious threat to global biodiversity associated with our growing human population.

In 2000 the World Conservation Union released their RED LIST of Threatened Species, compiled from the research of scientists around the world. They announced that one in four mammal species faces extinction in the near future. Extinction also threatens more than one thousand birds, hundreds of amphibians, reptiles and fish, and more than five thousand plant species.

In 2006 the RED LIST documented 784 complete extinctions and 65 extinctions in the wild, with some individuals remaining in captivity, since 1500 AD (when historical scientific records began), but this number doesn't account for the thousands of species that go extinct before scientists even have a chance to describe them. They consider a species extinct when exhaustive surveys in known or expected habitats fail to record any individuals. Previous extinctions were due to natural causes. However, experts believe that today most extinctions are caused by humans and total dozens per day; that's roughly one hundred to 1000 times higher than previous rates.

The Red List shows that most of the world's threatened species are suffering habitat loss where livestock are a factor. United Nations scientists point out that the meat industry is one of the most significant contributors to the most serious environmental problems, at every scale from local to global including problems of land degradation, climate change and air pollution, water shortage and water pollution, and loss of biodiversity.

Today it is estimated that 99 percent of threatened species are at risk from human activities. It is also believed that 16,119 species are threatened with extinction, but this may be a gross underestimate because fewer than 3 percent of the world's 1.9 million described species have been assessed by the Red List.

One animal that symbolizes this crisis is the Spix's macaw, a blue-gray Brazilian parrot of which only one remains in the wild. The macaw, which lives in the dry scrubland, has been driven to the brink of extinction by habitat destruction and the exotic pet trade.

The exotic pet trade also uses rare wildlife in meals and medicine, a centuries-old habit that is hard to break. Wild animals on the endangered-species list are continuing to find their way to specialty restaurants for diners willing to pay. The extravagant prices charged for wildlife dishes are no deterrent for those who have the money and power.

A recent report by the World Wildlife Fund found medicine containing rhinoceros horn and tiger bone still available in shops across China, three years after the government banned all commercial use of the products. An underlying problem is a general lack of compassion for animals.

Ian Warkentin, of Memorial University in Corner Brook, N.L., warns that humans are also eating frogs into extinction, as we harvest at least 400 million frog legs each year. He says that frog populations, already under pressure from disease, climate change, and habitat loss, could go the way of Canada's East Coast cod stocks.

Population growth, as E. O. Wilson says, is "the monster on the land."

In his AlterNet posting of 11 March 2009 Chris Hedges' article "Are We Breeding Ourselves to Extinction?" warns that we are experiencing an accelerated obliteration of the planet's life forms because, simply put, there are too many people. Most of these extinctions are the direct result of the expanding need for energy, housing, food, and other resources. The Yangtze River dolphin, Atlantic gray whale, West African black rhino, Merriam's elk, California grizzly bear, silver trout, blue pike, and dusky seaside sparrow are all victims of human overpopulation.

Hedges cautions that if the current rate of extinction continues, *Homo sapiens* will be one of the few life-forms left on the planet, its members scrambling violently among themselves for water, food, fossil fuels, and perhaps air until they too disappear.

I invite anyone to meet the great challenge of Professor Al Bartlett:

> *Can you think of any problem, in any area of human endeavor, on any scale, from microscopic to global, whose LONG-TERM solution is in any DEMONSTRABLE way aided, assisted or advanced by further increases in population, locally, nationally, or globally?*

No one has been able to meet Bartlett's challenge since he set it out on 8 January 1996. A. A. Bartlett is Professor Emeritus of Physics at the University of Colorado, Boulder.

> Anyone who believes exponential growth can go on forever in a finite world is either a madman or an economist.

Kenneth Boulding, Professor of Economics, University of Colorado, Boulder

According to the UN:

> Indeed, the livestock sector may well be the leading player in the reduction of biodiversity … Livestock now account for about 20 percent of the total terrestrial animal biomass, and the 30 percent of the earth's land surface that they now preempt was once habitat for wildlife.

Comic used with permission from Mike Keefe

CLIMATE CHANGE (Climate Disruption)

On 9 September 2009 Optimum Population Trust presented a news release entitled "Contraception is 'Greenest' Technology." Their research showed that contraception is almost five times cheaper than conventional green technologies as a means of combating climate change.

They added that each seven dollars spent on basic family planning over the next four decades would reduce global CO^2 emissions by more than a ton. To achieve the same result with low-carbon technologies would cost a minimum of thirty-two dollars. The UN estimates that 40 percent of all pregnancies worldwide are unintended.

I suppose one cannot address population without addressing the huge amount of air pollution produced by our growing population. However, I am not going to get caught up in the ongoing debates taking place in the realm of the skeptics. I don't need to dwell on the overwhelming scientific evidence, charts, graphs, or other convincing data. For me the most compelling evidence that mankind has managed to disrupt the natural flow of things is just one image. It is the heartbreaking image of a polar bear stranded on an ice flow in the middle of the Arctic. That is real. That is evidence. And that is testament to our disturbing disconnection to nature.

The plight of the polar bear has touched the hearts of people around the world, including Al Gore and Oprah. In fact, the polar bear has become the poster child for climate change, and rightly so. To deny that mankind played a role in this tragedy is extremely irresponsible and delusional.

> The Arctic is often cited as the canary in the coal mine for climate warming … and now as a sign of climate warming, the canary has died.
>
> Dr. Jay Zwally,
> NASA climate scientist,
> December 2007

We do know that the last decade has seen the most extreme weather conditions within recorded history, corresponding with the highest population levels in recorded history. This scenario has led to increased species extinction, the spread of arid regions, and stronger floods, droughts, and forest fires.

John Holmes—the United Nations Undersecretary General for Humanitarian Affairs and Emergency Relief Coordinator—addressed this issue in his "Disasters—the New Normal" presentation (blog posted on 4 September 2009). He had this to say:

> After the terrible human toll from natural disasters in 2008, people could be forgiven for thinking that the worst must be over. Surely we could not see such a year repeated? A year when the mudslides, wildfires, typhoons and volcano eruptions that usually make headlines became sideshows to the devastating cyclone Nargis in Myanmar, the Sichuan earthquake in China, droughts and floods in Africa and Asia, and successive hurricanes in Central America. Together

they killed three times as many people as the annual average.

But I fear any such optimists would be wrong. We already have enough data from the last decade to know that natural disasters kill and displace more and more people, year on year. The projections of more drought and reduced agriculture yields in Africa, widespread heavy flooding in Asia, more wildfires in Australia, stronger and more frequent storms in the Caribbean, are playing out right now. The number of people affected by drought alone is increasing by around 5 million every year.

The humanitarian community faces the challenge of responding more effectively than ever, with the same resources, when the evidence is unequivocal that climate change will increase the frequency and intensity of deadly hazard events. How best to help, when major disasters can already be overwhelming for even the richest, best equipped countries, let alone their poorer—and less prepared—counterparts? And when most of the catastrophes actually occur in the poorest countries, and affect the poorest people the most?

For a start, we must change our mindsets. While mitigating the advance of climate change through reducing emissions is the best way to protect future generations, that strategy has little to offer to the 164 million people who were affected by natural disasters last year, and the hundreds of millions more whom we know will be affected in the decades to come. The focus on mitigation must not obscure the dramatic impact that climate change is already having on millions of mainly poor and vulnerable people in developing countries.

> Those people need help now to adapt to their new reality ... **Extreme weather is the new normal in this century**. The sooner that is recognized, the sooner we can set about creating the tools and systems that can make extreme weather events less deadly.

In March 2009 parched Australia experienced one of these extreme weather scenarios. Melbourne thermometers topped forty-three degrees centigrade on a third successive day for the first time on record, while Adelaide hit a staggering 45.6 degrees centigrade. Ministers are blaming the heat—which follows a record drought—on global warming. Experts worry that Australia, which emits more carbon dioxide per head than any nation on earth, may also be the first to implode under that impact of climate change.

> It's the extremes, not the average, that cause the most damage to society and to many ecosystems. We now have the first model-based consensus on how the risk of dangerous heat waves, intense rains, and other kinds of extreme weather will change in the next century.
>
> Environmental News Service,
> 29 October 2006
> "Scientists Predict Future of Weather Extremes"

In the *State of the World 2002,* the Worldwatch Institute warned that there was already evidence that regional climate changes had affected a wide range of physical and biological systems. These changes include glacier shrinkage, permafrost thawing, later freezing and earlier buildup of ice on rivers and lakes, lengthening of mid- to high-latitude growing seasons, shifts of plant and animal ranges, declines of plant and animal populations, and earlier flowering of trees, emergence of insects, and egg-laying by birds. They add:

> Scientists have uncovered new knowledge about the vulnerability of various systems. Several natural systems are recognized as especially at risk of irreversible damage, including glaciers, coral reefs

> and atolls, mangroves, boreal and tropical forests, polar and alpine ecosystems, prairie wetlands, and remnant native grasslands. Climate change will increase existing risk of extinction of the more vulnerable species and the loss of biodiversity, with the extent of the damage increasing with the rate and magnitude of change.

Projected adverse impacts to human systems include:

- A reduction in potential crop yields in most tropical and subtropical regions for most temperature increases.
- Decreased water availability for populations in many water-scarce regions, notably in the subtropics.
- An increase in the number of people exposed to vector-borne and water-borne diseases (such as malaria and cholera) and an increase in heat stress mortality.
- A widespread increase in the risk of flooding for tens of millions of people, due to both increased heavy precipitation events and sea level rise.

Of course, the oil giants are not happy with these scientific reports regarding climate change, according to an article in the 19 May 2007 *Ottawa Citizen*. Reporter Mike De Souza cites a Greenpeace USA report that revealed grants from US oil giant ExxonMobil to forty-one think tanks that have questioned climate-change science or opposed government action to reduce greenhouse gas pollution with doomsday economic forecasts. Overall, Greenpeace estimates ExxonMobil has donated nearly $23 million to denial organizations since 1998.

> What do the following have in common: the carbon dioxide content of the atmosphere, Earth's average temperature and the size of the human population? Answer; each was, for a long period of Earth's history, held in a state of equilibrium. Whether it's the burning of fossil fuels versus the rate at which plants

> absorb carbon, or the heat absorbed from sunshine versus the heat reflected back into space, or global birth rates versus death rates—each is governed by the difference between an inflow and an outflow, and even small imbalances can have large effects. At present, all of these three are out of balance as a result of human actions. And each of these imbalances is creating a major problem.
>
> "This Planet Ain't Big Enough for the 6,500,000,000,"
> Published 27 June 2007
> *The Independent* by Chris Rapley

"Indigenous Communities Unite against Climate Change" is a news release that was posted on the NUNATSIAQ website on 17 April 2009. Many indigenous communities have come together to form a group, Many Strong Voices, which includes people from the Arctic and the tiny coral isles sprinkled throughout the globe's oceans. Nunavut, Niue, and Sahka are all populated by indigenous communities that are being adversely affected by climate change.

In April 2009, officials and scientists from these disparate lands met in Washington, DC to discuss how to bring attention to their common climate crises. Delegates at this conference included Nunavummiut along with Micronesians, Cook Islanders, Athabaskans, Barbadians, and Seychellans. The near-term goal of Many Strong Voices is to gain support for the greatest emissions reductions possible at the UN Climate Conference in Copenhagen in December 2009.

"We want to tell the world that the Inuit hunter falling through the ice and the Pacific Islander fishing on rising seas are connected," said Sheila Watt-Cloutier, former president of the Inuit Circumpolar Council and a nominee for the 2007 Nobel Peace Prize.

The fifteenth UN Climate Conference was held in Copenhagen on 30 November 2009. The Climate Camp website states that the facts are clear. Global climate change, caused by human activities, is happening, threatening the lives and livelihoods of billions of people and the existence of millions of species. Social movements, environmental groups, and scientists from all over the world are calling for urgent and radical action on climate change.

At this Climate Conference, governments of the world united at the biggest summit on climate change ever to take place. But will this event prove to be more successful than those of the past, which produced nothing more than business as usual?

Climate Camp is calling on all peoples around the planet to mobilize and take action against the root causes of climate change and the key agents responsible, both in Copenhagen and around the world. This mobilization begins now, until the COP-15 summit, and beyond. Get involved at *www.climatecamp.org.uk*.

> If any fraction of the observed global warming can be attributed to the action of humans, then this by itself is positive proof that the human population has exceeded the carrying capacity of the earth.
>
> As a result, it is an inconvenient truth that any actions or programs to reduce global warming that do not center on population reductions are what Mark Twain called "Silent Lies."
>
> A. A. Bartlett

GLOBAL DIMMING

On 15 January 2005, the BBC broadcast its weekly acclaimed *Horizon* documentary, which can be found at *www.globalissues.org/print/article/529*. This episode was about a dangerous phenomenon called global dimming.

According to this documentary, global dimming is caused by pollution in the atmosphere, such as sulphur dioxide, soot, and ash, creating more water droplets in the clouds. Those clouds then reflect more of the sun's heat back into space, so less is reaching the earth. This causes a cooling effect, until efforts to reduce pollution are successful, as they have been in some areas. Then the cooling reverses, and a warming trend returns with even greater intensity.

The pollutants that lead to global dimming also lead to various human and environmental problems, such as smog, respiratory problems, and acid rain. Therefore, it is imperative that we make every effort to reduce these pollutants to protect our health and ecosystems.

Climatologists studying this phenomenon believe that the reflection of heat has made waters in the northern hemisphere cooler. As a result, less rain has formed in key areas and crucial rainfall has failed to arrive over the Sahel in Northern Africa. In the 1970s and 1980s, massive famines were caused by failed rains, and climatologists never quite understood why they had failed.

The answers that global dimming models seemed to provide, the documentary noted, has led to a chilling conclusion: "What came out of our exhaust pipes and power stations (from Europe and North America) contributed to the deaths of a million people in Africa, and afflicted 50 million more" with hunger and starvation.

Scientists said that the impact of global dimming might not be in the millions, but billions of dollars. The Asian monsoons bring rainfall to half the world's population. If this air pollution and global dimming has a detrimental impact on the Asian monsoons, some 3 billion people could be affected.

Another source of heat reflection is contrails (the atmospheric condensation of vapor from the engines of aircraft flying high in the sky). During the aftermath of the 11 September 2001 terrorist attacks in the United States, all commercial flights were grounded for the next three days as a safety precaution. This had the fortunate effect of allowing climate scientists to look at the effect on the climate when there were no contrails and no heat reflection. What scientists found was that the earth's temperature rose by some one degree centigrade in that three-day period. They believe that global dimming is hiding the true power of global warming.

Currently, most climate change models predict a five-degree increase in temperature over the next century, which is already considered extremely grave. However, global dimming has led to an underestimation of the power of global warming.

Addressing global dimming alone, without addressing global warming, will lead to massive global warming—possibly an increase of ten degrees centigrade over the next hundred years.

"This is not a prediction," the documentary said, "it is a warning of what will happen if we clean up the pollution while doing nothing about greenhouse gases."

FOOD

> **I wish I could have a free lunch for every time I've heard someone declare "Malthus was wrong."** …
>
> Meanwhile, man-made forces are conspiring to put a ceiling on food production. Global warming and the resulting climate change may well be increasing the incidence of extreme weather events, as well as inflicting permanent damage on some farming regions. At the same time, our effort to slow global warming by switching from fossil fuels to biofuels is taking large tracts of land out of food production.
>
> Some people worry about peak oil—when we reach the peak of petroleum production. I worry about peak grain. With the world population growth outpacing food supply, say goodbye to the era of unlimited improvement.
>
> Niall Ferguson,
> *Los Angeles Times,*
> 30 July 2007

Thomas Malthus published the first edition of his "Essay on the Principle of Population" in 1798. His premise was that there must be a “strong and constantly operating check on population.” This would take two forms: “misery” and “vice,” by which he meant not only alcohol abuse but also contraception and abortion (he was, after all, an Anglican minister).

Although his predicted food shortages and mass starvation did not materialize as quickly as he had anticipated, there was good reason for this. Ferguson explains:

> The conventional explanation for this is the succession of revolutions in global agriculture, culminating in the postwar “green revolution” and the current wave of genetically modified crops. Since the 1950s, the area of the world under cultivation has increased by roughly 11%, while yields per hectare (about 2.5 acres) have increased by 120%. Yet these statistics don’t disprove Malthus. As he said, food production could increase only at an arithmetical rate, and a chart of world cereal yields since 1960 shows just such a linear progression, from below 1.5 metric tons to around 3.
>
> The agricultural advances of the “Green Revolution” made substantial contributions against hunger, bringing high-yield crops and new techniques to food production. Crop harvests increased more than two and one-half times between 1950 and 1984. But while highly successful, the Green Revolution also established environmentally harmful practices, causing land degradation and groundwater contamination to the point where future food production has been jeopardized.

Zero Population Growth points out that agriculture is the most intensive way in which humans affect the land, and through conventional agriculture much of that impact has been negative. In fact, there is increasing evidence that our resources are being depleted at a rate beyond which they can replenish themselves.

> *In effect, we are feeding ourselves at the expense of our children.*
>
> Lester Brown
> of the Worldwatch Institute, 1992

> *Modern agriculture is the use of land to convert petroleum into food.*
>
> A. Bartlet

Famine

> A new crisis is emerging, a global food catastrophe that will reach further and be more crippling than anything the world has ever seen. The credit crunch and the reverberations of soaring oil prices around the world will pale in comparison to what is about to transpire.
>
> Donald Coxe,
> global portfolio strategist at BMO Financial Group,
> April 2009, *National Post*

Wikipedia, the free encyclopedia, defines a famine as a widespread shortage of food that may apply to any faunal species, which phenomenon is usually accompanied by regional malnutrition, starvation, epidemic, and increased mortality.

Historically, famines have occurred among the poor because of agricultural problems such as drought, crop failure, or pestilence. A famine can be made worse by war, or economic policies that place the poor at a disadvantage. Epidemics can reduce available labor. Changing weather patterns and the ineffectiveness of medieval governments in dealing with crises, wars, and epidemic diseases like the Black Death helped to cause hundreds of famines in Europe during the Middle Ages, including ninety-five in Britain and seventy-five in France.

During the twentieth century, an estimated 70 million people died from famines across the world, of whom an estimated 30 million died during the famine of 1958–61 in China.

Canadians have been cushioned from the recent famines—and the food riots and hunger that are ravaging much of the planet at present. CBC news reported that, for the first time in recent memory, there were food riots in 2007 in a host of countries ranging from Zimbabwe and Morocco to Mexico, Hungary, and Austria. Russia and Pakistan introduced food rationing for the first time in decades (and Pakistani troops were sent out to guard imported wheat). To conserve dwindling stocks, India has banned the export of rice, except for high-end basmati, and other big rice-eating countries, notably the Philippines, are talking of a "rice crisis" and promoting drastic measures to guarantee supply.

According to the UN's World Food Program, the root causes of today's higher prices are rising energy costs, the almost decade-long drought in Australia (an important exporter), and the flourishing middle classes in China and India, who have developed a taste for grain-fed beef, pork, and chicken. Also, a large portion of our grain crops is going into the production of biofuels.

> **We've gone from competing with our animals for grain to competing with our cars.**
>
> Harriet Friedmann,
> Sociology Professor at University of Toronto,
> 2008

Friedman adds that the world has seen large-scale food shortages and spikes in commodity prices before, but this time could be different. We have made obtaining food much more income-dependent than ever before. She says:

> Even in the Depression in the 1930s, most people tended to know someone on a farm. They could barter for food. Doctors were paid in chickens. That

> is not the case anymore. If you don't have money, you won't eat well.

United Nations Secretary General Ban Ki-moon has described the current situation as the worst international crisis since the Second World War.

> Nothing will benefit human health and increase chances for survival for life on earth as much as the evolution to a vegetarian diet.
>
> Albert Einstein, 1921

Of course, you don't have to be an Einstein to know that a meat-based diet is having a devastating impact on our planet. There have been numerous books written about the many harmful effects of eating meat, to both our bodies and our planet. Two of my favorites are *Diet for a New America* by John Robbins and *Your Heart, Your Planet* by Harvey Diamond.

It always amazes me to see so many people who devote their entire lives to protecting wildlife and habitat. Yet, these same people give hardly a thought to the pain and suffering of domestic food animals that provide our society's meat-based diet. Having been a vegetarian for over twenty-one years now, I can't imagine returning to a lifestyle that causes such misery for our fellow beings. According to the UN:

> In all, livestock production accounts for 70 percent of all agricultural land and 30 percent of the land surface of the planet … 70 percent of previous forested land in the Amazon is occupied by pastures, and feedcrops cover a large part of the remainder … About 20 percent of the world's pastures and rangelands, with 73 percent of rangelands in dry areas, have been degraded to some extent, mostly through overgrazing, compaction and erosion created by livestock action.

Land Degradation

One of the most severe problems is degradation of land—the backbone of agriculture. According to the World Resources Institute, the productivity of 11 percent of Earth's vegetated land surface, an area equivalent to the combined size of India and China, has already been diminished by human activity.

James Howard Kunster, in *The Long Emergency* (2006), warns that our methods of food production are unsustainable. He says,

> As industrial agriculture reached its climax in the early twenty-first century, the fine-grained, hierarchical complex relations between the soil and the human beings and animals associated with food production have been destroyed or replaced by artificial substitutes. Farmland has in effect been strip-mined for short-term gain. Instead of soil stewardship achieved by acquired knowledge of practices such as crop rotation, manuring, and fallowing, corporate farmers just dump industrial fertilizers and toxins on ground that has been transformed from an ecology of organisms to a sterile growth medium for crop monocultures.

In developing nations, land is abandoned as harmful farming practices, exacerbated by rapidly expanding populations, cause insurmountable degradation. The American Farmland Trust calculates that the United States loses more than one million acres of productive farmland to urban sprawl each year—an area larger than the state of Delaware. And as humanity continues to expand its footprint, wetlands and other environmentally sensitive areas are further threatened by conversion to cropland. Conventional agriculture also ties into concerns about the loss of biodiversity and genetic material. As more and more open space is converted to farmland or cattle grazing, plant and animal species become endangered or extinct.

Zero Population Growth warns that new technology in agriculture has also brought new health risks. "Pesticide use has increased to more than 800 million pounds a year in the United States alone, and pesticides and fertilizers used in agriculture are among the largest sources of U.S. water pollution. In addition to polluting water supplies, modern agriculture's intensive water usage is depleting groundwater aquifers, resulting in water shortages and fostering reliance on energy intensive irrigation." Sustainable agriculture appears to be a long ways off.

In the June 2007 *Independent*, Chris Rapley ponders the remarkable population growth from 1 billion in 1800 to 6.5 billion in 2007. This is an average growth rate of 0.90 percent per year. He states,

> Impressive increases in the food supply have played a part, but the underlying driver has been the shift from an "organic" society, in which energy was drawn from the wind, water, beasts of burden (including humans) and wood, to a fossil fuel-based world in which most of our energy is obtained burning coal, oil, and gas. This transition has fuelled the changes in quality of life associated with modern technology, especially the major advances in hygiene and medicine. Although unevenly distributed, these bounties have seen life expectancy double and a corresponding reduction in mortality rates.
>
> But success in reducing mortality has not been matched by a lowering of the birth rate—and this has resulted in the dramatic increase in the human stock ... This is not comforting news. Even at current levels, the World Health Organization reports that more than three billion people are malnourished. And although food availability continues to grow, per capita grain availability has been declining since the eighties. Technology may continue to push back the limits, but 50 per cent of plants and animals are already harvested for our use, creating a huge impact on our partner species and the world's ecosystems.

> And it is the airborne waste from our energy production that is driving climate change.

FOOD AND NATIONAL SECURITY

> Food and security may not be a twosome that comes quickly to mind, but experts know that our food supply is particularly vulnerable. We're familiar with the hardships that follow spikes in the price of gas or the freezing of credit lines, but few of us in the U.S. have experienced the panic and privation of a broken food chain—so far. That's going to change in the decades ahead. Count on it, even if it seems as unlikely today as, for most of us, an economic meltdown did just one short year ago.

Alternet posting on 3 March 2009 by Chip Ward

"Our Worst Enemies Aren't Terrorists: Rethinking National Security on a Sinking Planet"

Ward recalls the shortages and ensuing food riots in thirty countries across the planet in 2008 as grim coming attractions for life on a planet with unpredictable extreme weather, booming populations, overloaded ecosystems, and distorted food economies. The spike in prices that put food staples out of reach of rioting masses of people was soon enough mitigated by the collapse of energy prices when the global economy tanked. He warns,

> Make no mistake, though: food shortages and the social unrest that goes with them will eventually return. The typical American meal travels, on average, 1,000 miles to get to your plate. The wheat in your burger bun may be from Canada, the beef from Argentina, and the tomato from Chile. Food shipped from that far away is vulnerable to all sorts of disruptions—a calamitous storm that hits a food-growing center; spikes in the price of fuel for fertilizer, farm machinery, and trucking; internecine

> strife or regional wars that shut down harvests or block trade routes; national policies to hoard food as prices spike or scarcities set in; not to speak of the usual droughts, floods, and crop failures that have always plagued humankind and are intensifying in a globally warming world.

Ward adds,

> When a severe drought in Australia led to plummeting rice production in the Murray River Basin last year, the price of rice across the planet suddenly doubled. The spike in rice prices, like the sudden leap in the cost of wheat, soy, and other staples, was primarily due to the then-soaring price of oil for farm machinery, fertilizer, and transport, though rampant market speculation contributed as well. At that moment, the collapse of Australian rice farming pushed a worsening situation across a threshold into crisis territory. Because the world agricultural trade system is so thoroughly interconnected and interdependent, a shock on one part of the planet can resonate far and wide—just as (we've learned to our dismay) can happen in financial markets.

China, with its 1.3 billion people, is also in grave danger of massive food shortages. In an interview conducted by Andreas Lorenz with China's Deputy Minister of the Environment on 7 March 2005, Minister Pan Yue said, "The Chinese miracle will end soon."

> China has dazzled the world in recent years with the economic strides being made, but it has come at a huge cost to the country's environment. Pollution and population will soon overwhelm the country and will create millions of "environmental refugees."

Minister Pan explained,

> Many factors are coming together here: Our raw materials are scarce, we don't have enough land, and our population is constantly growing. Currently, there are 1.3 billion people living in China, that's twice as many as 50 years ago. (This is an average growth rate of 1.39 percent per year.) In 2020, there will be 1.5 billion people in China. Cities are growing but desert areas are expanding at the same time; habitable and usable land has been halved over the past 50 years.

Farmland in California is also disappearing. California loses about 100,000 acres of productive farmland annually to urban growth, fueled by a search for cheap land to house the 350,000 to 700,000 new California residents each year

Of course, the food shortage is alarmingly apparent in Africa. In the *Economist*, 10 August 2006, the article "The Path to Ruin" gives a vivid description:

> Bossaso is an exit point from the Horn of Africa and it is bursting. This port in northern Somalia already has 300,000 people, up from 50,000 in the 1990s. More arrive each day. It is a raw place ... Several thousand Ethiopians sleep rough in Bossaso's dirt, like animals. They are sustained by Muslim alms: a free meal each day, paid for by Bossaso traders. Some of the Ethiopians arrive in town feral with hunger. They have to be beaten back with cudgels when the meal is served. The hope of all of them is to be illegally trafficked across the sea to Yemen. They slip out of town in the moonlight, cramming into metal skiffs that are death traps. Many drown in the crossing: the boat sinks or they are tossed overboard by traffickers when Yemeni patrols approach. Some of the men interviewed in Bossaso for this story have since drowned in this way. Refugee agencies say only

> a few of those who survive will find jobs in Saudi Arabia. The rest will drift, disappear, or die young.
>
> It wouldn't take much for famine to seize hold of the area. Humanitarian action has kept the starving alive, but it has not enabled them to recover their lives. The trend is an ever increasing need for food aid plus ever less money from donors to pay for it. The World Food Programme (WFP) is responsible for delivering most of the aid in the Horn. It says that the number of Ethiopians on its books has doubled since the 1990s, in bad years to as many as 10 million. The situation is not much better elsewhere. Some 1.7 million hungry people are reliant on food aid in south Somalia—when the WFP can get it to them. And 3 million people in Kenya, mostly in the country's arid north, will get some kind of food aid this year.

"Our Last Chance to Win the War on Hunger" by William Paddock in the *Carrying Capacity Network Handbook* (1994) has this to say about food:

> A Chinese proverb says unless we change direction, we will wind up where we are going. Where we are going in the War on Hunger lies defeat, a defeat assisted by plant pathologists, a defeat with the catastrophic consequences of a tripling of world population. Can we change direction? The record suggests not. Plant pathologists collectively have been unable to advance beyond our 1950s assumption on how to fight world hunger. Thus, we share responsibility for the spending of billions of dollars on a strategy that has resulted in more hunger, not less, and "threatens the very existence of mankind."
>
> If these are blasphemous words, they fit the axiom, "All great truths begin as blasphemy." Most plant pathologists believe the world food shortage

> should be fought by increasing food production. Unfortunately, the approach is fallacious. Every shortage of supply is caused by a longage of demand. Thus, the world food shortage will be solved only by reducing the longage.
>
> Like knowing the time the first nuclear device exploded (5:30 AM 16 July 1945), it is known when the fuse was lit on today's population bomb: February 1935.
>
> William Paddock, 1990

February 1935: the month Gerhard Domagk, a pharmaceutical chemist, discovered Prontosil, the first of the sulfa drugs. It was a turning point in medicine when it was learned that bacteria could be attacked within the living body. This was followed by the discovery of penicillin in 1939.

Paddock adds that simultaneously in 1939 another technological breakthrough came when the insecticidal properties of DDT were discovered by Paul Herman Muller. Again, World War II rushed the product into production. DDT became a major factor in the increase in food production during the next twenty years. It became a cornerstone of a worldwide effort to eliminate malaria.

Paddock points out:

> In the 40 years before 1940, the population of Mexico grew 52% (from 13 to 19.8 million—an average growth rate of 1.052 percent per year). A serious population growth? Yes, but manageable. However, in the next 40 years it grew by 251% (from 19.8 to 69.4 million—an average growth rate of 3.14 percent per year). A serious growth? No. *A frightening and unmanageable explosion.* What happened in Mexico happened in varying degrees throughout the developing world. The results of the wonder penicillin and the miracle DDT were 20th century

> equivalents of Ireland's 19th century potato. Muller, Chain, Florey, and Fleming all received the Nobel Prize for discoveries that ironically turned loose the unprecedented human growth rate now threatening the survival of much of humankind.

It is interesting to note that it was also within that next forty years that the Vatican gained veto status in the United Nations. It was in 1964 that the Vatican (Holy See) was granted the status of permanent observer state. In that capacity, the Holy See has been able to influence the decisions and recommendations of the United Nations with their relentless campaigns against family planning programs. Also, during that period there was a shift to petroleum-based energy for agriculture, allowing for increased food production.

Within fifteen years after inauguration of the United States foreign aid crusade, it became abundantly clear it wasn't working. Billions were spent to alleviate hunger and reduce poverty—but every year there was more hunger, and more poverty. Paddock advises,

> Because of our expertise and historical background, plant pathologists have an obligation to send an accurate message to world leadership. Governments must be told, in a way they can hear, that they are condemning their citizens to greater poverty when they leave to the future, action on the sticky problem of exponential population growth and that political tar baby: motivating their citizenry to have fewer children.

THE ENVIRONMENTAL COMMUNITY

The 1970s ushered in a new era of freedom of expression that manifested in various ways. Modern art, psychedelic music, the flower-power lifestyle, and a new awakening to issues of the day were all part of the "mod" scene. For many, these issues included the environment and population, as the hippie community searched for more meaningful and long-term solutions to world problems.

Protesters were demonstrating against the Vietnam War, and John Lennon's songs "Imagine" and "Give Peace a Chance" became part of the new peace movement that swept the planet. It was a time when anything seemed possible. The first heart transplant had just been performed, the first test-tube baby had been conceived, the first Boeing 747 jumbo jet had just been introduced, and the first man had walked on the moon. There was a new realization, after the Woodstock phenomenon, that by working together the 70s generation had the power to create their own destiny. Today, there are many people looking back at that time and wondering what happened to derail the momentum of the hippie era.

Alan Kuper, in his article "From Sentience to Silence" had this to say about it:

> In the heady days of the new environmental awareness, at the first big Earth Day celebration in April 1979, the ecological threat posed by U.S. population growth was part of every discussion. David Brower, executive director of the Sierra Club, had encouraged Paul Ehrlich to write "The Population Bomb," which became a runaway best-seller. The educational work of the new organization Zero Population Growth, or ZPG, became familiar to American school children. In 1972 the Sierra Club, the nation's premier conservation organization, adopted a ZPG platform, declaring as one of its objectives to "... bring about the stabilization of the population first of the United States and then of the world." Other groups made similar commitments.

Similarly, David Nicholson-Lord remembers back in his Internet Forum Article "Whatever Happened to the Teeming Millions?". Like many of us, he feels that when it comes to dealing with population issues, we are going backward. He states,

> In the 1960's and 70's, concern about population growth was a mainstream environmental issue. Paul Ehrlich wrote *The Population Bomb*: pressure groups flourished—Population Countdown in the UK, Zero Population Growth in the US. In 1973 a government-appointed panel declared that Britain's population could not "go on increasing indefinitely" and the government should "define its attitude" to the issue. The newly founded Ecology Party debated sustainable population levels, Oxfam publicly supported zero population growth and Greenpeace's slogans included "Stop at Two."
>
> Three decades later, the mainstream has largely abandoned the topic. Greenpeace says it's "not an issue for us," Oxfam doesn't list it on its website A-Z, the Greens didn't even mention it in their 2005 election manifesto. Population Countdown, worried about alienating funders, became Population Concern and, more recently, Interact Worldwide. Zero Population Growth, for similar reasons, morphed into Population Connection. As an issue, population is, in short, off the radar.

So, what happened?

Well, there were a number of factors involved in this disappearing act.

- Many people were distracted by the Vietnam war.
- Paul Erlich's prediction of mass starvation was too "time-specific" and was dismissed by many.
- The baby boomers became less idealistic.
- The rise of the religious right in North America put a damper on both environmental concerns and birth control.
- Many population myths arose to cloud the issue.

- The growth lobby became very active in supporting the growth ethic.

The Dreaded Three D's: Delusion, Denial, and Deception

Greg Wood

> All serious environmentalists know perfectly well that population growth, exploding in the 20th century, has been a key driver of every environmental problem. It's a fact, not an opinion, that total human impact is the average per person multiplied by the number of people …
>
> Yet for far too long, governments and environmental NGOs have observed a taboo—invented in the 1980s by a bizarre coalition of the religious right and the liberal left—on stating this obvious fact. So they keep on implying that our numbers can grow forever with no ill effects. It's a "silent lie" and by encouraging us to ignore the vital need to stabilize our numbers by humane means (contraception) before nature does it for us by inhumane, natural means (famine, disease, was) this absurd taboo betrays our children.
>
> David's breaking of this taboo should embolden others in the green movement to follow suit.

Roger Martin, Optimum Population Trust chair, news release, 13 April 2009

"Attenborough Is New OPT Patron: Greens Urged To Spell Out Population Dangers"

> I've seen wildlife under mounting human pressure all over the world and it's not just from human economy or technology—behind every threat is the frightening explosion in human numbers. I've never seen a problem that wouldn't be easier to solve with fewer people, or harder, and ultimately impossible,

> with more. That's why I support the OPT, and I wish the environmental NGOs would follow their lead, and spell out this central problem loud and clear.

Sir David Attenborough, Britain's best-known natural history film-maker, 13 April 2009, Patron of Optimum Population Trust, trustee of the British Museum and Royal Botanical Gardens, Kew, and a fellow of the Royal Society, knighted in 1985.

On 18 April 2009 *Newstrack India* posted an article, "Overpopulation Is World's #1 Environmental Issue." According to a survey of the faculty at the SUNY (State University of New York) College of Environmental Science and Forestry, overpopulation is the world's top environmental issue, followed closely by climate change and the need to develop renewable energy to replace fossil fuels.

According to this article, the faculty at the college, at which environmental issues are a primary focus, was asked to help prioritize the planet's most pressing environmental problems. Overpopulation came out on top, with several professors pointing out its ties to other problems that rank high on the list:

- "Overpopulation is the only problem," said Dr. Charles A. Hall, a systems ecologist. "If we had 100 million people on Earth—or better, 10 million—no others would be a problem," he added.
- According to Dr. Allan P. Drew, a forest ecologist, "Overpopulation means that we are putting more carbon dioxide into the atmosphere than we should, just because more people are doing it and this is related to overconsumption by people in general, especially in the 'developed' world."
- "But, whether developed or developing, everyone is encouraged to 'want' and perceive that they 'need' to consume beyond the planet's ability to provide," said Dr. Susan Senecah, who teaches the history of the American Environment Movement at SUNY.

ENVIRONMENT GROUPS:

AFRICAN WILDLIFE FOUNDATION

In 1961, the African Wildlife Leadership Foundation was founded at the height of the African independence movement to help newly independent African nations and people conserve their own wildlife.

Since then, this organization, now called the African Wildlife Foundation, has played a major role in ensuring the continued existence of some of Africa's most rare and treasured species, including the elephant, mountain gorilla, rhinoceros and lion. They are presently working in Congo, Virunga, Samburu, Kilimanjaro, Maasai Steppe, Zambezi, Kasungula, and Limpopo. Regarding population, they have this to say:

> For thousands of years, the wildlife and people of Africa co-existed in balance. In the 20th century, wildlife faced escalating pressure from a growing population and its effects, from habitat destruction to spread of disease, to overhunting. The balance was upset.

Audubon Society (Washington DC, USA)

> There is no issue of importance to the environmental community that is not affected by the increasing number of humans on the planet. Unless we can limit population growth, we cannot achieve ecological stability.
>
> Peter Berle,
> President, National Audubon Society
> From "Why Population Matters" handbook, 1991

There are numerous environment groups that have tackled the population issue in the past, but few of them are still working at it. One is the National Audubon Society. They believe that population is one of the single largest factors contributing to the degradation of the earth's environment, the alteration of its climate, and the loss of many plant and animal species. They warn that the dramatic and unprecedented reproductive success of our own species is now a major contributor toward worrisome and perhaps irreversible changes in that environment.

In their handbook, *Why Population Matters*, they say, "Homo sapiens, long thought to be the most intelligent life-form on Earth, is doing what few wild animals ever do: fouling its own nest."

As the cartoon character Pogo observed, "*We have met the enemy and he is us.*"

SIERRA CLUB (United States)

In 1969 the Sierra Club in the United States urged people to abandon population growth as a pattern and goal and to achieve a stable population no later than the year 1990. On 11 July 2008, when the Sierra Club promoted World Population Day, they continued their urgent plea for a reduction in population. They stated,

> If we are to tackle global challenges like global warming, poverty, and population growth, the United States must rise to the challenge and show leadership by investing in sustainable development solutions—solutions that prioritize global health initiatives, including family planning. Slowing population growth and addressing the over consumption and inequitable distribution of natural resources, is key to long-term environmental protection.

They encourage people to make the population-environment connection and support voluntary international family planning programs that improve the quality of life of people around the world and ensure an improved environmental future.

BIODIVERSITY FIRST (Ontario, Canada)

The new kid on the block, Biodiversity First, is a newly formed environment group that is trying to revive the population issue in

Canada. Formed in May 2008, this group provides an Internet forum for its members to participate in ongoing population/biodiversity discussions. Biodiversity First believes that biodiversity preservation is incompatible with our unsustainably high population. The group's president, Brishen Hoff, explains that their mandate is to educate the public through articles and letters to media and government decision makers. Biodiversity First bases their outreach strategies on the following premises:

1. Biodiversity is defined as the quantity, quality and variety of native species.

2. Preserving biodiversity is essential to preserving our quality of life and survival.

3. Human population size and growth represents the biggest threat to biodiversity.

4. Earth's human population is over ten times what is optimal.

5. Human overpopulation is responsible for hundreds of species extinctions.

6. Our unsustainably high population is incompatible with biodiversity preservation.

7. The more natural resources per capita, the higher our quality of life.

THE ALBERTA WILDERNESS ASSOCIATION (Alberta, Canada)

The AWA, founded in the 1960s, has from its beginnings recognized that the greatest threat to wild places and wildlife is the inexorable growth of human numbers and the resulting pressure on the environment to produce increasing resources for increasing numbers of people who produce increasing amounts of waste. AWA believes that society's ability to deal with the issue of growth is fundamental to our success in achieving an ecologically sustainable future.

ENGENDERHEALTH (U.S. and International)

EngenderHealth is an international nonprofit organization that has been working for sixty years to make reproductive health services safe, available, and sustainable for women and men worldwide. Based in New York City, they have twenty offices in the field, and more than 70 percent of their staff work in countries across Asia, Africa, and the Americas.

Their staff of highly skilled medical personnel, health care trainers, and public health professionals works around the globe in partnership with local governments and nongovernmental agencies to help health care workers, administrators, physicians, hospital staff, and counselors deliver high-quality health care services in some of the world's poorest countries. They estimate that their work has touched the health and lives of more than 100 million individuals in the ninety countries where they have worked.

CHILDFREE (International)

Childfree groups began to form in the 1970s, most notably among them No Kidding! and the National Organization for Non-Parents. There are now numerous childfree groups around the world that realize that parenting is not for everyone. Parenting is a lifetime commitment, and many women, especially those who also want to pursue a career, have no desire to take on this commitment. They do not feel that it is fair to the child if they cannot give it their full attention and the kind of love that every child deserves.

> "Childfree by Choice" is a group of adults who all share at least one common desire: we do not wish to have children of our own. We are teachers, doctors, business owners, authors, computer experts—you name it. We choose to call ourselves "childfree" rather than "childless," because we feel the term "childless" implies that we're missing something we want—and we aren't. We consider ourselves childfree—free of the loss of personal freedom, money, time and energy that having children requires.
>
> Childfree by Choice website

> "The world might, perhaps, be considerably poorer if the great writers had exchanged their books for children of flesh and blood."
>
> Virginia Woolf

Childfreedom, according to the "Happily Childfree" website, is choosing not to create or raise children. It's about wanting to devote one's life to other objectives. For some that is their career, for others hobbies (or volunteer work). Most childfree people recognize that parenting is a stressful, time-consuming, and often thankless job, and would rather do something else with their lives.

As they point out, making the choice to be childfree is not something that is chosen lightly. In many cases childfree people have thought longer and harder about why NOT to have kids than their counterparts have thought about why TO have kids.

I will be discussing this issue in more detail in Part 3.

OTHERS

Of course, there are numerous other environment and related groups who have addressed the issue of population, and many continue to do so. Some of these groups are:

- Conservation Council of Ontario—Ontario, Canada
- Association Anti-Pollution 2000—Brussels, Belgium
- Association Demographie et Ecologie—Bron, France
- Associazione Italiana per l'Educazione—Rome, Italy
- Catholics for a Free Choice—Washington DC, USA
- East Kootenay Environmental Society (now known as Wildsite)—Kimberley, BC, Canada
- Imagine a World of Unwanted Children—San Jacinto, CA, USA

- International Network of Feminists IN/FIRE—Washington DC, USA
- International Institute for Sustainable Development—Winnipeg, Man., Canada
- Mouvement Demographie—Ecologie—Bomal-sur-Ourthe, Belgium
- Stichting De Club van Tien Miljoen—Valkenswaard, Netherlands
- Planned Parenthood Federation of America—USA
- Federation For Sexual Health (previously Planned Parenthood Federation) —Canada
- Federation for American Immigration Reform—USA
- Centre for Immigration Studies—USA
- Numbers USA
- Earth Policy Institute—USA
- World Wildlife Fund
- Conservation International
- National Wildlife Federation
- Childfree—International
- National Wildlife Federation—USA
- Northwest Environment Watch—USA

We feel this issue is of crucial concern for successful conservation and sustainable development. Even while environmental goals can be met, conservation efforts will become secondary if population continues to grow at the present rate. The sheer number of people, forced to exploit the environment

> for extraction of finite resources to meet basic needs, impacts the limited amount of progress we have been able to make.
>
> Conservation International, 1999

POPULATION GROUPS

> The optimum population of a country is the one which is most likely to produce a good and sustainable quality of life for its inhabitants without adversely affecting the quality of life of people in other countries.
>
> Optimum Population Trust
> Manchester, England, 1995

Without the presence of the many dedicated population groups around the world, we would be in even more dire circumstances than we are today. There are numerous groups who have tirelessly endeavored to foster public awareness of the connection between our high population densities and the dangers to which our environment is being exposed.

This is being achieved by means of lectures, conventions, publications, education programs, letter writing campaigns, coalitions, raising funds for family planning programs, press releases, conducting research, providing a population perspective on social and environmental problems, etc. Here I will list some of these groups.

- Population Institute of Canada (also known as Global Population Concerns)—Canada

  This group, formed in the late 1980s, accepts the following premises:

1. Overpopulation is the chief cause of ongoing ecological damage.
2. Overpopulation is the fundamental cause of growing insecurity.
3. Overpopulation is the prime reason that sustainable development remains beyond reach.

- Optimum Population Trust—Manchester, England

  The Optimum Population Trust has two main aims:

  1. To promote and coordinate research into criteria that will allow the optimum population of a region to be determined
  2. To increase awareness, particularly among those who influence opinion, of the results of this research

They are especially interested in establishing the optimum population of industrialized countries. Of the very many possible criteria, they believe the three principal indicators for establishing optimum population are:

- The preservation of biodiversity
- The availability of fresh water
- The availability of land not only for agriculture, forestry, mining, waste disposal, building and recreation but above all for the conversion of renewable forms of energy.

- Zero Population Growth US (now known as Population Connection)

In 1991, ZPG produced the "Priority Statement on Population." They worked with a coalition of environmental groups who felt that what was needed was an affirmation of the relationship between population growth and environmental degradation and a call on public policy makers to address the issue.

The result of the core group's work was the "Priority Statement on Population." The first effort of its kind, the statement was endorsed by over 160 organizations and prominent individuals. From Nobel Prize winners to "Dear Abby" to national environmental, women's, scientific, civic, and education groups representing millions of members, the endorsement list is impressive evidence of widespread concern about the environmental impacts of overpopulation.

PRIORITY STATEMENT ON POPULATION

> Among the most important issues affecting the world's future is the rapid growth of human population. Together, the increase in population and in resource consumption are basic causes of human suffering and environmental degradation and must become major priorities for national and international action.
>
> Because of its pervasive and detrimental impact on global ecological systems, population growth threatens to overwhelm any possible gains made in improving human conditions. Failure to curb the rate of world population growth will magnify the deterioration of the Earth's environment and natural resources and undermine economic and social progress. A humane, sustainable future depends on recognizing the common ground between population and the environment.
>
> Current national and international efforts to address the world's rapidly expanding population are not sufficient. A new commitment to population programs which enhance human rights and conditions is urgently needed. The United States and all nations of the world must make an effective response to the issue of population growth a leading priority for this decade.
>
> Zero Population Growth,
> 1991

- Population Media Center

The Population Media Center works worldwide using entertainment-education for social change. PMC's programs encourage positive behavior change among the audience. This group was founded in 1998 by William Ryerson. In the ten years since PMC's inception, the organization has been a pioneer in the use of new methodologies for informing people about reproductive health issues and promoting behavior change.

PMC works in underdeveloped nations that have a national television network. They work with local writers, actors, producers, etc., to develop soap operas in which family planning is part of the storyline. They have had demonstrated success in reducing fertility rates in countries where they have worked.

PMC works worldwide from its headquarters in Shelburne, Vermont (USA). It has representatives in California and Oregon, as well as overseas offices in Brazil, Ethiopia, India, Jamaica, Kenya, Malawi, Mali, Mexico, Niger, Nigeria, the Philippines, Rwanda, Saint Lucia, Senegal, and Sudan.

- William and Flora Hewlett Foundation

The Hewlett Foundation embarked upon their funding program in 1967. Their mission remains essentially unchanged: to promote voluntary family planning and good reproductive health for all because of the benefits to individuals, societies, and the entire global community.

- Global Population Speak Out

The Global Population Speak Out is a project that was initiated in 2009 by John Feeney, urging people to break down the barrier to public discussion of population issues during the month of February. The 2009 effort was a great success – including over 200 blog articles, 46 letters to the editors, 20 scholarly articles, and 24 news articles and radio interviews. For 2010 John Feeney will be teaming up with the Population Institute to help him expedite the 2010 GPSO, which is also scheduled for the month of February. Let's hope that this effort becomes an annual event! To participate, you can contact the Population Institute at www.populationinstitute.org, or email them at gpso@populationinstitute.org.

I will not discuss every population-related group, but I have listed most of the major ones below:

- Carrying Capacity Network—Washington DC, USA
- Australians for an Ecologically Sustainable Population—Canberra, Australia
- Negative Population Growth—Teaneck, NJ, USA
- EcoPop (Ecologie et Population)—Zollikofen, Switzerland
- Population-Environment Balance (Balance)—USA
- Diversity Alliance for a Sustainable America—USA
- Population Connection (formerly Zero Population Growth)—USA
- Equilibres et Populations—Levallois-Perret, France
- Ministry for Population Concerns—Glendale, CA, USA
- National Optimum Population Commission—Corvallis, OR, USA
- Population Action International—Washington DC, USA
- Population Council—New York, NY, USA
- Population Information Program, John Hopkins Univ.—Baltimore, MD, USA
- The Population Institute—Washington DC, USA
- Religious Consultation on Population—Washington DC, USA
- Population and Quality of Life Independent Commission—Paris, France

- Population Reference Bureau Inc.—Washington DC, USA
- Population Reference Bureau—USA
- Action Canada for Population and Development—Canada
- German Foundation for World Population—Germany
- PopPlanet website
- Pathfinder International—USA and thirty-seven countries
- World Overpopulation Awareness
- Overshooting Australia—Australia
- Population Countdown—Internet Worldwide
- Californians for Population Stabilization
- Andrew W. Mellon Foundation—USA
- Buffet Foundation
- Ted Turner Foundation—USA
- Bill Gates Foundation—USA
- Population Health
- Tamara C. Fox Foundation
- Canadian Association of the Club of Rome—Canada
- International Family Planning Coalition
- National Abortion and Reproductive Rights Action League
- Center for Reproductive Law and Policy
- Margaret Sanger Center International (Planned Parenthood—New York)
- Doctors For a Sustainable Population—Australia

RELIGIOUS INFLUENCES

One might expect that the biggest opposition to reducing population would come from the great religions of the world. Not so. With the exception of the Vatican, claiming to represent the position of the Roman Catholic Church, most religions are quite open to addressing the issue of population control and family planning. It is not the religions that oppose family planning, but rather certain representatives of religions who oppose family planning to further their own agenda. When it comes to addressing population and religion, the Worldwatch Institute has this to say in their book *State of the World 2002*:

> Many religious leaders are coming to realize that there is no inherent conflict between family planning and religion, and that in fact lack of reproductive rights represents a grave social injustice. In Iran, Islamic clerics have even issued *fatwas*, or religious edicts, approving family planning methods—from oral contraceptives and condoms to sterilization. This approval, along with the integration of family planning services with primary health care, the provision of free contraceptives, and the strengthening of men's role in reproductive health, resulted in the total fertility rate in Iran dropping from 5.6 children in 1985 to 2.8 children in 2000—among the most precipitous declines in family size in the modern demographic transition.
>
> Where religion continues to hamper efforts to give people greater control over their reproductive lives, the world's religious leaders may need to reconcile their actions with their humanitarian ideals.

An Alternet posting by Tana Ganeva on 1 April 2009 had this to say:

> The Catholic leadership continues to render itself more and more irrelevant with out-of-date and loudly proclaimed stances on abortion, reproductive rights, gay rights, AIDS policy, stem cell research—the list can go on and on, until the End Times. But a new Gallup poll reveals that most American Catholics appear comfortable existing in the new millennium.
>
> The poll shows that the views of practicing Catholics on a range of social issues are more or less in line with American non-Catholics. In fact, Catholics today are actually more liberal than the non-Catholic population on a number of moral issues like abortion, homosexuality, and stem cell research, according to Gallup's data.
>
> 40% of Catholics find abortion morally acceptable, compared to 41% of the general population … But it also points to the fact that often the most vocal spokespeople for a religion are not the most representative of that denomination's adherents as a whole, but rather a crazy fringe given a platform by our sensationalist media.

~

> I believe that the Vatican has availed itself of the fact that racists and xenophobes exist in our society to categorize as racism any arguments for limiting population growth and any objections to unlimited immigration. Many people who would otherwise speak out are intimidated into silence by this form of intellectual terrorism.
>
> Dr. Madeline Weld, 1995
> Population Institute of Canada

In the June 1994 newsletter of the Canadian Population Action Network appeared the work of a religious group called the Religious Consultation on Population, Reproductive Health and Ethics.

This group facilitates the contribution of religious leaders to international dialogue about development and population issues, including poverty, women's health and rights, the environment, and materialism.

The Consultation, whose participants represent diverse faith traditions, provides publications and convenes symposia and conferences for the religious, ethics, and policy communities. Three authoritative presentations at a panel discussion held during the second preparatory committee meeting of the ICPD (International Conference on Population and Development) have been published in a booklet titled, *Religious and Ethical Perspectives on Population Issues.*

1. The first author, Azizah Y. al-Hibri, explains the Islamic law and school of thought, concluding that, "The majority view is that a Muslim family is permitted to engage in family planning."

2. In the second presentation on poverty, population, and the Catholic tradition, Daniel C. Maguire articulates "dominant views of Catholic theology" that differ from those of the Vatican. He says, "Catholics can regard artificial contraception and voluntary abortion as morally permissible options." He asks for understanding of the harsh measures taken in China, which can be harbingers of our own future, if or when we arrive also at the *draconian critical mass.*

3. The third, by Lutheran James B. Martin-Schramm, sees the appropriate Christian response to population growth as an attack on poverty and injustice, but advocates as the most important measure improving the lives of women, including fulfilling their fundamental right to family planning. He views legal access to abortion as necessary due to the way many women are treated.

   "Only after the last tree has been cut down,

> Only after that last fish has been caught,
>
> Only after the last river has been poisoned,
>
> Only then will you realize that money cannot be eaten."
>
> Cree Indian Prophecy

In his interview in *Le Soir* (5 June 1999) the Dalai Lama answered a question about the principal challenge to man in the twenty-first century:

> I think that the damage caused to the environment, the pollution will become more and more disturbing. Also the problems caused by overpopulation. People have a difficult time apprehending those two problems. Things will get worse unless we take specific and effective measures regarding the environmental and population problems.
>
> Dalai Lama, 1999

So, it would appear that the Vatican, as well as the more religiously compliant countries it controls, is holding out the strongest religious opposition to population control. The residents of these countries, living in poverty and being less educated, are more easily controlled and terrorized than those in industrialized countries where family planning programs are available and widely accepted. I believe that it is extremely racist to refuse women in underdeveloped countries the same right to family planning programs that is enjoyed in developed countries.

Although representing only a tiny minority, the Vatican has a great deal of influence on global decision-making because of the unique position given to them by the United Nations. The Vatican (also known as the Holy See or Roman Catholic Church) is the only religious entity that has been granted the privilege of veto status in the UN, allowing them to derail family planning initiatives at UN conferences.

The Catholics for a Free Choice have explained how this came about. They pointed out that Permanent Observer status is a matter of custom: there is no provision for it in the UN Charter. They added that the custom originated in 1946, when Switzerland named a "permanent observer" to the UN and the UN secretary general accepted this designation. To become a Permanent Observer, a state must be a member of at least one specialized agency of the UN system (such as the International Atomic Energy Agency), must be "generally recognized" by UN member states, and must apply to the UN secretary general for the status.

Permanent Observers may address the General Assembly and participate in its debates. They can take part in UN conferences. These conferences are increasingly central to the work of the UN and often determine the allocation of resources. The UN agency organizing each meeting decides what level of participation to allow observers, and non-member states typically are granted full status enjoyed by UN member states, including a vote on any question.

Recent General Assembly resolutions have called for all "states" participating in conferences to be accorded "full voting rights." This enables the Holy See (Vatican) to exercise a presence equal to that of any member state—including some power to block consensus—at recent conferences including:

- 1992 Conference on the Environment and Development in Rio de Janeiro
- 1994 International Conference on Population and Development in Cairo
- 1995 World Summit for Social Development in Copenhagen
- 1995 Fourth World Conference on Women in Beijing

Despite its designation as a non-member "state" Permanent Observer, in international law the Holy See is not a state and therefore should not have veto power in the UN. It is a religious entity without defined temporal territory. Diplomatically, however, many countries treat the Holy See as a state because of the influence of the pope as leader of Catholics worldwide. That is not to say that Catholics worldwide agree with the pope or the Vatican regarding population—quite the contrary. In fact, there have been a number of actions taken against the Holy See's unfounded privilege at the UN.

- In 1995, Catholics for a Free Choice (CFFC) initiated a petition asking the United Nations to reconsider the status of the Holy See. Hundreds of NGOs from around the world signed the petition, along with approximately 2,000 individuals who signed the petition at the Fourth World Conference on Women and the NGO Forum.

- In 1996, Mouvement Ecologie-Demographie in Belgium forwarded a petition, or "Call to the UN organization to reconsider the status of the Holy See," sponsored by USPDA (case postale CH-3052, Zollikofen, Switzerland) along with various women's organizations, including (surprisingly) the National Coalition of American Nuns.

- In 1999, CFFC launched the "See Change" campaign to change the Holy See's status at the UN. This initiative included an international postcard campaign to the secretary-general of the UN and is endorsed by a large coalition of women's, religious, and reproductive rights organizations.

- In 1999, the editor for the Women's International Network wrote, "The Vatican opposed the very organization of UNFPA at the 1974 Population Conference in Bucharest, Romania, where members of the Vatican disguised as representatives of various institutions, lobbied against every positive move to make contraception available. The day before the Conference opened the Vatican delegation called a special press conference to announce that the meeting should be canceled as the subject was not fit to discuss at an international meeting. Since then the Vatican has continuously opposed UNFPA (the United Nations Fund for Population Activities) and its programs for women."

- In 2000 the government of Brazil, the world's largest Catholic country, blasted the local Roman Catholic church for opposing condom use to prevent the spread of AIDS. The National Bishop's Association reiterated its stance against Catholics using condoms, despite internal opposition from some clergymen.

In the June 1996 newsletter of the Canadian Population Action Network, Andrew Macpherson notes that the Vatican's status at the UN is facing increasing challenge. At the 4WCW in Beijing in 1995, health group chair Mervat Tallawy of Egypt at one point announced that she would not recognize the Holy See on yet another point of order, but later backed down. In apologizing, however, she cautioned the Holy See: "Please don't abuse this right too much."

On 12 August 1995 the *NY Times* published the article "Catholic Church Resists Family Planning." It outlined the heated debate between the Roman Catholic Church and President Alberto K. Fujimori of Peru. Mr. Fujimori stated, "It is hypocrisy to pretend not to see that different methods of birth control are applied for families of different social classes. It is only fair to disseminate thoroughly the methods of family planning to everyone. The women of Peru have to be the owners of their destiny … It is especially important to assure that those at the lowest end of the economic scale have the same access to services as those at the upper levels."

Mr. Fujimori, a Catholic representing a country that is 90 percent Roman Catholic, was the only male president who spoke at the Fourth United Nations Conference on Women in Beijing. No other Latin American president had put birth control at the forefront of a national agenda—in open defiance of the Roman Catholic Church. He stated that he believed the first step in reducing poverty was decreasing the size of low-income families.

So, why shouldn't the pope and the Vatican have veto power in the United Nations conferences? Well, according to Madeline Weld, with the Population Institute of Canada (1995), there are plenty of reasons:

The Vatican, under various popes, has sabotaged all efforts to address the population crisis right from the inception of the UN. As a result of strong pressure from the Vatican on the World Health Organization, family planning programs were excluded from that organization. By keeping family planning separate from general health care initiatives, the Vatican has been able to impede the development of family planning programs in a large number of countries. It greatly influenced U.S. population policies during the Reagan and Bush eras. The Vatican managed to keep population off the agenda during the UN Conference on Environment and Development in 1992 (also known as the Earth Summit), and to tie up the International Conference on Population and Development. Not only does the Vatican oppose contraception, it also strongly opposes any limits to immigration.

It would seem that while the Vatican is not very concerned about the health of the planet, it is very concerned about the health of its power. Many believe that the Vatican has more or less lost hope about controlling the wayward west. Even Catholics in the developed world don't take the Pope too seriously, at least when it comes to practicing what he preaches. In Latin America, much of Africa and parts of Asia, however, the Vatican's efforts to sabotage contraceptive services have been hugely successful.

Don't you think that the irresponsible behavior of men is caused by women?

Pope John Paul II

In 1997 Carl Bernstein and Marco Politi wrote an article entitled "The Angry Pope." This article describes what occurred when

John Paul II met with the head of the UN Population Fund, Nafis Sadik, shortly before the International Conference on Population and Development in Cairo in 1994. At this UN conference a Program of Action would be approved, one that would focus on the reproductive rights of both couples and individuals and guarantees of reproductive health. It stressed the obligation of government to provide health services while granting the greatest possible freedom of contraceptive methods.

Pope Wojtyla feared a global policy encouraging the massive distribution of birth control pills and condoms. But what alarmed him most was the program's insistence that abortion be performed under safe and legal conditions. Bernstein and Politi explain the view of the Vatican:

> In the files prepared for the pope, the Vatican Secretariat of State stressed how much political conditions had changed since the previous conference ten years before in Mexico City. During the Reagan administration the United States had pushed "prolife" policy with a view to pleasing the pope and reinforcing the strategic alliance with the Vatican. But now the winds in Washington had shifted. The Clinton administration favored a woman's right to choose and defend individual sexual rights, including those of homosexuals. It also favored the availability of safe and legal abortions.
>
> The pope found this intolerable. He suspected that the United States and an American feminist lobby wanted to impose Western-style sexual lifestyles on the developing countries.

When the pope looked at his guest, Nafis Sadik, she was wearing the costume of her native Pakistan, and her face had a calm and determined expression. She explained that the conference's Program of Action dealt mainly with children and mothers—that is, the group most vulnerable to the consequences of over-sized families and sexual abuse. She added that in many societies, and not just in the developing world, women don't have equal status with men. There's a lot of sexual violence within the family.

Nafis Sadik pointed out that women are quite willing to practice natural methods and abstain, as the pope had recommended, because they're the ones who get pregnant and don't want to be. But they can't abstain without the cooperation of their partners.

At this point Pope John Paul II interjected, "Don't you think that the irresponsible behavior of men is caused by women?"

> Sadik froze when she heard this statement, but then replied, "In most of the developing countries men look on marital relations as their right, and the women have to comply. Men come home drunk, have sexual relations with their wives, and the wives get pregnant. Or they get HIV without having any control over their partner's behavior and their own situation.
>
> "Violence within the family, rape in fact, is very common in our society. The most upsetting thing about all this is that only women suffer the consequences. Many women, you know, wind up abandoned. Latin America is full of abandoned families, full of women who are left as the heads of households, with children to look after, while the men go off and start another family somewhere else."
>
> The Pope, however, showed no compassion for the suffering of women, causing Sadik to wonder how he could be so hard-hearted. She later told her friends, "He doesn't like women. I expected a little more sympathy for suffering and death."

Well, the pope did attend the International Conference on Population and Development a few months later. And he did, indeed, manage to derail any meaningful progress on the issues of family planning, reproductive health, and women's rights. Once again the Vatican (Holy See) accomplished its mission to block consensus on the major objectives. Since UN decision-making is based on consensus rather than majority vote, this was easily accomplished.

In 1993 Zero Population Growth reported that organizations such as the Ministry for Population Concerns, Catholics for a Free Choice, and the International Coordinating Committee for Religion and the Earth were concerned that the goals and strategies of the religious right did not correlate with religious faith in general.

The Religious Right "challenges us to retake and reclaim religion," says Laurie Shepard of the Religious Coalition for Abortion Rights. "Diverse individuals know how to make their own moral decisions."

> It can be said that the family planning movement is one of the important social changes of this century, and especially of the last half-century ... No country except the Holy See objected to the services provided by the family planning movement.
>
> Roderic Beaujot, 1995
> Professor of Sociology at the University of Western Ontario
> Member of the Canadian National Advisory Council for the ICPD and of the Canadian Delegation at Cairo

On 18 December 2006 the Indo-Asian News Service reported, "Mosques in Pakistan to Preach Family Planning." They advised that mosques would be distributing contraceptives and spreading awareness about the importance of family planning and safe sex. Around 22,000 clerics, including 6,000 women, would be appointed to spread the message of the benefits of a small family. There would also be programs to make university-level students aware of these norms. The move was borrowed from Bangladesh, adopting the slogan "small family, happy family." Clerics would inform people about the significance of family planning in their sermons.

This is a great example of a country taking positive steps to deal with the population crisis in a comprehensive, humane manner. With government, religious representatives, women, and educational institutions working together toward a similar goal, they are bound to be successful. This is the kind of cooperation we need at the United Nations level but unfortunately have never achieved.

In 1995 the Center for Research on Population and Security in North Carolina was circulating a petition "To Withdraw UN Observer Status from the Holy See" similar to the See Change postcard previously mentioned. They wanted to inform the United Nations that an informal coalition was forming to help combat the opposition of the Catholic Church to desperately needed national and international family planning and population growth control programs. They stated,

> With its history of service to humanity, its extraordinary organization and its wealth, the Roman Catholic Church could have contributed greatly to containment and solution of the current crisis of world population growth. Instead, because of its intransigent opposition to modern methods of family limitation, based on the 1968 papal encyclical *Human Vitae* banning birth control, its role has been just the opposite: it has contributed greatly to the overpopulation dilemma itself—and thus also to continuation of the servile status of women in many countries, to failure of efforts to improve the health of women and their infants, to the spread of hunger and serious malnutrition, to depletion of our planet's natural resources and destruction of the environment.
>
> We are convinced that the position of the pope and his church is quite simply *immoral*, and *wrong*, and will continue to cripple national and international programs designed to bring humanity's population growth under control. We say this in the context of our own deep beliefs and espousal of family values.
>
> We believe the billions of couples the world around who want to limit their family size by safe, effective and humane means, *hold the high moral ground* in this dispute. We also resent, and will mobilize to

> resist, the undemocratic means by which papal power has harassed and intimidated governments at all levels in their efforts to provide family planning services.
>
> The Church's dogma of papal infallibility has precluded any effective efforts to rescind or modify the ban on contraception imposed by *Humanae Vitae.* (World population has increased by 1,000,000,000 since the encyclical was released just 26 years ago.) One recent liberalizing effort within the Church—an effort that naturally failed—was the recommendation of the Pontifical Academy of Sciences urging limits on family size to avert "insoluble problems" caused by runaway growth; the Academy recommended that family size be limited to about two children per couple.
>
> Demands of the Vatican that the edicts of *Humanae Vitae* be followed are made to ensure survival of the principle of infallibility and the institution of the papacy. The price of these demands in human terms—in suffering, illness and premature death—is so great as to make such demands immoral. *On these grounds, we believe the "non-member state permanent observer status" of the Holy See in the United Nations, as well as its similar relationships with specialized agencies in the UN system, is inappropriate and should be terminated as soon as possible.*"

I recall that petition very well, since I circulated it in my community in 1995, gathering pages of signatures to send to the United Nations. I never did receive a response from the United Nations and can't help but wonder if the issue was ever discussed by UN members.

Reverend Martin Luther King Jr.

In 1963 Rev. Martin Luther King Jr. gave his "I Have a Dream" speech, which inspired a generation and changed the course of history. Now, forty-five years later, we are still celebrating his legacy as we pause to honor his message of hope.

On 19 January 2009, Martin Luther King Day, celebrities and working folk alike paid tribute to this legend of a man. Oprah dedicated a show to him, noting the sacrifices he had made and the significance of her hero's life. He was the youngest person ever awarded the Nobel Peace Prize and was remembered for his supreme intelligence and his dedication to the civil rights movement.

However, what most people choose not to remember is one of his most captivating and stirring speeches given in 1966, the one about "family planning." He believed that overpopulation was a special and urgent concern even at that time, when our population was far less than today's 6.7 billion. He pointed out that we spend paltry sums for population planning, even though our spontaneous growth is an urgent threat to life on our planet. He passionately stated,

> There is no human circumstance more tragic than the persisting existence of a harmful condition for which a remedy is readily available. Family planning, to relate population to world resources, is possible, practical and necessary. Unlike plagues of the dark ages or contemporary diseases we do not yet understand, the modern plague of overpopulation is soluble by means we have discovered and with resources we possess. What is lacking is not sufficient knowledge of the solution but universal consciousness of the gravity of the problem and education of billions who are its victims.

It seems to me unfortunate that his most important message has been forgotten by our society at a time when it so desperately needs to be heard.

SPIRITUAL RENAISSANCE

> The Indigenous people of Mother Earth who still have a connection to their land, language, culture, history and spiritual traditions are the poorest and

> most socially and politically marginalized people in every country in which they reside …
>
> Since the mid-seventies there has been a Native Spiritual Renaissance throughout the Indigenous world. Not only have young people learned again from their elders, but tribes across the continents have learned from each other. According to an ancient prophecy, this is the time when the Eagle meets the Condor. This Indigenous cultural and spiritual awakening comes just at a time when western culture and spirituality has gone bankrupt.
>
> Hank Zyp
> In the Alberta Council for Global Cooperation Newsletter
> (Spring 2002)

At one time ancient native spirituality was called animism, shamanism, witchcraft, ancestor worship, and superstition by sociologists. However, it has come a long way since then.

Today, our indigenous people are not the only ones seeking out spirituality, as we have been reminded on Oprah, with her "Remember Your Spirit" programs. Record numbers of people are shifting away from structured religions and turning to spirituality instead. This kind of belief system is gaining popularity because there is no middleman to negotiate with, you do not have to deal with the "guilt" ethic or make large monetary contributions, and you can express your spirituality in any way you wish. It could involve bonding with nature, practicing a ritual, dancing, meditation, yoga, or numerous other forms of participation. Many of the forms explored on the *Oprah* show involved giving from your heart, healing practices, volunteering, and sharing your joy for life.

ATHEISM

> The U.S. population continues to show signs of becoming less religious, with one in five Americans failing to indicate a religious identity in 2008.

American Religious Identification Survey (ARIS), 2009

The last few decades have seen a lot of doors opening, and a lot of suppressed people coming out of the closet. Gay and lesbian couples are now speaking freely about their relationships. Cross-gender people are now being allowed to make choices regarding what sex they really want to be. Many women around the world are beginning to demand their rightful status and equal rights in the work place. Many survivors of abuse by priests, teachers, medical staff, etc., are now speaking out. And finally, atheists are coming out of the closet to proclaim their right to believe or not believe as they wish.

Atheists are also a quickly growing sector of the population. In reality, millions of people who had claimed to be of a specific religion did not in fact practice it in any way or attend any church. They often just adopted that religion from their parents and had never given changing it much thought. Or they were reluctant to claim that they were spiritual or atheist, rather than religious, in fear of harsh judgment from society. Well, society is now removing that taboo and encouraging all individuals to feel free to claim their own belief system without ridicule.

> Cheer up friends. Do not be appalled if life seems to have no purpose. If there is no apparent purpose in evolution or in the scheme of things and you are despondent about it you can do something about that too. You can put a purpose into your life. You can go about doing good. Do something that needs to be done. Without a god there is plenty to do. The world needs you. Have a goal. Have a philosophy. No religion or church has a monopoly on morals or ethics despite what the clergy say.

G. Vincent Runyon, *Why I Left the Ministry and Became an Atheist*

> It's often said that people "need" something more in their lives than just the material world. There is a gap that must be filled. People need to feel a sense of purpose. Well, not a BAD purpose would be to find out what is already here, in the material world, before concluding that you need something more. How much more do you want? Just study what is, and you'll find that it already is far more uplifting than anything you could imagine needing.
>
> Richard Dawkins,
> "Science, Delusion, and the Appetite for Wonder"
> The Obligatory Quotes Page, *www.gaydeceiver.com/quotes/*

"Personal God Going the Way of the Dodo?"

Ronald Aronson, posted on alternet.org, 5 May 2009

From article "40 Million Nonbelievers in America? The Secret is Almost Out"

Aronson points out that according to the latest American Religious Identification Survey of more than 54,000 adults, between 2001 and 2008 the number willing to identify themselves as atheist and agnostic has gone from under 2 million to 3.6 million. This is a rise of 85 percent of those willing to describe themselves as living without God during the years of the most overtly religious presidency in U.S. history! Aronson continues:

> Consider: If these numbers are correct, nonbelievers amount to more than the highest estimates of African Americans or gays. Secularists are one of America's largest minorities. It is no longer possible to proclaim, as the Gallup Poll announced fifty years ago: "Nearly all Americans believe in God." That is today's most significant change.
>
> If a new confidence is in the offing it is also visible in the American Humanist Association's scandalous

Christmastime bus ads in Washington DC ("Why believe in a god? Just be good for goodness' sake."). No less striking is the "Out" campaign (Come Out, Reach Out, Speak Out, Keep Out, Stand Out) especially among students and young people.

UNITED NATIONS / GOVERNMENTS

Remember, population growth in America is not an act of God—it is an act of Congress.

Edward C. Hartman
From his book *The Population Fix*, 2006

We have a situation in this country, as in most others, where government policies are subsidizing and abetting the trend to overpopulation, implying that policy is in agreement with the inevitable consequences to people and planetary systems. Governments and their traditional economic advisors espouse their usual philosophy on the glories and benefits of increasing human numbers in this country while being blinded to the enormous negatives of such advice and policies. Neither the well-being of people down the road nor the ecological health of the nation are factored in. Notwithstanding the writing on the wall, the country's economists/politicians remain disconnected from their planetary roots and act as if humans are exempt from the laws of nature.

Ted Mosquin, 1992

At the third preparatory conference for the International Conference on Population and Development in 1994, the objectives of the UN were defined: the goal would be to stabilize world population at 7.27 billion by 2015. The means would be threefold:

- Filling unmet demands for contraceptive services
- Increasing educational opportunity, particularly for girls
- Providing basic health services, particularly for infants and mothers

Obviously none of these objectives made it through the International Conference on Population and Development intact or were ever fully implemented. Now, over a decade later, the situation has gotten even more serious and more difficult to remedy.

Meanwhile, in Canada in 1994, the Canadian Population Action Network (formerly Sustainable Population Society) was concerned about the population situation in Canada. They stated,

> The Government has no comprehensive population policy. There are Ministers of Environment, Immigration, Human Resources, Health, etc., but each seems to act as if these were independent portfolios. They do not appear to recognize the links between population increase and environmental degradation in Canada, but only in the Third World. High Canadian consumption rates do not appear to register as problematic. We have repeatedly pointed out that, if we consume 25 times as much per capita as Africans, as has been estimated, our 28.5 million Canadians consume (and pollute) more than all 680 million Africans. And when we add one percent to our population we add slightly more consumption potential (285,000 x 25 = 7,125,000 units) than when Africans add one percent (6,800,000 units) to theirs.

In 1994 a draft Canadian Biodiversity Strategy was issued by the Federal-Provincial-Territorial Working Group. It acknowledged that:

> [t]he impact of human activities on natural ecological processes is the primary cause of biodiversity loss worldwide. As the human population grows and consumes an increasing share of the planet's

> resources to meet its needs, the impact on current levels of biodiversity also increases. To conserve biodiversity and use biological resources sustainably, a better balance must be struck between our use of the Earth's resources and the Earth's capacity to produce them, recognizing that these resources must be shared with millions of other species.
>
> Our governments should be taking a leading role in addressing the population problem, both globally and federally. A U.S. population group that was founded in 1972, "Negative Population Growth," is very concerned about our society's refusal to recognize that population size and growth are the central problems confronting us. They state, "That issue is also ignored by almost all segments of our society, including, to mention a few of the most important, our Federal government, the academic community, the major environmental organizations, the mass media, and the current crop of presidential candidates. They are all shamefully derelict in their duty.

In 1972, following two years of research and public hearings, the final report of the President's Commission on Population Growth and the American Future (the Rockefeller Commission Report) was released. The commission was established by Congress in response to a proposal by then President Nixon. Its mission was to assess the social, economic, and environmental impacts of continued population growth in the United States. What was its major conclusion?

> We have looked for, and have not found, any convincing economic argument for continued national population growth. The health of our economy does not depend on it. The vitality of business does not depend on it. The welfare of the average person certainly does not depend on it.

In fact, it was found that the US economy could actually benefit from a move toward a stable population. Key points regarding advantages of reducing population included:

- Per capita income would rise. Due to age shifts, in a move to a stable population there would be more people of working age as a proportion of the total US population.
- The dependency ratio would decrease. With a stable population, there would be fewer youth "dependents" for workers and the economy to support (education, teenage pregnancy, etc.). At the same time, elder dependents would increase, but the commission found that the decrease of youth dependents would more than offset the increase in older dependents.
- Quality of life would improve. Lower levels of economic activity would lessen the demand and competition for resources and ease the stress on the environment.
- Pressure on the labor force would be eased. The need for increased production, employment, and consumption would decrease, and correspondingly lessen the problems associated with the social and environmental consequences of growth.

So, whatever became of these recommendations, and why was this not the impetus for a drastic reduction in population? The findings of this government commission made it very clear that all indicators pointed toward a limit to growth to improve quality of life. Well, in his book *The Population Fix*, Edward Hartman explains, "Six months prior to seeking reelection, reportedly under immense pressure from religious leaders, President Nixon simultaneously received and renounced the report."

I can't help but wonder who really funds and influences the Vatican? How does the Vatican in turn manage to influence world governments even outside of the UN arena?

Although the influence of the Vatican in the United Nations is not the only barrier to reducing our population to a sustainable level, I believe it is by far the most powerful force working against achieving a sustainable population level. Yet this obstacle would be the easiest removed.

All it would take to stop the Vatican from having veto power in the UN would be for the UN officials to revoke this special privilege given the Vatican, a privilege which is being sadly abused. This in turn would reduce the Vatican's influence on the World Bank, World Health Organization, and individual governments. It would also contribute to a decreased opportunity for religious terrorism to occur in poor countries depending on these agencies for aid.

However, there are a number of other reasons, based mainly on myths, for the "population explosion" dialogue that was so popular in the '70s being dropped from our vocabulary:

1. Controversies over what is considered "coercive" population control programs, such as China's.
2. The fact that mass famine predicted by Paul Ehrlich and others didn't materialize by his predicted date due to the "green revolution."
3. Opposition from pro-life groups.
4. Opposition from various feminist groups.
5. Opposition from the growth lobby.
6. A media ban on the population issue.
7. Government's refusal to discuss this taboo issue.

> If humanity expects to flourish into the 21st century, it must take action with its intellect rather than its emotional and religious paradigms that prove outdated, outmoded and irrelevant.
>
> Bob Woodruff
> Earth 2100, *www.earth2100.tv*

THE SOUTH-SOUTH INITIATIVE

1994 was a busy year for countries of the south, as well as those of the north. In the 1998 *Earth Times*, Erin Trowbridge writes about the "South-South Initiative." At the 1994 United Nations International Conference on Population and Development, the Partners in Population and Development were formed. This was an intra-governmental coalition of developing nations who intended to address the changing paradigms of population issues and the inverse relationship between a nation's state of development and the size of its population. The more people living in a country, the harder it is to provide proper services and health care to all.

Trowbridge adds that the Partners were founded by ten countries, Zimbabwe, Kenya, Mexico, Colombia, Thailand, Indonesia, Bangladesh, Morocco, Egypt, and Tunisia, which had gained expertise in the fields of reproductive health and development. The idea was to create a forum for the leaders of these countries to share experiences and exchange technical information that would help other countries learn from their successful programs.

By 1998 the Partners had grown to fourteen nations, with the admissions of China, India, Pakistan, and Uganda.

Going back to where they had begun, the Partners held their fourth annual board meeting in Cairo, where they set down concrete plans of action and programs of exchange. Cairo again became a hot seat as political leaders, nongovernmental organization representatives, and private sector donors gathered to discuss just how well those ideas borne of the first conference were taking seed.

"The baby is out of the incubator," said Steven Sinding, director of the population and science division of the Rockefeller Foundation, which provided $1.3 million of funding to cover the core activities of the Partner's Secretariat.

The goal of the Partners was to foster cooperation and exchange of technical information between developing countries, rather than follow the development strategies sent out from the industrial nations. They discussed their greatest successes and illuminating aspects of their programs that they would like to see better developed. Indonesian representatives said they would like to replicate the all-inclusive clinics they saw run by Profamilia n Colombia; Chinese officials said they'd like to work with Thai officials to develop AIDS awareness programs; and many nations voiced a desire to work with Bangladesh's micro-credit loan programs.

One of their biggest challenges was to raise funding for their programs. Much of this funding could have come from United Nations programs, if a consensus had been reached on implementing these recommended programs.

> And to ensure a healthier and more abundant world, we simply must slow the world's explosive growth in population. We cannot afford to see the human waste doubled by the middle of the next century. Our nation has, at last, renewed its commitment to work with the United Nations to expand the availability of the world's family planning education and services. We must ensure that there is a place at the table for every one of our world's children. And we can do it.
>
> President Bill Clinton
> United Nations, New York
> 27 September 1993

> I consider the dramatic growth in the world's population to be the greatest challenge currently facing the environment … The effects of this rapid increase are felt around the globe. Starvation, deforestation and lack of clean water are just some of the problems.
>
> Al Gore
> US Vice President

Of course, when President Clinton and Al Gore talk about **the world's population**, they are talking about all countries of the world—developed countries as well as Third World countries. All countries are contributing to the consumption of world resources, and the production of enormous human waste in the form of garbage, excrement, pollution, and CO^2.

> In the long run the problem of overpopulation of the countries of the South can be fully resolved only through their development. But action to contain the rise of population cannot be postponed.
>
> Julius Nyerere,
> President of Tanzania and Chair of the South Commission,
> 1990

Shortly after the so-called "global gag rule" was reversed in 2009, this statement was made:

> For too long this unwarranted ban has been used as a political wedge issue, the subject of a back and forth debate that has served only to divide us ... It has undermined efforts to promote safe and effective voluntary family planning in developing countries ... I have no desire to continue this stale and fruitless debate.
>
> President Obama, 2009

CHINA

China's family planning effort remains perhaps the most controversial, complex, and misunderstood on our planet. In their desperate attempt to deal with their burgeoning population, which was nearing one billion, the government finally took action. In 1980 the State Council, China's highest governmental body, issued an open letter to all Communist officials ordering that they could have only one child. China's provinces and major cities passed laws and regulations limiting births. The one-child policy had begun.

The official government statement of justification was that population growth interferes with economic development. They have proven this to be correct.

Barbara Crossette, in her 1999 article "Rethinking Population at a Global Milestone," pointed out:

> Even as they issued the harsh decree that families could have only one child, the Chinese also put together a comprehensive package of changes in the economy, rural land ownership and social services—and the country began to take off. Lamentably, Western experts often emphasize, political democracy was not part of the package. But the sweeping changes paid off in many other ways.
>
> Semi-socialist India, on the other hand, lagged in introducing fundamental economic and social reforms to match China's—perhaps, ironically, because in a democracy such measures have to have some popular support. There was also history: India's legendary first Prime Minister, Jawaharial Nehru, set his sights on big industries, not village schools or rural doctors.
>
> If current trends continue, India will surpass China as the most populous nation in the next half century. It enters a new millennium with work still to be done on a gigantic scale that the world cannot ignore … Could it be true that democracy is not the most efficient way to bring a country out of poverty? Or is it that political leadership, more than the political system, matters most?

"Democracy Cannot Survive Overpopulation"
Isaac Asimov

"The key in talking about population growth," said Lester Brown, president of the Worldwatch Institute in Washington in 1999, "is not whether India is a democracy or not, but whether there is leadership. By leadership, I mean leaders who will talk about the problem, discuss it and what it means to the next generation and the generations to follow."

> Population must be stabilized and rapidly. If we don't do it, Nature will, and much more brutally.
>
> Maurice Strong
> Secretary General at Rio Earth Summit, 1992

WORLDWATCH INSTITUTE—STATE OF THE WORLD

In 1984 the Worldwatch Institute began producing an annual report on progress toward a sustainable society. Each year this report is presented in the form of a book entitled *State of the World*, which is translated into all major languages. In the absence of a comprehensive annual assessment by the United Nations or any national government, this book is now accorded semi-official status by national governments, UN agencies, and the international development community. More than 1,100 US college and university courses—ranging from biology to geography to political science—use the volume. As the New York Review of Books points out, *State of the World* "deals with calamitous events rationally and constructively, and always offers logical solutions.

SCIENTIFIC COMMUNITY

> *Of course human numbers are at the very core of our crisis. The explosive rate of growth simply can't continue.*
>
> *Dr. David Suzuki*

> Globally, and in Canada, population problems result from failure to recognize and act in accordance with one of Nature's fundamental characteristics. Every

> species is endowed with a reproductive potential which, if uncontrolled, will result in its population exceeding the carrying capacity of its environment.
>
> Dr. C. Fred Bentley, 1994
> Professor Emeritus of Soil Science,
> University of Alberta, Canada

> We must stabilize population. This will be possible only if all nations recognize that it requires improved social and economic conditions, and the adoption of effective, voluntary family planning. We must ensure sexual equality, and guarantee women control over their own reproductive decisions.
>
> The Union of Concerned Scientists, 1993

Established in 1969, the Union of Concerned Scientists (UCS) has created a unique alliance between many of the nation's leading scientists and thousands of committed citizens. As of 1993 over 1670 scientists, including 104 Nobel laureates—a majority of the living recipients of the prize in the sciences—had signed onto their Global Resources Project, producing "The World Scientists' Warning to Humanity." This partnership addresses the most serious environmental and security threats facing humanity.

The project's goal is to increase awareness of the threat that global environmental degradation poses to humanity's life-support systems. The campaign's mandate is to organize efforts in professional academies to address this issue and to use scientists' voices to educate their fellow citizens and world leaders. UCS is currently working to:

- encourage responsible stewardship of the global environment and life-sustaining resources
- promote energy technologies that are renewable, safe, and cost-effective
- reform transportation policy

- curtail weapons proliferation

An independent, nonprofit organization, UCS conducts technical studies and public education and seeks to influence government policy at the local, state, federal, and international levels.

> We the undersigned, senior members of the world's scientific community, hereby warn all humanity of what lies ahead. A great change in our stewardship of the earth and the life on it is required, if vast human misery is to be avoided and our global home on this planet is not to be irretrievably mutilated.
>
> Union of Concerned Scientists, "Warning," 1993

The UCS believes that human beings and the natural world are on a collision course. Human activities inflict harsh and often irreversible damage on the environment and on critical resources. They warn that if not checked, many of our current practices put at serious risk the future that we wish for human society and the plant and animal kingdoms and may so alter the living world that it will be unable to sustain life in the manner that we know. Fundamental changes are urgent if we are to avoid the collision our present course will bring about.

They join many other scientists, such as David Suzuki and Jacques Cousteau, in lamenting the irreversible loss of species, which by 2100 may reach one-third of all species now living. We are losing the potential these species hold for providing medicinal and other benefits, and the contribution that genetic diversity of life-forms gives to the robustness of the world's biological systems and to the astonishing beauty of the earth itself.

Our massive tampering with the world's interdependent web of life—coupled with the environmental damage inflicted by deforestation, species loss, and climate change—could trigger widespread adverse effects, including unpredictable collapse of critical biological systems whose interactions and dynamics we only imperfectly understand. Uncertainty over the extent of these effects cannot excuse complacency or delay in facing the threats.

Regarding population, the UCS points out that the earth is finite. Its ability to absorb wastes and destructive effluent is finite. Its ability to provide food and energy is finite. Its ability to provide for growing numbers of people is finite. And we are fast approaching many of the earth's limits. Current economic practices that damage the environment, in both developed and underdeveloped nations, cannot be continued without the risk that vital global systems will be damaged beyond repair.

Pressures resulting from unrestrained population growth put demands on the natural world that can overwhelm any efforts to achieve a sustainable future. If we are to halt the destruction of our environment, we must accept limits to that growth.

These world scientists believe that acting on this recognition is not altruism, but enlightened self-interest: whether industrialized or not, we all have but one lifeboat. No nation can escape from injury when global biological systems are damaged. No nation can escape from conflicts over increasingly scarce resources. In addition, environmental and economic instabilities will cause mass migrations with incalculable consequences for developed and undeveloped nations alike.

It was back in 1993 that the UCS warned that developing nations must realize that environmental damage is one of the gravest threats they face, and that attempts to blunt it will be overwhelmed if their populations go unchecked. The greatest peril is to become trapped in spirals of environmental decline, poverty, and unrest, leading to social, economic, and environmental collapse. Unfortunately, mankind refused to heed that warning, and we are seeing signs of the scientists' predictions today.

> If the people will lead, the leaders will follow.
>
> Dr. David Suzuki

> No matter how distracted we may be by the number of problems now facing us, one issue remains

> fundamental: Overpopulation. The crowding of our cities, our nations, underlies all other problems.
>
> Paul R. Ehrlich
> Honorary President,
> Zero Population Growth

Dr. Cuker, professor of Marine and Environmental Science at Hampton University (2008) had this to say:

> Our children will live in a much better world if human population growth is checked by the rational decision to reduce family size, rather than by famine, epidemics and war. So where is our national leadership on this issue? For six years the Bush administration worked to dismantle both national and global population control efforts, cutting funding to these programs over the issues of abortion and birth control in deference to conservative evangelicals and the Catholic Church. The administration directed resources to support abstinence-only sex mis-education programs that failed to deter unwanted teen pregnancies.
>
> All species, including humans, must reproduce in order to survive. It is absurd to build a population control policy based upon the notion that older teens and adults will abstain from sex. The official position of the Catholic Church is that sex is a sin outside of marriage and so is any form of marital birth control (including condoms) other than abstinence during times of peak female fertility.
>
> The Catholic position not only thwarts effective family planning but also blocks the most important weapon in the fight to stop the AIDS/HIV epidemic. Yet, according to Catholic Church publications, some 80 percent of Catholics defy the church and use contraception. Frankly, I don't think it any of

> my business as to the sex life or lack thereof, of the pope, priests (as long as it does not include child abuse), nuns, or lay Catholics. But I do object to the pontiff's decree interfering with a rational public policy that will protect Earth from the ravages of overpopulation. And ditto for AIDS/HIV and a woman's right to control her own reproduction. We need realistic public policy that promotes family planning and safe sex, not one designed to capture votes from the religious right.

Support for reducing population to a sustainable level is almost unanimous from the science community. Every credible scientist has come to the realization that we must bring environmentally damaging activities under control to restore and protect the integrity of the earth's systems we depend on.

THE GROWTH LOBBY

> We see here, baldly, the conflict between an implacable human urge and the calculations of science. To say which approach is rational is not to predict the likely winner. The scientists are wrestling with an 800-pound gorilla: GREED.
>
> Lindscy Grant,
> "The Economists' Myths,"
> October 2007

James Sinnamon, an environmental and political writer, is greatly concerned about the way the Australian government, and others in the western world, deliberately encourage population growth. He is puzzled as to why this push for growth continues when common sense and intuition, not to mention the hard evidence, tell us that a larger population cannot possibly be in the interests of the current inhabitants of his country or of the rest of the planet. He points to the growth lobby, which is profiting off the human suffering, chaos, and loss of wildlife habitat and diversity. He explains,

> That group is the growth lobby. It is really a group of land speculators and landlords operating in an organized way at a corporate level. Land speculators and landlords openly welcome the way that growing demand increases the price of resources and services which include water, land, power, housing, roads, food production and transport, which each one of us needs in order to live a dignified life, or even simply to live.
>
> As one consequence, in Brisbane at the start of 2009, many are being impoverished by insatiably greedy landlords, who exploit these circumstances to increase rents at every possible opportunity.
>
> The growth lobby also includes property developers, financiers, building companies and suppliers of building materials. There are also others that gain from population growth through high immigration, such as immigration lawyers, employment agencies and some employers.
>
> While these activities may provide a façade of economic prosperity, none are capable of increasing the underlying ability of this society to provide for its own needs. At some point such "growth" has to end … but the growth lobby wants this situation to continue indefinitely. To ensure that the forced march to dystopia continues, the growth lobby pours funds into the coffers of Australia's major political parties, including Anna Blight's Labor Party.

Sinnamon warns that this situation creates obligation and dependency in our political parties and governments. In turn, our governments endlessly facilitate the real estate economy, in the face of every democratic objection, merely to keep themselves in government. He warns that if we are to hope for any kind of a decent future for ourselves and our children, these corrupt arrangements must be brought to an end and the power of the growth lobby must be broken.

Mr. Sinnamon is not alone in his thinking, as our current economic system seems to depend on an ever-increasing population. Actually, with increased density, some people benefit while the majority suffer. All non-human life suffers from human increase, but economic systems ignore that cost since it doesn't have a price tag, at least not yet.

A large, expendable work force benefits business owners, but it places labor at a disadvantage. Workers with dependents can't afford to hold out on strike or take chances on being permanently replaced. High unemployment reduces wages, while high demand for workers increases wages and benefits. The rich need a large supply of the poor, and what better way to continue this cycle than to promote an increasing population? Or better yet, pay your governments to do it for you.

In Canada, the taxpayers are subsidizing this influx of cheap labor to the tune of about $20 billion in program resources that could have been used to reduce some of our many home-grown problems, according to John Meyer (2009). He believes that environmentally, mass immigration is an ongoing disaster, with urban sprawl taking over our best agricultural land.

Immigrants are a boon to the cheap labor employers, developers, and media corporations for whom they constitute a cash cow. Immigration is now responsible for almost all of our population growth, which is great for the above mentioned lobbies but bad for the average Canadian. Who want more people in the country? Most Canadians don't.

Immigration-driven population growth is responsible for 80 percent of Canada's overshoot of our Kyoto 2012 carbon emissions target of 560 megatons. That's right, mass immigration is out-polluting the Alberta tar sands by three or four to one. We are about 30 percent over the 560mt goal now and headed higher. Meyer concludes that we need to bring immigration policy into the twenty-first century.

In addition, the forces of globalization have only complicated the situation.

The forces of globalization centered in the institutions and programs of the International Monetary Fund, the World Bank, and large, mostly American corporations, as well as funds flowing through many so called aid and development programs, are seen to reinforce, and in many ways drive the policies of the wealthy and powerful, who are creating and perpetuating the intolerable conditions with which Indigenous people are now living.

Chief Phil Lane
of Lethbridge, Alberta,
in *Listening to the Excluded* by Hank Zyp

The number of national governments, as well as national and international agencies, aggressively trying to encourage people to limit their reproduction has increased very markedly during the past two or three decades. Unfortunately the archaic myth that more people is axiomatically good, desirable, beneficial, necessary and in the public interest persists. That is particularly the case in Canada where politicians, chambers of commerce, businesses of most kinds and individuals with personal agendas constantly preach the need for more people in Canada.

So we have a selfish, myopic immigration policy that blindly disregards global and Canadian population problems which are truly future-endangering because of the environmental deterioration and resource depletion (e.g. cod stocks) they cause. Moreover there is a strong tendency for internal conflicts to increase with rising density of population, as in Rwanda.

Dr. Fred Bentley,
Sustainable Population Society
Professor Emeritus of Soil Science at University of Alberta, 1994

MEDIA

No sector of our society has been more negligent in addressing the population issue than the media, with few exceptions. It is the media to which we look for balanced reporting on world events and the state of our planet. Yet, by making this a taboo topic, they have managed to undermine any efforts to have open and meaningful debate regarding population issues. It is especially irresponsible for our public broadcasting networks like CBC and BBC to refuse to deal with population (as I discussed in Part 1) when so many citizens have expressed their concern about the issue.

There are numerous programs on TV, like the *Nature of Things*, which vividly show the devastation our growing population is causing. However, they stop short of actually pointing out that it is caused by overpopulation or mentioning that reducing population would be a viable solution. TV talk shows are eager to interview celebrities who are pregnant, glorifying parenthood and promoting big families. Yet, they seldom mention the realities of how difficult parenting is, and the many neglected and abused children resulting from the lack of family planning. They don't mention the burden that overpopulation puts on society or the environment.

News reports daily mention the effects of growth and the need for spending billions of dollars on expanding, building, replacing, or updating our infrastructure and increasing our energy supply, housing, schools, prisons, etc. Yet seldom do they give the other side of the story, including suggestions that we reduce the demand by reducing population. The news is constantly quoting the Vatican on the virtues of being celibate or avoiding the use of birth control or family planning. Yet never do they balance this out with views from family planning or population groups.

On the other hand, the population movement on the Internet, reflecting the discontent of the average citizen, is growing by leaps and bounds. This underground movement is using the increasing number of Internet sites, blogs, discussion groups, and speak-outs to let their voice be heard.

> Today, the news media uncommonly deal with the material on overpopulation and depletion of natural resources. Thus, if the media does deal with the issue of population, the material almost always suggests that there are benefits from increased population, reflecting the biased interests of say, the real estate industry. The real estate industry, and other business interests, in the absence of scientific evidence to the contrary, always or almost always promote population growth. The media always desire to sell more newspapers, and thus also commonly promote high immigration and high fertility levels.
>
> Doctors for a Sustainable Population (Australia), 2009

Now, with racism on the mind of many political leaders, we are up against a situation where journalists and other media people are anxious to be politically correct in their commentary and writings on immigration. This means ever more immigration is being advocated or defended in a context entirely excluding what is happening to larger and larger areas of the planet and its health.

However, there are organizations trying to encourage media involvement in population coverage. The Population Institute is an international educational organization that was established in 1969. It now has members in 172 countries and is headquartered in Washington, DC.

The Population Institute's Global Media Awards are designed to encourage greater media coverage of population and development issues. They honor those who have contributed to creating awareness of population problems through their outstanding journalistic endeavors. The awards serve to encourage editors, news directors, and journalists to acquire a more in-depth knowledge of population issues to stimulate high standards for journalism.

There are twelve categories for awards, including magazine, TV shows, radio, news, editorials, online, and films. Prof. A. A. Bartlett won the award for Best Magazine Article on Population in 2008.

LANDMARKS IN POPULATION HISTORY

The baby boomers will no doubt remember the findings of the Club of Rome, published in 1972 from their "Project on the Predicament of Mankind." The technical part was written by a Massachusetts Institute of Technology project team, which built an elaborate computer model to track a number of variables from 1900 to 1970 and project their paths to the year 2100. The results were disturbing, to say the least.

The variables in the model were resources, population, pollution, industrial output per capita, and food per capita. The model gave rather similar pictures under all of the scenarios where population was not controlled. Population, industrial output per capita, pollution, and food per capita all grew exponentially. Natural resources declined with the growth of population and industrial output.

Since the time of the Club of Rome project in 1970, there have been numerous events, reports, conferences, etc., that have reinforced its findings and a few that have offered opposition.

- 1970: Two months after the first "Earth Day," the First National Congress on Optimum Population and Environment convened in Chicago. Religious groups—especially the United Methodist Church and the Presbyterian Church—urged, for ethical and moral reasons, that the federal government adopt policies that would lead to a stabilized US population. President Nixon addressed the nation about problems it would face if US population growth continued unabated.

- 1970: Paul Ehrlich's book *The Population Bomb*, which was written in 1968, was being widely read and discussed.

- 1970: Title X of the Public Health Service Act was established as the single largest source of federal US funds for domestic family planning programs. Title X supports approximately

4,000 family planning clinics serving low-income individuals and teenagers.

- 1972: Stockholm Conference on Population

- 1972: The "Rockefeller Commission" issued its 186-page report concluding that further population growth would do more harm than good.

- 1973: Roe v. Wade Supreme Court decision prohibited states from restricting access to abortion and protected a woman's right to choose to terminate a pregnancy prior to fetal viability. Prior to this decision, between 15 and 20 percent of all recorded maternal deaths in the United States during this century were attributed to illegal abortion.

- 1974: The United Nations designated 1974 as World Population Year. The aim of this was to focus the attention of governments, organizations, and individuals on the possible effect on various aspects of life that the size and growth of the world's population would have.

- 1974: President Nixon, recognizing the gravity of the overpopulation problem, directed in National Security Study Memorandum 200 (NSSM) that a new study be undertaken to determine the "Implications of World Population Growth for U.S. Security and Overseas Interests."

- 1974: International Population Conference in Bucharest, Romania

- 1975: *Our planet was host to 4 billion people*

- 1975: President Ford completed the 1974 NSSM study, which recommended that America should try to reach population stability by 2000. This would have required a policy of encouraging one-child families!

- 1981: The Global 2000 Report—The US Department of State and Council on Environmental Quality presented to President Carter the following recommendation: "The

United States should develop a national population policy which addresses the issues of population stabilization as well as just, consistent, and workable immigration laws."

- 1984: At the United Nations International Conference on Population held in Mexico City, President Reagan initiated the "Mexico City" policy (also known as the "global gag rule"). This policy withheld US funding from any private organization that provided information, counseling or health care related to abortion, such as the International Planned Parenthood Federation.

- 1986: The Reagan administration withheld its contribution to the United Nations Population Fund (UNFPA) over allegations that UNFPA was participating in the management of China's controversial "One Child Policy," despite verification of the fact that UNFPA was not involved in any coercive activities.

- 1987: The Brundtland report of the World Commission on Environment and Development was released.

- 1987: *Global population reached 5 billion*

- 1989: World Population Day was established on 11 July by the Governing Council of the United Nations Development Program. It was inspired by the public interest in Five Billion Day on 11 July 1987, approximately the date on which the world's population reached five billion people.

- 1992: One of Bill Clinton's first acts as president was to sign a Presidential Memorandum overturning the "Mexico City" policy of 1984.

- 1992: UN Conference on Environment and Development, Earth Summit at Rio

- 1993: President Clinton created the "President's Council on Sustainable Development" and charged it with helping to "grow the economy and preserve the environment," objectives that some may see as conflicting.

- 1994: International Conference on Population and Development in Cairo
- 1994: South-South Initiative—Countries of the south formed the Partners in Population and Development
- 1995: Fourth World Conference on Women in Beijing.
- 1999: *World population reached 6 billion*
- 1996: The President's Council on Sustainable Development called for a "Move toward stabilization of U.S. population." Yet, funds for population programs were slashed by nearly 90 percent.
- 1999: President Clinton and Congress ended a three-year standoff and agreed to pay nearly $1 billion in back dues owed to the UN, which included funding for family planning programs. A concession the Clinton administration was forced to make to the Republican-dominated House of Representatives was to restrict funding to programs that advocated abortions in foreign countries.
- 1999: The Catholics for a Free Choice launched the "See Change" campaign to change the status of the Holy See (Vatican) at the United Nations.
- 2000: On 14 July Governor Gray Davis signed a proclamation declaring the week of 22–28 October 2000 as World Population Awareness Week in California. WPAW is an intense educational campaign designed to create public awareness about the trends in world population growth, the detrimental effects they have on our planet and its inhabitants, and the urgent need for action in order to change this situation.
- 2001: President Bush cut funding to family planning programs, promoting abstinence as the most effective

form of birth control. He continued to enforce the Mexico City "gag rule" dictates and consistently vetoed legislation overturning the policy.

- 2009: On his third day as president, President Obama reversed the "global gag rule" for family planning, which had been imposed by Bush eight years earlier. Obama also proposed that Family Planning provisions be included in his stimulus bill that would have expanded eligibility for Medicaid-funded family planning services. However, the Democrats caved in to Republican outrage, and this proposal was not adopted.
- 2012: *World population will reach 7 billion*

OBAMA

More than 250 health and human rights organizations from around the world sent Obama a letter, thanking him for ending a policy "which has contributed to the deaths and injuries of countless women and girls." A World Bank reporter stated that women in developing countries, where access to contraception is poor, often turn to abortion as a means of birth control.

Secretary of State Hillary Clinton said Obama's repeal of the ban was "a welcomed and important step" that would help ensure women and children have full access to health information and services.

Each of the above events, conferences, or reports greatly affected the population movement. Many supported the notion that population and consumption could not keep on growing indefinitely, and that change was both urgent and mandatory. However, over the years support for the "global gag rule" went up and down like a yo-yo, with each new president. Could Obama be the president to finally make the "gag rule" a thing of the past and open up a new era of candid debate about overpopulation and the need for a population policy? Perhaps all he needs is the public's support to turn Martin Luther King's dream for universal family planning programs into a reality.

The preceding list of events came from numerous sources, including the Canadian Population Action Network, Edward C. Hartman's book *The Population Fix*, and Zero Population Growth US.

I have outlined some of the circumstances and people who have brought us to the present population dilemma. If we are to learn anything from our history, I hope that it will be to rectify our past mistakes and insist that our leaders deal with population in an honest and meaningful way.

(In response to this question by Bill Moyers: What do you see happening to the idea of dignity to human species if this population growth continues at its present rate?)

> It's going to destroy it all. I use what I call my bathroom metaphor. If two people live in an apartment, and there are two bathrooms, then both have what I call freedom of the bathroom, go to the bathroom any time you want, and stay as long as you want to for whatever you need. And this to my way is ideal. And everyone believes in the freedom of the bathroom. It should be right there in the Constitution. But if you have 20 people in the apartment and two bathrooms, no matter how much every person believes in freedom of the bathroom, there is no such thing. You have to set up, you have to set up times for each person, you have to bang at the door, aren't you through yet, and so on. And in the same way, democracy cannot survive overpopulation. Human dignity cannot survive it. Convenience and decency cannot survive it. As you put more and more people into the world, the value of life not only declines, it disappears. It doesn't matter if someone dies.
>
> Isaac Asimov

> Which is the greater danger—nuclear warfare or the population explosion? The latter absolutely! To bring about nuclear war, someone has to DO

something; someone has to press a button. To bring about destruction by overcrowding, mass starvation, anarchy, the destruction of our most cherished values—there is no need to do anything. We need only do nothing except what comes naturally—and breed. *And how easy it is to do nothing.*

Isaac Asimov
Found on *www.BetterWorld.net* website

PART 3: CONTRIBUTING FACTORS

THE STORY OF THE HUNDREDTH MONKEY (*www.hundredthmonkey.net*)

The Japanese monkey, *Macaca fuscata*, has been observed in the wild for a period of over 30 years. In 1952, on the island of Koshima scientists were providing monkeys with sweet potatoes dropped in the sand. The monkeys liked the taste of the raw sweet potatoes, but they found the dirt unpleasant.

An 18-month-old female named Imo found she could solve the problem in a nearby stream. She taught this trick to her mother. Her playmates also learned this new way and they taught their mothers, too.

This cultural innovation was gradually picked up by various monkeys before the eyes of the scientists. Between 1952 and 1958, all the young monkeys learned to wash the sandy sweet potatoes to make them more palatable. Only the adults who imitated their children learned this social improvement. Other adults kept eating the dirty sweet potatoes.

Then something startling took place. In the autumn of 1958, a certain number of Koshima monkeys were washing sweet potatoes—the exact number is not known. Let us suppose that when the sun rose one morning there were 99 monkeys on Koshima Island who had learned to wash their sweet potatoes.

> Let's further suppose that later that morning, the hundredth monkey learned to wash potatoes.
>
> THEN IT HAPPENED!
>
> By that evening almost everyone in the tribe was washing sweet potatoes before eating them. The added energy of this hundredth monkey somehow created an ideological breakthrough!
>
> But notice.
>
> A most surprising thing observed by these scientists was that the habit of washing sweet potatoes then jumped over the sea. Colonies of monkeys on other islands and the mainland troop of monkeys at Takasakiyama began washing their sweet potatoes!
>
> Thus, when a certain critical number achieves an awareness, this new awareness may be communicated from mind to mind. There is a point at which if only one more person tunes-in to a new awareness, a field is strengthened to the point where this awareness is picked up by almost everyone!

The Wikipedia free encyclopedia states the "Hundredth Monkey Effect" is a supposed phenomenon in which a learned behavior spreads instantaneously from one group of monkeys to all related monkeys once a critical number is reached. By generalization it means the instant spreading of an idea or ability to the remainder of a population once a certain portion of that population has heard of the new idea or learned the new ability. The story behind this supposed phenomenon originated with Lawrence Blair and Lyall Watson, who claimed that it was the observation of Japanese scientists.

This story was further popularized by Ken Keyes, Jr., with the publication of his book *The Hundredth Monkey*. Keyes presented the "Hundredth Monkey Effect" story as an inspirational parable, applying it to human society and the effecting of positive change therein. Since then, the story has become widely accepted and even appears in books written by some educators.

The hundredth monkey story may be a myth, but the capacity to spread ideas around the world with lightning speed in the age of email and the internet is no myth. We even have a phrase for it—emails, You Tube videos, or blogs are said to "go viral." The concept of overshoot is one that desperately needs a critical mass of people to trigger a response in the general population that will put pressure on politicians to act. Sitting at our computer, each of us can be that hundredth monkey to help create the momentum that will motivate citizens around the globe to make a sustainable population a goal.

Your awareness is needed in saving the world from overpopulation. You may be the "Hundredth Monkey" …

In Part 3 of this book, I intend to explore ways that we can do just that. For one thing, it is extremely important that we empower couples to say no to unwanted parenthood. In some cases, where there is no access to family planning programs, the focus will be on providing funding for these programs.

Since I became aware of the population crisis in 1971, I have taken notice of the many various reasons that people have children. Over the years many parents have confided in me regarding their motivation to have children, and even regarding their regret for having children. I have also read about the many unwanted and unplanned children that enter this world unloved and are often abandoned or sold into slavery or the sex trade. All too often the reasons people have children have nothing to do with truly wanting a child to cherish and love. I will be looking at some of these reasons and myths next.

REASONS FOR HIGH BIRTH RATES

1. Having Babies is the Natural Thing To Do—Expected by Society as an Honored Tradition

> Once it was necessary that the people should multiply and be fruitful if the race was to survive. But now to preserve the race it is necessary that people hold back the power of propagation.
>
> Helen Keller

In the past, tradition and ignorance dictated what the family norm should be, and this conditioned value system we used when planning for a family often went unquestioned. Girls had been conditioned to believe that their only purpose was to grow up, have children, and be good mothers and wives. However, with changing times, busy lifestyles, and a rapidly growing population, it is imperative that we rethink this premise. In fact, many women now are choosing to be childfree. In these troubled and more knowledgeable times, not everyone sees having children as a blessing.

Now, many women do have a choice. There are also more reasons that families are choosing to be childfree. Birth control is more reliable, people are marrying later, marriages seem less stable, our world is a scarier place to raise children, and women are more reluctant to give up their careers. According to the National Center for Health Statistics, in 1975 about one in eleven women was childless by the age of forty-four. By 1993, that number had risen to about one in six.

JUST SAY NO TO COERCED PARENTHOOD

> If motherhood doesn't interest you, don't do it. It didn't interest me, so I didn't do it.
>
> Katherine Hepburn

Many more couples are weighing all the pros and cons and deciding to be childfree. However, this is only possible where family planning programs are available and where couples are encouraged to recognize the benefits/options of a childfree lifestyle.

After a baby is born, marital satisfaction declines, says Ralph LaRossa, a professor of sociology at Georgia State University. When researchers chart this decline, it's a U-shaped curve that rises only as children get older and leave home.

Many *Childfree* couples claim that they give their decision to be childfree more thought than most parents give to having children. It is apparent, given the numerous cases of abandoned babies, child neglect, and abuse, that far too many people give inadequate thought to having and raising children. On a recent *Oprah* show, she discussed the growing issue of child neglect, saying that it is at epidemic proportions. With the growing cost of raising a family, and the increasing number of working mothers, both parents and children are losing out.

Some people feel that childfree couples are being selfish, but in reality the opposite is true. Dr. Bonnie Bukwa, retired Chemistry Instructor at Cranbrook's College of the Rockies, points out:

> Those without children make more opportunities and resources for the children of those who do breed. In effect the non-breeders are denying their own genes for the benefit and opportunities of the genes of others. It actually is a VERY selfless act, genetically equivalent to taking a bullet to protect another or throwing oneself on a grenade in combat! The really selfish ones are those having many children on purpose! That is right in there with overconsumption.
>
> And while I'm at it, the worst are those having children carelessly who they then abuse, neglect, or expect others to support. (2009)

We often hear parents say that they both work because they want to give their children all the things they could never have. What they are really talking about is material things. But in order to do that, they are sacrificing the truly important things like spending time with their children, not the least of which is sharing experiences of nature with them.

The vast majority of today's children suffer from nature deficit disorder, which renders them disconnected from the land and unsympathetic to the plight of our disappearing wildlife. Instead, many children grow up in artificial environments dominated by electronic gadgets and in front of electronic babysitters. Far too large a part of our society has given up quality time for material things, and we are often bribing our children in order to ease our feeling of guilt for neglecting them.

While many mothers look forward to being parents and celebrate the birth of their babies, not all mothers are in such a fortunate position. Childbirth can be a very agonizing and dangerous time for the mother. In developing countries especially, it is still quite common for mothers to die during this ordeal. Poverty, malnutrition, and the presence of various diseases can complicate the birthing process. With AIDS so prevalent in many of the poorest countries, this disease can also be passed on to the child, putting both mother and child at risk.

Although modern medicine in developed countries has greatly reduced complications at childbirth, there are other risks that are greatly underestimated and seldom discussed. A growing number of mothers are experiencing postnatal distress (also known as post-partum depression) and at a greater intensity than previously thought.

"Postnatal distress may be rather broader-based than we had previously thought," says Pauline Slade, a British psychologist whose research suggests that labor and childbirth can trigger post-traumatic stress symptoms usually associated with war.

The Dr. Phil Show of 11 May 2009 discussed cases of young mothers who had been overwhelmed by their children to the point of actually murdering them. There are many young mothers who become depressed for a variety of reasons and eventually snap. They were just unprepared for the demands of motherhood, and with the addition of post-partum depression they could not cope.

2. Lack of family planning programs.

According to the Population Institute of Canada, over 350 million women around the world would like to limit their family size but are denied access to safe, affordable family planning programs. The United Nations and participating countries have failed time and again to provide adequate funding for these family planning programs. It seems that governments can always find funding to continue senseless wars or unnecessary space missions, but not for this basic necessity that should be every woman's right.

Of course, there are many illegitimate (and many so-called legitimate) businesses that benefit from overpopulation and that would not want to see an end to the surplus of poor women and children available for the sex trade and child slavery. These powerful entities are among those male-dominated forces working against population control, as it would hinder their commercial interests. The strong patriarchal influence, including male-dominated forces such as organized crime, the Vatican, the growth lobby, the War Machine, and the United Nations, will be discussed later in Part 3.

> "Every single day, tens of millions of children work in conditions that shock the conscience ... We must wipe from the earth the most vicious forms of abusive child labor."
>
> President Clinton,
> BBC News Online,
> 16 June 1999

Clinton spoke these words at an International Labor Organization conference in Geneva seeking to end the worst forms of child labor—slavery and bondage, prostitution and pornography, drugs and hazardous work. But since that time, little has changed.

According to Ms. Tomita, the campaigns coordinator with the International Secretariat of the Global March Against Child Labor, there are an estimated 246 million child laborers (about one out of every six children in the world in 2009). Estimates of the number of child slaves and bonded child laborers in India alone amount to 60 million in 2009. Many children in Asia are kidnapped or otherwise trapped in servitude, where they work in factories and workshops for no pay and receive constant beatings. She added,

> They have been burned, branded with red hot brands, starved, whipped, chained up, raped and kept locked in cupboards for days on end. These children are robbed of their childhood because they have to toil up to 18 hours a day, seven days a week." (*www.anti-slaverysociety.com*)

In Africa more than 200,000 children are sold each year into slavery, principally for seasonal work such as harvesting cocoa (for chocolate) and other cash crops, according to the website *www.anti-slaverysociety.com* (2009).

On BBC News, 20 February 2003, a United Nations official described the trafficking of women and children across Asia as *the largest slave trade in history.*

In fact, human trafficking has replaced the drugs trade as the world's largest illegal business. According to the BBC News, 20 June 2002, the people trade has become a multi-billion-dollar business, with millions of men, women, and children bought and sold every year. The Organization for Security and Cooperation in Europe says that the trade is rising, apparently because traffickers feel there are fewer risks involved in trading humans compared with drugs.

> The transfers are made using even more cruel and devious means than the original slave trade ... The victims are usually teenage girls who end up working in sweat shops or brothels ... But ending the trade in humans is virtually impossible given the level of corruption among government officials. In some countries, police, who are supposed to stop these crimes, are involved in crimes by offering protection to criminals. Pimps and middlemen get protection from the police ... Officials need to be trained and made more accountable.
>
> Unicef's Kul Gautum at International Symposium on Trafficking of Children, Tokyo (2003)

Like thousands of progressive people in the world, Mr. Gautum believes that a combination of poverty, globalization, organized crime, and discrimination against women encourage the trade.

> *The rich require an abundant supply of the poor.*
>
> *Voltaire*

According to the Anti-Slavery Society, the international trafficking of women and children is a growing phenomenon, as thousands of women and children are trafficked by businessmen into dens around the world.

Surprisingly, many follow the same slave routes used in the Middle Ages or the Renaissance, when the Slav women and children were sold in slave markets and purchased by buyers from Italy and France. Similarly, we are now, after a lapse of twenty-five years, seeing the revival of the once thriving slave trade routes across West Africa—except now, the camels have been replaced by trucks, jeeps, and aircraft.

The children are kidnapped or purchased for twenty to seventy dollars each by slavers in poorer states and sold into slavery in sex dens or as unpaid domestic servants for $350 each in wealthier oil-rich states. Their lives are at the mercy of their masters, and suicide is often the only escape.

Brokers in cross-border operations scout for children from poor families who are simply playing outside. They then kidnap the children or tell the parents that their children will receive a good education with a wealthy family and persuade the parents with a little cash. Of course, in reality the children are sold into slavery and never see their families again. Most of the young girls end up pregnant, contributing greatly to the overpopulation crisis.

> *About half the modern world doesn't have the same basic amenities the ancient Romans took for granted.*
>
> Peter Gleick

About half of all pregnancies in the world are unplanned, and many of those are the product of rape. For the millions of women around the world who do not want more children, but who are being given no alternative, there may be new hope. Recently a new, non-surgical method of voluntary female sterilization has been developed. A compound called quinacrine, in the form of a pellet, is inserted directly into the uterus to prevent future pregnancy. Many women and health-care workers in the Third World, desperate for cheap, easy-to-administer birth control, see the two maverick developers as saviors.

Stephen D. Mumford and contraceptive researcher Dr. Elton Kessel are the sole distributors of quinacrine, which is manufactured in Switzerland. It is now being distributed in about twenty countries through a network of doctors, nurses, and midwives. However, it has not been approved in Canada and the United States.

> One outspoken quinacrine advocate is gynecologist Naseem Rahman. On a Sunday in late January, she threads her way through a Dhaka, Bangladesh, slum inhabited by stonecutters and rickshaw pullers and speaks to women about birth control. She says she will send her health workers back here soon to spread the word about the free quinacrine sterilizations that she provides at her private clinic.
>
> She believes that the developed world's cautious standards of medical ethics and safety have no place in the lives of women for whom repeated pregnancies bring nothing but deprivation and danger. Quinacrine, she points out, is dramatically less expensive than any alternative she can provide.
>
> Panindigan.tripod.com/quinacrine, website,
> "Americans Export Sterilization to the Third World"

In 2003, the International Federation of Gynecology and Obstetrics announced in a 159-page publication that the quinacrine method is safe, effective, and simple enough to be provided in a basic clinic setting in resource-poor areas of the world. Indeed, earlier concerns about increased ectopic rates and carcinogenicity have not been borne out by the data so far accumulated.

According to the *www.quinacrine.com* 2009 article "Permanent Female Contraception," this publication, which includes twenty-five articles from fourteen countries and reports on 40,242 cases, was distributed at the FIGO World Congress, November 2003, in Santiago, Chile—a conference attended by some 8,500 obstetrician-gynecologists.

3. There are many girls and women who have children to fill a void in their life.

This was the case with the "Octomom," and as Dr. Phil stated numerous times on his TV show, children should not be "born with a job."

Comic used with permission from Mike Keefe

Kara Jesella, in her article "The New Eugenics," May 2009 put it this way:

> Octomom Nadya Suleman is a bogeyman to moralists of all breeds. Religious fundamentalists may approve of big families, but a husbandless

> woman with fourteen children epitomizes feminism gone wild. To proponents of small government, she is a modern-day reincarnation of the Reagan-era welfare queen. And to environmentally-friendly progressives, she is something else: the human equivalent of a Hummer.

Jesella points out that Suleman is not the only woman whose reproductive choices are inciting eco-anxiety. The reaction to the Octomom illuminates a conversation that is happening about the relationship between women's childbearing choices and the environment. It's certainly not uncommon to hear women in their twenties and thirties say that they are not sure they want to have children partly because they're worried about being earth-friendly.

With nearly 7 billion people on this planet, you'd think a couple would feel blessed that they could not add any more "consumers" to our already struggling planet. Yet women continue to use fertility treatments recklessly, often resulting in multiple births. As Dr. Phil and Dr. Oz both pointed out, multiple births often cause birth defects and great difficulties for both the babies and parents.

> We have a couple of billion more people on this planet than we need. What are we doing trying to figure out new ways to let couples have more babies?
>
> George Annas, Boston University

> For me the fundamental issue is one of what, for lack of a better word, I'd call planetary responsibility. I don't care if it's a poor single mom or Melinda Gates: I don't think anyone has the right to make reproductive choices that result in overpopulation. There are too many people already and the planet just can't support more of us. The result will be dwindling resources, vanishing habitat, all of which will cause unimaginable harm and suffering.
>
> Peaco Todd, Cartoonist, May, 2009

> Desperation to have a child comes from neediness, not instinct. It comes from the expectation that a child will fill an existing hole in our heart. Children, or anything else out there, can't fill that empty space. A feeling of wholeness comes from within.
>
> Susan Jeffers

This void that many parents are trying to fill can often be caused from parents not accomplishing their own goals in life, so they then pass those goals onto their children. If the parent was not successful as an athlete, painter, doctor, etc., they then set that goal for their child. We all know parents who have a career already planned for their child before he or she is even out of diapers. These children were born to fulfill the unmet dreams of the parents.

And it isn't just the women who are at fault here. The *Huffington Post* reported on 1 June 2009 that Desmond Hatchett, a twenty-nine-year-old who lives in Knoxville, Tennessee, has fathered twenty (maybe twenty-one) children with at least eleven different mothers. The website *www.Huffingtonpost.com* points out that the kids, who are between eleven months and eleven years old, require food, clothing, etc., which doesn't come cheap. That's a problem for their minimum-wage-earning father.

"I had four kids in the same year. Twice," Hatchett says.

He was called to court last week where he appeared on the docket eleven times to answer for fifteen of his twenty-one children who haven't received child support recently. The mothers of Hatchett's children are supposed to get anywhere from $25 to $309 a month, but the government is only allowed to take up to 50 percent of his pay check, and when that's split so many times some women only get a $1.98 a month.

Global opinion and law are far too lenient on men who feel free to impregnate as many women as they like, often with no consequences. In fact, the men are often seen as "macho" or "studs," while the women are condemned as "whores." This is true even in the case of rape—including statutory rape, date drug rape, war rape, or child rape. The men are seldom held accountable morally or legally. It is the women or our social systems (the taxpayers) that are usually held accountable and left with the responsibility of caring for the child.

Sometimes the reasoning for wanting large families is for parents to have someone to take care of them when they get old—a security blanket. This is a very selfish reason, as many of these children are born in third world countries and end up starving to death before they have a chance to grow up. They were born with the job of taking care of their parents at a very young age and often don't have the resources to fulfill their purpose, if they survive at all.

Of course, if families had far fewer children, there would be far less poverty. Even in the animal kingdom, mothers often put their young ones first, even fighting to the death for them. Have we, as a species, really become so far removed from nature?

Because humans off-load the cost to government, other family members, or strangers, they are able to cheat the biological and evolutionary rules of survival. These are people sociologists call "cheats" because they garner greater advantage than they are prepared to pay for.

> *When the family is small, whatever little they have they are able to share. There is peace.*
>
> Philip Njuguna,
> pastor,
> Nairobi, Kenya

4. To hold a marriage together.

You probably know someone who was having marital problems and thought that maybe having a child (or another child) would bring the couple closer together. However, most often this tactic backfires, they end up divorced anyhow, and now the child has only one parent.

Using a baby as a pawn in a marital relationship is cruel and senseless. Not only that, but being a parent is a very demanding job that not everyone is suited to. Oprah often says that it is the hardest job in the world. We all seem to have this preconceived, and often unrealistic, notion about having a perfect family like the Waltons or Partridge Family. We think that we won't make the same mistakes that our parents made, but it rarely works out as we planned. For some parents it is a rude awakening and a great disappointment.

> Having children brings much trouble and numerous responsibilities, and no matter how much care you give your children there is never any guarantee that they will not bring you great pain and heartbreak.
>
> Men and women are like other living creatures: they bring children into the world with little or no thought about the matter and then they suffer and toil as best as they can to rear them. Men and women think that it is necessary to have children. It is not. It is their animal nature and social custom, rather than reason, which makes them believe that this is a necessity.
>
> Democritus (460–370 BC)

Having children that aren't properly planned for, or that are unwanted, is a double misdemeanor. It is terribly unfair to the child and equally unfair to the environment. For every extra child that is born, a plant or animal has to be sacrificed to make room for it. Species are disappearing at an alarming rate as our population continues to grow and encroach on wildlife habitat.

> Pressures resulting from unrestrained population growth put demands on the natural world that can overwhelm any efforts to achieve a sustainable future. If we are to halt the destruction of our environment, we must accept limits to that growth.

> "World Scientists' Warning to Humanity," signed by 1600 senior scientists from seventy countries, including 102 Nobel Prize laureates

5. Addictions—Drugs or Alcohol.

We often see cases on TV where an addicted mother is not sufficiently aware to take precautions and often gets pregnant with an unwanted baby. When that baby is born, it usually has Fetal Alcohol Syndrome or a drug addiction. These babies often end up in the system for government agencies to care for at the taxpayers' expense, or they may be left in a single-parent situation, quite possibly with a life-long disability.

Needless to say, being a parent is a very demanding job for the best of us, so if the addicted mother decides to keep the child, this could mean a life of great hardship for both the mother and child. Unfortunately, it is also common for these babies to end up in a dumpster or one of the many drop-off stations now being provided for unwanted babies.

6. The grandparents want grandchildren.

Grandparents can place tremendous pressure on their married children to produce offspring. When parents have children just to please their own parents, they often end up resentful and unhappy with their situation. This frustration is often passed on to the children, who may be neglected or abused.

> Human beings, who are almost unique in having the ability to learn from the experience of others, are also remarkable for their apparent disinclination to do so.
>
> Douglas Adams

Of course, not all grandparents insist on having grandchildren.

My uterus, husband and I all agree—no children

Alternet posting by Juniper, 25 March 2009

Juniper states,

> I am a woman. I have all the biological requirements to have a child. Yet, I do not have the instincts or rational desire to do so. Does that make me less of a woman to not want to have a child either by using my body, my eggs, or my money to adopt?
>
> My parents are the only people who, when I said I didn't want to have kids, responded with, "sounds like a good idea." They married because I was on the way and had two more after me. They know how hard it is to raise kids.
>
> How many times have I heard after saying that I don't want children:
>
> * "Oh, I'm sorry." Sorry for what? I've made a conscious choice and I'm proud to have the courage (because that's what it takes in this society) to say no.
>
> * "Don't you like kids?" LOVE 'EM! They're cute, huggable, sweet smelling, curious, and all that. I just don't want one in my home relying on me.
>
> * "You'll change your mind." Isn't it possible that as an adult, I've learned how to make a decision and stick to it?
>
> My husband and I talked about kids before marriage. We both agreed we didn't want any … Why choose to be childfree? Well there are the selfish reasons (that's what you tell me, I'm selfish) such as wanting a clean house, peace and quiet, financial and personal

freedom, as well as an identity that isn't bound to someone much younger than you.

Then there is the "carbon footprint," impact on society, society's impact on the child, and overpopulation. Those are real concerns.

7. To trap a husband.

This is a trick that has been used for centuries, usually with devastating results. Women who fear that their partner will leave them will often purposely get pregnant in hopes that it will convince their partner to stay and perhaps marry them. This desperate tactic is not as successful as it once was, and it is the child (and often the parents too) who suffer the consequences.

Photo is courtesy of Jenny Cummer

Just as a woman should not be forced to have a baby she doesn't want, a man shouldn't be forced to support a child he doesn't want either. We should not have double standards here when it comes to freedom of choice. It is not fair to trick a man into being a father in situations where he is led to believe that they are engaging in safe sex, but where the woman intentionally tries to get pregnant. Both men and women should be cautious when entering into a sexual relationship, and open communication is extremely important to ensure that there are no surprises for either partner.

8. Teen pregnancies.

According to the *Pregnant Teen Help* website, the United States has the highest rates of teen pregnancy and births in the western industrialized world. Teen pregnancy costs the United States at least $7 billion annually. *Although billions of dollars are spent taking care of teenage mothers and their children, only millions are needed to provide good prevention programs.*

Every year about 750,000 girls in the United States will get pregnant, and more than two-thirds of them will not graduate from high school. Unmarried teenagers having children account for 24 percent of all unmarried expectant mothers.

PILLS, RINGS, PATCHES, SHOTS: WHAT'S NEW IN HORMONAL BIRTH CONTROL?

Louise Sloan, lead writer on *www.health.com* (15 May 2008) tells us that there are so many different ways to get hormonal birth control into your body now:

- The oral birth control pill comes in many variations now, with different kinds and ratios of hormones (estrogen and progestin).
- Then there are the hormonal methods that don't involve swallowing anything: implants, hormone-infused vaginal rings, and birth control patches.
- The patch is ideal for women who don't want to take the pill every day, and it has a higher success rate than the pill (you have to remember to take the pill).
- The ring delivers hormones gradually.

Sloan points out that this is great news for women because it gives them the opportunity to find a "method of delivery" that works best for their bodies and lifestyles.

For emergency birth control, the morning-after pill (MAP) is available. The active ingredients in this pill are similar to those in birth control pills; the MAP simply contains higher doses. The morning-after pill is designed to be taken within seventy-two hours of intercourse, with a second dose taken twelve hours later. According to the manufacturers, the MAP (also known as Plan B or Emergency Contraceptive Pill) is more than 80 percent effective in preventing pregnancy. The MAP is not the same as the French abortion pill RU-486.

With so many unplanned pregnancies, abortion is also an important consideration when women and teens think about their future plans. Many teens do not want to enter parenthood alone, and they often do not feel that they can afford it. This kind of responsibility at such a young age is often overwhelming for any teen. However, abortion has been a touchy and personal subject for years and the cause of ethical and medical debates around the world.

People do make mistakes, some knowingly, others unknowingly, and legal abortion is an ethical, safe solution to a destructive situation (which any pregnancy that is unwanted or places the female in a state of uncertainty/anxiety is). The *decision* represents a powerful and positive perspective for young people who think life has more to offer than raising children. Part of the population control argument should be to help relieve the existing stigma from the act of choosing an abortion. Having the choice to have an abortion emphasizes the mental, physical, and lifelong liberating consequences that are associated.

The website *www.Pregnantteenhelp.org* tells us that there are about 1.38 billion women in the world who are in the childbearing years (ages fifteen to forty-four). About 6 million women a year become pregnant. Many teenagers are also sexually active throughout the world. By age twenty:

- 77 percent of women in developed countries have had sex.
- 83 percent of women in Sub-Sahara Africa have had sex.
- 56 percent of women in Latin American and the Caribbean have had sex.

And a lot of unplanned pregnancies result. More than 25 percent of women in the world get an abortion. Compare this with the United States, where nearly 40 percent of women who get pregnant have an abortion.

- *About half of all pregnancies are unplanned.*
- 1.29 million abortions took place in 2002.
- More than 42 million abortions were carried out from 1973 to 2002.
- Two out of every one hundred women have an abortion each year.
- More than 52 percent of abortions obtained are by women who are under twenty-five.
- Around 66 percent of all abortions are obtained by single women.
- Teenagers obtain 19 percent of abortions.

Pregnant Teen Help points out that these statistics are hardly surprising when you consider that, according to the Guttmacher Institute, by the age of nineteen, 70 percent of teenagers have engaged in sexual intercourse. So, parents have a unique window of opportunity, and a responsibility, to educate their children about sex before the age of fifteen. While it can be uncomfortable, parents need to talk to them about contraceptives and sexually transmitted illnesses (STIs) and encourage safe sex.

If a sexually active teen does not use contraceptives, there is a 90 percent chance that she will become pregnant inside a year.

When one looks at the teen sex statistics, it is clear that most teenagers have sex, despite the intense moralizing by conservatives and the religious factions around the world. It also appears that education, the prevention of rape, and access to family planning options can help delay unwanted teen pregnancy and prevent the need for abortion.

Regarding teen pregnancy, Hollywood is also responsible for encouraging teens to become parents. By glamorizing motherhood, the media is portraying unrealistic life situations and providing poor role models. For example, the movie *Juno* has been accused of glamorizing unwed teen motherhood and encouraging irresponsible behavior. Also, talk show hosts have become obsessed with pregnant celebrities who are having babies as "accessories." The average teen could never hope to bring up a child in a similar fashion with the same kind of maturity and resources. This kind of coerced parenthood is very irresponsible.

The website *www.Standupgirl.com* is a website that invites girls to share the truth about their unexpected pregnancies. On 13 May 2009 Missy shared a common story:

> I am 17 turning 18 next week. I should have gotten my period last Wednesday, but it never showed … Turning 18 for my birthday I was going to get my license and look for a car and start school at a community college this Summer. I have no job, and neither does my boyfriend. I'm scared to disappoint my parents and not being able to come up with money as well. Not being able to care for myself how would I care for another person? My boyfriend and I really don't want to do abortion but it looks like we are going to have to.
>
> Don't look now, but the front lines of the abortion battle are shifting. Thanks to advances in medical technology and the introduction of the drug mifepristone (aka RU 486), which gives women the option of having safe, early abortions in private

> locations instead of public clinics, the raving crazies who tape pictures of bloody fetuses to their bodies, stalk Planned Parenthood and howl "murder" at anyone who walks through its doors, may suddenly find themselves all dressed up with nowhere to go—and no one to terrorize.

Private RU-486 Confounds Anti-Abortionists: Who Can We Harass Now?
by Sara Robinson, Group News Blog, posted 14 February 2008, *www.alternet.org*

The religious right's thirty-year campaign of violence against US and Canadian medical clinics has resulted in the following domestic terrorism numbers:

- Seven murders, including three doctors, two clinic employees, a security guard, and an escort
- Seventeen attempted murders
- 383 death threats
- 153 incidents of assault and battery
- Three kidnappings
- Forty-one bombings
- 173 arsons

One-third of all abortion clinics in 1981 were gone by 2005.

Robinson adds that according to the *Washington Post*'s Rob Stein:

> At a time when the overall number of abortions has been steadily declining, a new survey reported that RU-486-induced abortions have been rising by 22 percent a year and now account for 14 percent of the total—and more than one in five of early abortions performed by the ninth week of pregnancy.

> This option of drug-induced medical abortions is putting more abortion providers back in service. This medical abortion gives women the dignity of going through the process in the privacy and comfort of their own homes, rather than having to hunt down a clinic, face a hysterical mob, and endure a painful and invasive surgery.

The Women's International Network states that at least one woman dies every minute from causes related to pregnancy and childbirth. In developing countries, a woman's lifetime risk of dying from pregnancy and childbirth-related causes is thirty-eight times higher than the risk for a woman in more developed regions.

Family planning can prevent at least 25 percent of all maternal deaths. It allows women to delay motherhood and prevents unplanned pregnancies and unsafe abortions. In addition, the use of condoms protects women from sexually transmitted diseases. Family planning also prevents abortions. An estimated 20 million unsafe abortions take place each year in places where access to safe abortion is limited. Unsafe abortions result in at least 76,000 deaths every year, mostly in developing countries.

Voluntary family planning is a low-cost way to prevent much of the suffering women endure on this planet every day due to unwanted pregnancies. Another important benefit of reproductive choice is control over one's life. By exercising this choice, a woman is better able to take advantage of opportunities for education and employment and contribute more to her community.

9. Many couples will not give up until they have a son.

Sometimes this is to continue patriarchal tradition or carry on the family name, and sometimes it is to ensure a primary provider for the parents. This is a tradition that is more common amongst the wealthy in so-called first world countries, and in countries like China, where it is now having devastating effects.

On *www.OneNewsNow.com*, Charlie Butts has posted an article "Chinese Policies at Root of Gender Imbalance," 18 April 2009. He points out that China now has 32 million more males than females. There are reasons for the gender disparity. One of the reasons, according to Steven Mosher of the Population Research Institute, is due to sex-selection abortion.

Mosher explains that the parents will go in at eighteen weeks gestation and have an ultrasound—and if it reveals that they're carrying a boy, they'll continue the pregnancy. If it reveals they're carrying a little girl, they'll schedule an abortion. This kind of gender discrimination is common, to a lesser degree, in many countries around the world.

10. Rape.

This is one of the saddest situations of all, especially if the mother is forced to go through with having the baby due to lack of abortion opportunities. Statistics are not available on the number of rapes occurring every day around the world, or the number of rapes that result in pregnancies. However, **rape is a leading cause, if not the number one cause, of unwanted pregnancies.**

WHO ARE THE VICTIMS? Published on RAINN—Rape, Abuse & Incest National Network

- One out of every six American women have been the victims of an attempted or complete rape in their lifetime (14.8 percent completed rapes; 2.8 percent attempted rape).
- 17.7 million American women have been victims of attempted or completed rape.
- Nine of every ten rape victims were female in 2003.
- While about 80 percent of all victims are white, minorities are somewhat more likely to be attacked.
- About 3 percent of American men—or one in thirty-three—have experienced an attempted or completed rape in their

lifetime, and 2.78 million men in the United States have been victims of sexual assault or rape.

- 15 percent of sexual assault and rape victims are under age twelve.
- In 1995, local child protection service agencies identified 126,000 children who were victims of either substantiated or indicated sexual abuse. Of these, 75 percent were girls.

An AlterNet article written by Alisa Valdez-Rodrigues on 9 May 2009 asks the question, "Is Porn That Depicts the Subjugation of Hispanic Women Tied to the Rise of Hate Crimes Against Latinos?"

Rodriguez points out that while few users of the Internet will admit to using pornography, facts published by *www.Familysafemedia.com* suggest that nearly half of all Internet users seek pornography online.

There are 4.2 million porn sites on the Web, totaling more than 400 million Internet pages. An astounding 25 percent of all search engine requests are for pornography. Pornography profits each year exceed the profits of NBC, ABC, and CBS combined.

Is there a link between pornography and violence against women?

Ms. Rodriguez found a very disturbing trend on a popular free porn site that is essentially the X-rated version of YouTube:

> Day after day, week after week, month after month, videos claiming to depict the rape of Latina maids or Mexican women seeking green cards, etc., have appeared in the top five videos of the day, often in the No. 1 spot, with high ratings from the site's users.
>
> Often, these videos depict women crying, begging for mercy and enduring unwanted anal sex … It is no coincidence that as hate toward Latinos and immigrants rises, Hispanic women are being presented in a very popular, profitable (and, we

> pretend, invisible) media outlet as the ideal rape victims.

The Federal Bureau of Investigation tells us there has been a steep rise in hate crimes against Latinos in the United States in the past six years—a rise of 35 percent between 2003 and 2006.

Human Rights Watch (15 November 2007) reported, "Saudi Arabia: Rape Victim Punished for Speaking Out." A court in Saudi Arabia doubled its sentence of lashings for a rape victim who had spoken out in public about her case and her efforts to seek justice. The court also harassed her lawyer, banning him from the case and confiscating his professional license.

An official at the General Court of Qatif, which handed down the sentence on 14 November 2007, said the court had increased the woman's sentence because of "her attempt to aggravate and influence the judiciary through the media." The court sentenced the rape *victim* to six months in prison and 200 lashes, more than double its earlier verdict. A gang of seven men had attacked and raped both her and a male acquaintance multiple times. Four of them were sentenced for kidnapping, as apparently prosecutors could not prove rape. The judges reportedly ignored evidence from a mobile phone video in which the attackers recorded the assault.

> "A courageous young women faces lashing and prison for speaking out about her efforts to find justice," said Farida Deif, researcher in the women's rights division of Human Rights Watch. "This verdict not only sends victims of sexual violence the message that they should not press charges, but in effect offers protection and impunity to the perpetrators."

Abdel Rahman al-Lahem, her lawyer, told the BBC Arabic Service:

> My client is the victim of this abhorrent crime. I believe her sentence contravenes the Islamic Sharia law and violates the pertinent international

> conventions. The judicial bodies should have dealt with this girl as the victim rather than the culprit.

To a lesser degree, this is true of many rape cases where the rape victim is treated as the culprit in court. Perhaps this is why only a small minority of rape cases are ever reported.

These rapes all too often result in unwanted children that have little chance of living a decent, productive, secure, and reasonably happy life. This situation of government-condoned rape also produces too many children and people for the earth's resources to support.

Marital Rape

"An Afghan law which critics say would legalize marital rape has been placed on hold pending review and revision after it fell under intense International Criticism," says an article filed by David Edwards and Stephen C. Webster on the website *www.rawstory.com* 6 April 2009.

The law was signed by Afghan President Hamid Karzai in early April 2009, but it was not put into effect immediately. US Secretary of State Hillary Clinton expressed her intent to see the law halted:

> I was deeply concerned because I do not think it reflects the values of the vast majority of the people of Afghanistan. This was a law, as I understand it, that was aimed at a minority of a minority, and it does impose harsh restrictions on women and children.
>
> I've expressed my concerns and objections about this law directly to President Karzai, and our president, President Obama, has spoken about the fact that it truly is not in keeping with the direction that Afghanistan has been following.

Critics say the law legalizes marital rape, and some lawmakers allege Karzai signed it hastily because he faces a crucial election on 20 August and wants to curry favor with Shiite voters, who could help swing the contest.

A spokesman for the British Embassy in Kabul said it was "dismayed" that the Afghan government had used its legislative power in such a retrogressive manner. He said, "This bill would have a significantly detrimental impact on the rights of women."

Date Rape

Wikipedia defines Date Rape as "Rape or non-consensual sexual activity between people who are already acquainted, or who know each other socially—friends, acquaintances, people on a date, or even people in an existing romantic relationship—where it is alleged that consent for sexual activity was not given, or given under duress."

Survivors of date rape know it as a major crime against women. The effects are long term and can leave a victim's life ripped apart, and it can possibly leave them pregnant. Post Traumatic Stress Disorder is a common problem for rape survivors.

According to the website *www.Loyola.edu/campuslife*, date rape is an often-heard phrase on college campuses, for it occurs with alarming frequency. It is estimated that one in four women has been a victim of rape or attempted rape. Of those who are raped, about 85 percent report that they know their attacker.

Rape is not a crime of sexual passion, or lust, or of love, but rather a crime of violence against another. Most people imagine a rapist as someone who lurks in the bushes, awaiting an unsuspecting stranger. Although this scenario does occur, rape is more often committed by a seemingly "nice guy" that the woman thought she knew well and even trusted. That is what makes this crime all the more devastating.

Date rape may also involve "date rape drugs" like GHB, Rohypnol, or Ketamine. These are common drugs used to facilitate sexual assaults, since they can render a victim helpless and vulnerable to sexual abuse. Victims are often fifteen to twenty-five years old because those are the common dating years.

Although men are sometimes the victims of rape, most victims are women and most perpetrators are men. According to *www.*

hopeforhealing.org, the devastation for the victim can be far reaching, and the conviction rate is poor because **only 5 percent of date rapes are ever reported**. So there is no way of knowing how many unwanted pregnancies result from date rape.

Child Rape

> A 64-year-old man found guilty of raping an eight-year-old girl is a church pastor.
>
> BBC News,
> "Liberia's child rape victims,"
> 18 January 2007

BBC news reports that Africa's first female president, Ellen Johnson-Sirleaf, came to power in Liberia in 2006, promising to tackle the problem of rape, which had become increasingly common during the previous fourteen years of conflict in the country.

Will Ross has been traveling around Liberia to assess whether that war on rape is being won but found little to smile about. News had just reached the office that an eleven-year-old girl called Janjay had died after being raped six months earlier. Janjay's mother said the rape had left her so badly injured she was incontinent and had to wear nappies.

Then there is the case of Arthur Blackie, a sixty-four-year-old man who was found guilty of raping an eight-year-old girl, Josephine. Arthur Blackie is a church pastor.

Each month the clinic treats several babies for rape, but from all the cases that have been recorded by the clinic since 2003, one can count the number of men convicted on one hand.

> What happens if a Catholic priest molests children? Usually, he's protected by the Church hierarchy. Maybe he'll eventually have his parish or diocese taken away, or be switched to another one—often

> after years of serial abuse. But there's a good chance he'll stay in the Church.
>
> "The Vatican's Perverted Sense of Justice" by Bill Frogameni, *Ms.* Magazine, April 2009

"Nearly 5000 Catholic priests (in the US) have sexually abused over 12,000 Catholic children ... but they were not excommunicated," says Father Roy Borgeois in August, 2008.

While there are no reliable annual surveys of rapes and sexual assaults on children, the Justice Department estimates that 44 percent of rape victims are under the age of eighteen.

> Grim tales are emerging from an investigation of the Irish Catholic Church. For years, they've been running reform schools which sound more like hellish work camps, where sadistic priests were given free rein. I found it ironic that some of these workhouses were used to make religious paraphernalia, like rosaries, that were sold to the faithful. I wonder haw many hail marys have been said on beads assembled by child-slaves who were raped or beaten as a reward? It does add a rather sinister gloss to Catholic prayers ... Can we stop equating religion and morality now? They never seem to have much to do with one another.
>
> "Grim Tales of Abuse Emerge from the Irish Catholic Church," AlterNet posting by PZ Myers, 21 May 2009

Some of the findings from the investigation include:

- A history of official cover-ups of pedophiles within the church since the 1930s.
- A pattern of beatings, abuse, and molestation in church-run workhouses.

- Molestation and rape were "endemic" at the boys' workhouses.
- Cases of children being falsely told that their parents or siblings were dead.
- A continuing insistence on protecting the child molesters in their ranks.
- A case of the Irish government cutting a deal with the Catholic church to cap their losses to lawsuits at $175 million … which is only a tiny part of the full cost.

Ipas is an international organization that is working to protect the world's youngest rape victims. They believe that child rape survivors must have the right to abortion, according to an October 2006 article on the website *www.ipas.org*.

In 2003, Ipas noted that the case of a nine-year-old Nicaraguan girl had made headlines around the world. Living in Costa Rica with her migrant worker parents, the girl known only as "Rosita" had been raped and impregnated by an adult attacker. Her parents and women's advocates struggled against the state and doctors who tried to force Rosita to bear a child—even though she was still a child herself.

Ipas points out, "While Rosita's plight may seem unique, it was hardly an isolated case. In August, an eleven-year-old had the first legal abortion in Colombia, after having been raped by her stepfather. Bolivia was also recently polarized when judges refused to approve pregnancy termination for a ten-year-old violated by a teenage cousin. In some parts of Latin America and the Caribbean, where abortion is typically tightly restricted, advocates are campaigning to make sure the youngest victims—sexually abused minors—can have therapeutic abortions, or those performed to preserve the girls' health or life."

However, these provisions are under fire, as opponents—including powerful interests from the Roman Catholic Church and other religious denominations—lobby for a total abortion ban.

The International Convention on the Rights of the Child says that countries "shall take all appropriate legislative, administrative, social and educational measures to protect the child from all forms of physical or mental violence, injury or abuse, neglect or negligent treatment, maltreatment or exploitation, including sexual abuse, while in the care of parents, legal guardians, or any other person who has the care of the child."

Statutory Rape

According to *West's Encyclopedia of American Law*, statutory rape is sexual intercourse by an adult with a person below a statutorily designated age.

The criminal offense of statutory rape is committed when an adult sexually penetrates a person who, under the law, is incapable of consenting to sex. Minors and physically and mentally incapacitated persons are deemed incapable of consenting to sex under rape statutes in all US states.

Statutory rape is different from other types of rape in that force and lack of consent are not necessary for conviction. A defendant may be convicted of statutory rape even if the complainant explicitly consented to the sexual contact and no force was used by the actor.

> It is one of the fastest growing problems in the country and here in Missippi … Statutory rape. Men and women who prey on children as young as 10 and 11 for sexual relationships. We have been told one out of every five children is a victim of statutory rape. We talk with a mother and her 14 year old daughter who is a victim. This mother is fighting back for justice and to make other parents aware of what is going on.
>
> Maggie Wade,
> "Statutory Rape Victim Speaks Out,"
> 8 May 2008

The mother says her daughter was a virgin. She says when she called police one of her biggest battles was convincing them this was not consensual and even if it had been it was still a crime. Her child was only fourteen. The age of consent in Mississippi is sixteen years old.

In 2006 according to the US Department of Health and Department of Human Services, there were more than 7,500 births to teenagers; the father was guilty of statutory rape in 102 of these births. Some of the girls were as young as twelve. According to statistics it is becoming more common for men nineteen to thirty to pursue girls from ten to fifteen years old.

Mittie Willians, a Catholic Charities court liaison for victims, says, "It is a crime, I don't think that as a society we have come to realize it's a crime, I think we have not quite accepted it."

War Rape

> War Rape describes rape committed by soldiers, other combatants or civilians during armed conflict or war. Rape in the course of war dates back to antiquity, ancient enough to have been mentioned in the Bible. During war and armed conflict rape is frequently used as means of psychological warfare in order to humiliate the enemy and undermine their morale. War rape is often systematic and thorough, and military leaders may actually encourage their soldiers to rape civilians ...
>
> When part of a widespread and systematic practice, rape and sexual slavery are now recognized as crimes against humanity and war crimes. Rape is also now recognized as an element of the crime of genocide when committed with the intent to destroy, in whole or in part, a targeted group. However, rape remains widespread in conflict zones.

From Wikipedia,
the free encyclopedia,
19 May 2009

Valnora Edwin, CGG Human Rights Programme Manager, warns, "The Silence has to be broken, the closed doors opened. We need to move away from thinking that sexual violence and other discriminatory practices against women should be kept private and not made public. Neither can we hide behind the shroud of traditions, customs, or tradition."

Edwin points out that human rights values speak about human dignity, which every human being has a right to. Blaming women/girls who are sexually abused is not the solution to the problem. She questions how perpetrators can justify the abuse of minors such as nine-month-old babies and two- and five-year-olds.

"Sexual violence is a crime! It is wrong and an evil perpetrated against women that demeans the value and respect of those women. We should no longer sit by and allow this to happen," says Edwin.

Edwin is referring to the civil war in Sierra Leone, which directed the world's attention to the problem of sexual violence in Sierra Leone, as women were raped and sexually violated in shocking and destructive manners.

> The *Telegraph* of London broke the news—because the U.S. press is in a drugged stupor—that the photos President Barack Obama is refusing to release of detainee abuse depict, among other sexual tortures, an American soldier raping a female detainee and a male translator raping a male prisoner.

AlterNet news article "Why the Pentagon is Probably Lying About its Suppressed Sodomy and Rape Photos," by Naomi Wolf, posted 30 May 2009 from Independent Media Institute

Wolf adds:

As I wrote last year in my piece on sex crimes against detainees, "Sex Crimes in the White House," highly perverse, systematic sexual torture and sexual humiliation as original documents reveal, directed from the top:

- President George W. Bush, Vice President Dick Cheney, Defense Secretary Donald Rumsfeld and Secretary of State Condoleezza Rice were present in meetings where sexual humiliation was discussed as policy.
- The Defense Authorization Act of 2007 was written specifically to allow certain kinds of sexual abuse, such as forced nakedness, which is illegal and understood by domestic and international law to be a form of sexual assault.
- Rumsfeld is in print and on the record consulting with subordinates about the policy and practice of sexual humiliation, in a collection of documents obtained by the ACLU by a Freedom of Information Act filing compiled in Jameel Jaffer's important book *The Torture Administration.*

And scores of detainees who have told their stories to rights organizations have told independently confirming accounts of highly consistent practice of sexual torture at U.S.-held prisons, including having their genitals slashed with razors, electrodes placed on genitals, and being told the U.S military would find and rape their mothers.

All forms of rape are ugly and inexcusable, but the fact that senior leaders of our governments are condoning this behavior is a travesty.

In Sierra Leone, the soldiers and generals who used rape as an instrument of war have been tried and many convicted. In Bosnia, likewise. Wolf asks, "When will we convict our very own global rapists, the ones who gave the U.S. the hellish distinction of turning us into the superpower of sex crime? ... **Women especially, who understand how sexual abuse and rape can break the spirit in a uniquely anguishing way, should be raising their voices loudly!"**

11. To receive social assistance, and not have to work.

At one time it was a common theme, often for generation after generation, to continue having children as an excuse to stay home and receive social assistance. Unfortunately, this government funding was often misspent and not used to properly feed and clothe the children as it was intended. However, recently in Canada Social Services is discouraging this behavior and making mothers go out and work instead of staying home. This has reduced the abuse of this service a great deal in Canada, although some provinces are more lenient than others regarding this policy.

The Carrying Capacity Network in the U.S. tells a different story:

WELFARE REFORM

> As U.S. population continues to grow both by natural increase and high levels of immigration, law and policy makers are struggling with rising demands for welfare services, spiraling costs, and increasing competition for limited financial resources. With local, state, and federal budgets already overburdened, government leaders on all levels are being forced to recognize limits to spending and to make difficult decisions on how to fund essential programs. Within this context, the question of who will pay for welfare reform has become an increasingly divisive, high stakes issue.
>
> At the center of the controversy are the legal immigrants, refugees, asylees, and other non-citizens who are eligible for federal public assistance funds in four major categories: Supplemental Security Income, Medicaid, food stamps, and Aid to Families

> with Dependent Children. Most immigrants can qualify for benefits after an initial three-year period during which their sponsors are liable for support.

Carrying Capacity Network asks the crucial question: "How many of 1992's approximately 1.4 million new immigrants directly compete with the native poor, minorities, and disadvantaged for low-skill jobs as well as contributing to wage depression in areas where income is needed most? Those looking closely at how to fund welfare reform are asking whether U.S. immigration policy is based more on accommodating special interest rather than realistically considering the capacity of our economy and welfare system to take care of citizens and immigrants already in the country."

12. For religious or moral reasons.

This is often a form of religious terrorism, as was discussed in Part 2. Poor and vulnerable people are often persuaded to follow the unfounded and outdated beliefs of the representatives of that religion, not necessarily the religion itself. Often, foreign aid is linked to compliance to these religious orders, and options are very limited. In most of these cases, family planning programs are denied, even for the prevention of AIDS or in the case of rape.

> To surrender to ignorance and call it God has always been premature, and it remains premature today.
>
> Isaac Asimov

The most powerful religious entity that opposes family planning is the Vatican. Although the Catholic religion itself (and many priests, nuns, and practicing Catholics) often support family planning, the Vatican does not. As a representative of the Roman Catholic Church, the pope refuses to give up this outdated and unpopular stance. This was discussed in much greater detail in Part 2.

In the *Philippine Daily Inquirer*, Philip C. Tubeza reported on a condom protest that took place on 27 September 2002 in Manila. Tubeza explained that instead of raising clenched fists, a militant group and pro-choice advocates waved condoms and lighted sky rockets wrapped in prophylactics during a picket in front of the US embassy in Manila to protest the US government's withholding of $34 million in family planning funds.

Women Rage spokeswoman Rhodz Espinola said,

> When President Bush ran and won with a pro-life platform, he actually declared war against the poor and working women all over the world. This forced international organizations to forego US funds intended for family planning programs … The administration is vigorously pushing for natural family planning methods, but tests have proven that these are not effective.
>
> It is the fundamental right of every woman to control her own body, and this includes the choice of whether to have or not have children, how many children to bear, to use or not to use contraception, and even what contraception to use, " Espinola added. "The state, church and society in general should not put pressure on the woman to choose either way. The woman has the right to make the choice on her own or in consultation with whoever she chooses.

Espinola condemned the Macapagal administration for bowing to the wishes of the Catholic Church when it comes to family planning. A major supporter of the Macapagal administration, the Catholic Church frowns on artificial contraception. About 80 percent of the population of the Philippines is Catholic.

Many groups and individuals, including myself, believe that the Vatican's position is simply criminal. It seems that some forces want to keep the Third World poor so that they can dominate it and ensure a continuous supply of humble supporters in the future. This situation was covered in great detail in Part 2.

13. Oops!

Did you ever forget to take a pill on schedule? Well, sometimes that is all it takes for some women to get pregnant. We often hear a parent refer to a child as their little "mistake" or their "surprise" child. Although the birth control pill is quite safe and effective if taken as prescribed, most other forms of birth control aren't so reliable and often leave women pregnant. In countries where family planning programs are not available, women often use the rhythm method to try to ensure safe sex. This involves trying to be sexually active only when they are least fertile. Of course, this method is not very reliable, since women are seldom in control of what time of the month they have sexual relations. Globally, over half of all pregnancies are unplanned.

If parents have decided that they do not want more children, the most effective form of birth control is a tubal ligation or vasectomy. Also, in some countries, quinacrine is available as a safe, effective, and inexpensive form of birth control.

> On the morning of May 1, 2007, 25-year-old Lee Wing Hin got her tubes tied. After the surgery was over, and she could be sure she would never bear children, what Lee felt was an overwhelming sense of relief. Six months later, she's still feeling it. "Pregnancy is something I've been anxious about for a very long time," says Lee, a graduate student at Toronto's York University. "I felt this was right for me—this is how I want to live."
>
> "Tying the Knot,"
> *www.macleans.ca*,
> by Kate Lunau, 31 October 2007

Lunau points out that tubal ligation is a surgical procedure that requires general anesthesia and lasts about thirty minutes; recovery takes a week. With one in one hundred patients experiencing complications, tubal ligation is riskier than male sterilization (vasectomy). And while tubals can sometimes be reversed, to do so requires a difficult operation that's not always successful. For that reason, experts insist, it should be considered permanent.

Lee isn't alone in not wanting kids. A 2001 survey found seven percent of Canadians aged twenty to thirty-four felt the same. While many among them might not seek a permanent solution, some insist other birth control methods are too invasive, untrustworthy, and altogether temporary.

"While Lee's own doctor was 'supportive,' women who are young, single and childless frequently have trouble finding a willing doctor," reports Ottawa-based sex therapist Sue McGarvie. "The view exists that you don't do that to a single women; they'll find a man and want to have babies. I find it incredibly patronizing."

Some hospitals ask that childless women under thirty get a second (or third) opinion. Others might be sent to see a psychiatrist first. Catholic hospitals could even require the approval of an ethics committee—one young mother who was denied the surgery by a Catholic-run hospital in Saskatchewan recently received a $7,875 settlement after complaining to the province's human rights commission.

> Good news (and long overdue, depending upon how you look at it) on women's access to health care. Remember the FDA's dragging of their heels on a decision to allow emergency contraception to be made available without a prescription during the era-of-non-scientific-thought-and-reasoning also known as the Bush administration? The U.S. District Court ruled today that the FDA did in fact act improperly.
>
> Amie Newman, posted on alternet.org, 24 March 2009
> "Court Rules on Emergency Contraception:
> Is Long Reign of Un-Science, Un-Reason Over?"

Newman added that the US District Court ordered the Food and Drug Administration (FDA) to make emergency contraception (EC) available without a prescription to women aged seventeen and older within thirty days. Physicians for Reproductive Choice and Health issued the following statement:

> Today's ruling restores science to its rightful place at the Food and Drug Administration. Numerous studies have shown that women of all ages can use emergency contraception safely and effectively, but political maneuvering led to unnecessary restrictions on this medication. I am grateful that the court listened to the medical experts in this case and expanded non-prescription access to 17-year-olds.

REASONS FOR LOW DEATH RATES

Although the greatest increase in population is due to high birth rates, low death rates also play a role in maintaining a high population. In some instances we will go to any length or expense to keep a patient alive, often against his or her will. It is unfortunate that the heroic measures we often take to extend human life were not similarly taken to prevent unwanted births.

> It's not because people started breeding like rabbits. It's that they stopped dying like flies.
>
> Nicholas Eberstadt, a demographer at the American Enterprise Institute on the World Population Awareness website.

The World Population Awareness group is responsible for founding World Population Awareness Week. They began the Green Umbrella Walk to create awareness for the need for worldwide family planning. They point out that only in recent history has humankind discovered the means with which to increase the average human life span and reduce infant mortality rate: sanitation practices and modern medicines. With these improvements, we have multiplied our numbers faster than ever before, causing the world population to quadruple in the twentieth century to over 6 billion people.

THE RIGHT TO DIE

Dying is not a crime. How could anyone think it is a crime to help a suffering human end his or her agony?

Dr. Jack Kevorkian (born 26 May 1928) is a controversial American pathologist. Nicknamed "Doctor Death," he is most noted for publicly championing a terminal patient's "right to die," aiding those who wanted to die to reach their goal without suffering. He has claimed to have assisted at least 130 patients to that end. Unfortunately, Kevorkian was convicted for his beliefs about the right to die and served eight years of a ten- to twenty-five-year prison sentence. He was released in June of 2007 on parole due to good behavior.

On 7 February 2008 CBC Radio interviewed Debra Hamilton, a nurse in intensive care in a Vancouver hospital. She said that the most difficult part of her job was "to nurse the living dead." She pointed out that this goes against what she is taught as a nurse—to keep people pain-free, in comfort, and living with dignity. She talks of the horrors of treating people with little hope of surviving, and the tortuous event of using CPR breathing tubes in intensive care. Patients often fight these tubes, and their arms have to be restrained.

Hamilton recommends that the families of these patients have an obligation to take part and see what is happening to their loved ones. She is not alone in having to witness the horror of having to watch a patient or loved one suffer for months or even years, and being denied *death with dignity*.

This has become a very controversial issue in recent years, with numerous books and movies dealing with the dilemma. However, in the movie version the person assisting with the death is the hero, and there are no negative consequences. In the movie *Million Dollar Baby*, for example, Clint Eastwood helps Hillary Swank end her suffering and walks out of the hospital room a hero. He is not arrested or condemned by society for his selfless and humane act.

In reality, however, this would have played out much differently. Clint Eastwood would have been held accountable for her death, and legal action would have been taken. This is the reality of our outdated and inhumane legal system.. Having a *living will* can allow one to refuse being kept alive artificially on a life-support system, but is of little use in granting a person the *right to die*.

The Sue Rodriguez story honestly portrays the horrors a person who is terminally ill and suffering has to go through to seek death with dignity. In her case, which went to court, she was unsuccessful in convincing the court to grant her the right to end her life. There are millions of people around the world in this same position who are being kept alive and suffering against their will.

In the CBC's *The Final Legal Word*, broadcast on 20 May 1993, this Sue Rodriguez update was broadcast:

> After losing in both the B.C. Supreme Court and the B. C. Court of Appeal, Sue Rodriguez takes her case to the highest court in the land. Rodriguez asks the Supreme Court of Canada to grant her the right to assisted suicide. On May 20, 1993, as shown in this special CBC Television coverage, Chris Considine once again pleads Rodriguez's case.
>
> Considine asks the court to grant Rodriguez the right to exercise control over her own body by allowing her to die with dignity with the aid of a doctor. On Sept. 29, 1993, Rodriguez loses her final legal battle. The Supreme Court judges rule against Rodriguez but by the narrowest of margin. They deny her request in a split 5–4 decision.
>
> In writing the majority judgment, Justice John Sopinka expresses the "deepest sympathy" for Rodriguez, but ultimately rules that she cannot be exempt from the law. "No consensuses can be found in favor of the decriminalization of assisted suicide.

> To the extent that there is a consensus, it is that human life must be respected."

The four dissenting justices who sided with Rodriguez wrote in the minority judgment that "the right to die with dignity should be well protected as is any other aspect of the right to life." They also wrote that the Criminal Code prevents people like Rodriguez from exercising autonomy over their bodies available to other people.

> A generation ago, in 1980, a number of people in France formed an Association for the Right to Die with Dignity (ADMD), which now has over 40,000 members. As medical care improves and people live longer, one can expect to see more such associations around the world, and eventually a change in perspective. At present, the law focuses on the act of the physician or nurse, and not on the rights of the patient. As that focus shifts so that the right of the patient to die with dignity becomes paramount, one can expect to see the law proclaim a fundamental right.
>
> Ronald Sokol, former lecturer in law at University of Virginia—he now practices law in France—21 March 2007 *New York Times* article

Sokol adds that within the next century, perhaps much sooner, the right to choose to die with dignity will be as widely recognized as the right to free speech or to exercise one's religion. It will cease to be called euthanasia or mercy killing. It will not be viewed as killing, but as a fundamental human right.

Sokol points out: "In Europe, euthanasia is already sanctioned by law in Belgium, the Netherlands and Switzerland. In the United States, the State of Oregon has also allowed it."

Patricia Hewitt from Leicester UK wants the right to kill herself. The former Health Secretary is not remotely ill. Rushing from meeting to meeting, she was frantic with energy. But for many years she has been "troubled" when contemplating her mortality and the dilemmas of people whose relatives find life unbearable. Two years since leaving her cabinet post, she has mounted her first big campaign to get a legal right for people to assist their own death. Why?

> What has really helped me make my mind up on this is thinking: what would I want if I found myself diagnosed with a crippling illness that I knew to be terminal? I don't know what decision I would make, whether I would want to die, but I absolutely know that I would want that choice.
>
> The website *Timesonline.co.uk*, 2009

There is a new perspective coming from the Center for Ethics, Philosophy and Public Affairs, Department of Moral Philosophy, University of St. Andrews, Edgecliffe, UK, 2007.

They point out:

> It is widely accepted in clinical ethics that removing a patient from a ventilator at the patient's request is ethically permissible. This constitutes voluntary passive euthanasia. However, voluntary active euthanasia, such as giving a patient a lethal overdose with the intention of ending that patient's life, is ethically proscribed, as is assisted suicide, such as providing a patient with lethal pills or a lethal infusion.
>
> Proponents of voluntary active euthanasia and assisted suicide have argued that the distinction between killing and letting die is flawed and that there is no real difference between actively ending someone's life and "merely" allowing them to die … If a patient is mentally competent and wants to die, *his body itself constitutes unwarranted life support unfairly prolonging his or her mental life.*

Currently, in Canada, euthanasia is considered an act of murder, regardless of whether or not the deceased person gives consent. On 15 June 2005 Francine Lalonde, Bloc Quebecois member, introduced a private member's bill (C-407) in the House of Commons. If it had passed, it would have legalized both euthanasia and assisted suicide. However, Canada's House of Commons refused to pass it.

There is still hope for Canadians though, as we are a member of the World Federation of Right to Die Societies, presently consisting of thirty-seven member organizations from twenty-three countries. The Federation was founded in 1980 at Oxford, England, at the third international conference of national right-to-die societies, as noted on the website *www.worldrtd.org*. The first meeting was held in 1976 in Tokyo, after the formation of what is now the Japan Society for Dying with Dignity.

The Federation believes that individuals should have the right to make their own choices as to the manner and timing of their own death. Each of their member societies is working in its own way to secure this right. They meet every two years at an international conference hosted by one of the member societies. The most recent meeting was held in Toronto, Canada, and was hosted by Dying with Dignity (Toronto, Canada).

THE GREEN MACHINE—THE "PERFUSOR"

> One press of a button and you can end your life with a swift injection of potassium chloride. That is the boast of Roger Kusch, once one of Germany's most promising conservative politicians and now the improbable promoter of a mercy-killing machine.
>
> "Death for hire—suicide machine lets you push final button," *The Times*, 29 March 2008
> By Roger Boyes

Boyes notes that if the "Perfusor," designed to sidestep strict laws banning assisted suicide, goes into production then Germany rather than Switzerland could soon become the destination of choice for those seeking to take their own lives.

Some 700 patients, including several terminally ill Britons, have traveled to Zurich, where the self-help organization Dignitas arranges suicide. Assisted suicide has been legal in Switzerland since 1942, providing a doctor has been consulted and the patient is aware of the consequences of his decision.

"The machine is simply an option for fatally ill people," said Dr. Kusch, fifty-three, presenting the green machine that looks like a cross between an electric transformer and a paint spray gun. "Nobody is forced to use it but I do believe that it will contribute to a debate that is moving thousands of people."

Boyes explains that the machine would be lent or rented so that the patients could insert the needles themselves and then push the button releasing the potassium chloride, used to execute death row prisoners in some US states. Supporters say the machine will bring about death in seconds. One of the responsibilities of the organization lending the machine will be to consult with doctors about the exact dosage.

Legal experts say that merely lending the machine to a prospective suicide is not against German law. Gerhard Strate, a defense lawyer from Hamburg, said,

> As long as the sick person is fully conscious and aware, then lending the machine to him is no more illegal than lending him a kitchen knife or a razor blade. It becomes illegal only if the potential suicide asks someone in the room to press the button for him.

It is great that more options are becoming available for the terminally ill. But what about others with diminished life quality, such as the elderly, the sick or the handicapped? Many people in this condition have given a great deal of thought to how they might wish to die. They say that control, peace and dignity are what count.

Fiona Stewart, on the website *onlineopinion.com*, posted 10 May 2005, discusses curtailing our right to know about the right to die with dignity. Stewart says, "If the new Spanish film *The Sea Inside* teaches us anything, it is that no amount of law and legislation can prevent a person who wants to die from devising the ways and means to take their own life."

This movie is about the life and death of lead character and real-life person Ramon Sampedro, who had been a cause célèbre in Spain. Paralyzed from the neck down from a diving accident at twenty-six, Sampedro spent his next twenty-eight years as, in his words, a head attached to a corpse.

Deeply resentful of being forced to live a life that he defined as having little quality, Sampedro repeatedly petitioned the Spanish and European courts. Repeatedly, Sampedro was denied permission to ask for assistance to die, a request he believed he had the right to make. The law disagreed.

Stewart adds, "Most people believe in death with dignity. In this, Sampedro was not exceptional. At the end of the day it is of little importance that he was not terminally ill. Rather, what mattered to him was that his life had so little dignity, that death was a preferable option. And on this latter point, Sampedro still cannot be singled out. For he was neither the first—nor shall he be the last—person to take matters into his own hands when the law fails."

> It seems important to point out that even if other states had followed the Northern Territory's lead and had legislated for voluntary euthanasia, a person in Sampedro's situation would never have qualified to use it. To benefit from the act, you had to be terminally ill. Sampedro's self-determined poor quality of life would not have entered the equation. This raises the question of what's law got to do with it, if such constraints apply? Well very little—as long as you know what to do.

> While everyone knows that rope is available and hanging works—one need only look at the national suicide statistics that show hanging as the most common means of suicide for all ages—the real question is, WHO WANTS TO DIE BY HANGING WHEN THEIR TIME COMES? NOT I, NOR ANYONE I KNOW.

Thankfully, best-selling books such as Derek Humphry's *Final Exit*, available at your local bookstore, contain all that the Sampedros of this world need to know.

The more recent case of Hannah Jones, a terminally ill thirteen-year-old in Britain, is another case where the threat of court action was necessary before she won her battle to die with dignity. Since this schoolgirl had been diagnosed with a rare form of leukemia at the age of four and later a heart condition, she had been in and out of hospitals nearly her entire life.

When doctors told Hannah that she needed a life-saving transplant, she decided that she had had enough. After discussing the high-risk operation with doctors, she knew it would only provide temporary respite, if it worked at all, and would be followed by constant medication.

"I just didn't want to go through any more operations," she told ABC News.

But her request to spend her last precious days at home turned into a legal battle when the hospital threatened her family members with court action if they didn't bring her back to the hospital for treatment.

The hospital finally dropped the court action after Hannah appealed to health officials, insisting that she was fully aware she could die and wished to spend her remaining days at home.

And so the struggle continues for the millions of victims suffering from illnesses that allow them no dignity and political systems that allow them no rights.

PATRIARCHAL INFLUENCES

Patriarchy is men making the decisions and telling women what to do.

According to the Webster's dictionary, *patriarchy* is defined as "social organization marked by the supremacy of the father in the clan or family."

As women, we like to think that we have made a great deal of progress in gaining equality and improving women's rights. After all, what were all those protests for in the 1970s? Women in most countries can vote now thanks to our persistence and bravery. In some jobs, women are even getting paid the same wages as men, and about 10 percent of politicians are women. Gosh, a few countries are even ruled by women, and Hillary Clinton could possibly be president some day. Oprah is one of the wealthiest people on the planet, and the Queen is still highly respected in many circles. This is all pretty darn good, right?

Well, who am I to burst the bubble? Yes, we have come a long way, but when it comes right down to it this is still a world dominated by men. Men still wield most of the power, make most of the major decisions affecting women, and in many countries have the right to keep women in a submissive and obedient state. The major decision-making entities on this planet are made up mainly, if not totally, by the male persuasion. This is especially true when it comes to decisions regarding reproductive rights and population growth. The United Nations, the growth lobby, the Vatican, the war machine, organized crime, and the thriving slave trade industry are run predominantly by men. They all need a steady supply of the poor to continue doing business as usual.

In Part 2, I explained how the United Nations had intentionally allowed the Vatican veto power that greatly interfered with decisions to promote family planning programs. I have also outlined the slave trade industry and how it benefits organized crime and others invested in this travesty. Of course, the growth lobby benefits greatly from increased population, which results in increased demand for housing, food, etc. All of these patriarchal sectors of society have a vested interest in population growth.

Now I would like to briefly discuss the War Machine, and how this male-dominated entity benefits from a steady supply of poor children, women, and men. War also perpetuates the sexual abuse of millions of women, resulting in untold numbers of pregnancies, and it takes funding away from more important causes, such as family planning programs.

WAR MACHINE

> The developed nations are the largest polluters in the world today. They must greatly reduce their overconsumption, if we are to reduce pressures on resources and the global environment. The developed nations have the obligation to provide aid and support to developing nations, because only the developed nations have the financial resources and the technical skills for these tasks.
>
> Acting on this recognition is not altruism, but enlightened self-interest: whether industrialized or not, we all have but one lifeboat. No nation can escape from injury when global biological systems are damaged. No nation can escape from conflicts over increasingly scarce resources. In addition, environmental and economic instabilities will cause mass migrations with incalculable consequences for developed and undeveloped nations alike.
>
> Developing nations must realize that environmental damage is one of the gravest threats they face, and that attempts to blunt it will be overwhelmed if their populations go unchecked. The greatest peril is to become trapped in spirals of environmental decline, poverty, and unrest, leading to social, economic, and environmental collapse.

> Success in this global endeavor will require a great reduction in violence and war. Resources now devoted to the preparation and conduct of war—amounting to over $1 trillion annually—will be badly needed in the new tasks and should be diverted to the new challenges.
>
> "World Scientists' Warning to Humanity,"
> Union of Concerned Scientists

> The embrace by any society of permanent war is a parasite that devours the heart and soul of a nation. Permanent war extinguishes liberal, democratic movements. It turns culture into nationalist cant. It degrades and corrupts education and the media, and wrecks the economy. The liberal, democratic forces, tasked with maintaining an open society, become impotent.
>
> "The Disease of Permanent War,"
> by Chris Hedges,
> *www.alternet.org*, posted 19 May 2009

Hedges tells us that it was a decline into permanent war, not Islam, that killed the liberal, democratic movements in the Arab world, ones that held great promise in the early part of the twentieth century in countries like Egypt, Syria, Lebanon, and Iran. It is a state of permanent war that is finishing off the liberal traditions in Israel and the United States. The moral and intellectual trolls—the Dick Cheneys, the Avigdor Liebermans, the Mahmoud Ahmadinejads—personify the moral nihilism of perpetual war. They abolish civil liberties in the name of national security. They crush legitimate dissent. They bilk state treasuries. They stoke racism.

Hedges warns that massive military spending in the US, climbing to nearly $1 trillion a year and consuming half of all discretionary spending, has a profound social cost. Bridges and levees collapse. Schools decay. Domestic manufacturing declines. Environmental protection is virtually ignored. Trillions in debts threaten the viability of the currency and the economy. The poor, the mentally ill, the sick and the unemployed are abandoned. Human suffering, including our own, is the price for victory.

A permanent state of war keeps citizens in a state of fear, as the corporations behind the war on terrorism must keep us afraid. Fear means that we will be willing to give up our rights and liberties for security. Fear stops us from objecting to military spending that is out of control.

Hedges points out that in *Pentagon Capitalism* Seymour Melman coined the term *permanent war economy* to characterize the American economy. He wrote that since the end of the Second World War, the government has spent more than half its tax dollars on past, current, and future military operations. It is the largest single sustaining activity of the government. The military-industrial establishment is a very lucrative business. It is gilded corporate welfare. Defense systems are sold before they are produced. Military industries are permitted to charge the federal government for huge cost overruns. Massive profits are always guaranteed.

Foreign aid is given to countries like Egypt, which receives some $3 billion in assistance and is required to buy American weapons with $1.3 billion of the money. The taxpayers fund the research, development, and building of weapons systems and then buy them on behalf of foreign governments. It is a bizarre, circular system. It defies the concept of a free-market economy. These weapons systems are soon in need of being updated or replaced. They are hauled, years later, into junkyards where they are left to rust. It is, in economic terms, a dead end. It sustains nothing but the permanent war economy.

The late Sen. J. William Fulbright described the reach of the military-industrial establishment in his 1970 book *The Pentagon Propaganda Machine*. Fulbright explained how the Pentagon influenced and shaped public opinion through multimillion-dollar public relations campaigns, Defense Department films, close ties with Hollywood producers, and use of the commercial media. The majority of the military analysts on television are former military officials, many employed as consultants to defense industries, a fact they rarely disclose to the public.

Unfortunately, this continual state of war that is being funded and promoted by the United States and other western countries is taking its toll on Gaza and Israeli Youth Soldiers.

> As the world decries Israel's attempt to defend itself from the rocket attacks coming from Gaza, consider this: When Hamas routed Fatah in Gaza in 2007, it cost nearly 350 lives and 1,000 wounded. Fatah's surrender brought only temporary stop to the type of violence and bloodshed that are commonly seen in lands where at least 30% of the male population is in the 15-to-29 age bracket.
>
> In such "youth bulge" countries, young men tend to eliminate each other or get killed in aggressive wars …In Arab nations such as Lebanon (150,000 dead in the civil war between 1975 and 1990) or Algeria (200,000 dead in the Islamists' war against their own people between 1999 and 2006), the slaughter abated only when the fertility rates in these countries fell from seven children per woman to fewer than two. **The warring stopped because no more warriors were being born.**
>
> "Ending the West's Proxy War Against Israel"
> by Gunnar Hein Sohn,
> *Wall Street Journal Europe*
> 12 January 2009

In Gaza, however, there has been no demographic disarmament. The average women still bears six babies. And so the killing continues.

This is just a brief glimpse of the patriarchal influences that are perpetuating overpopulation and adding to the pain and misery on this planet. All global citizens who genuinely care about the future of this planet must speak out for civility and justice. We can no longer pretend that we don't know what is happening. We can no longer stand by and allow this travesty to continue. As a woman, I can see that we have a lot of unfinished business to take care of.

WOMEN'S MOVEMENT— UNFINISHED BUSINESS

> The Elizabeth A. Sackler Center for Feminist Art, housed at the continually surprising and alive Brooklyn Museum, celebrated its second anniversary last weekend with a speak-out called "Unfinished Business." As the title suggests, the aim was to bring a diverse range of feminists together in one auditorium to talk about the future of our so-called movement. The lineup of official speakers was indeed, admirably diverse—both ethnically and generationally; it included activist and researcher C. Nicole Mason, labor organizer Ai-jen Poo, Grit TV host Laura Flanders, novelist and rabble-rouser Esther Broner, and hip-hop artist Toni Blackman.
>
> Most of the voices from the audience, however, sounded eerily similar. They spoke longingly about the exuberant past, characterized by abundant energy and "sisterhood." They lamented that no locatable movement exists anymore, that no one is organized, that no one is out in the streets. At one point, Broner even admitted, "I interpret everything through that time."
>
> Courtney E. Martin,
> "The End of the Women's Movement,"
> posted 6 April 2009,
> *www.alternet.org*

Martin pointed out that this approach is at the center of contemporary feminism's biggest challenge. We are intergenerationally fractured, right down to the most foundational of questions: *Is there a formal feminist movement anymore? Does there need to be?*

I think that many women feel that the radical, spunky, '70s-style of women's movement is dead and needs to be revived. There is a growing discontent with the dire state of our planet, and changing the world is becoming a priority again. Women need to be heard and seen in a very real sense, conducting protests and getting the attention of the media. There has never been a time when the need for women to unite to effect change has been more compelling.

Behavior left unchallenged too soon becomes acceptable. Behavior oft repeated becomes the norm. And there is no shortage of behaviors that desperately need to be challenged, including the lack of empowerment of women, the existence of child slavery, the lack of universal family planning programs, etc. Fortunately, we do have a number of inspiring role models to get us motivated.

There have been a number of heroes in the women's movement who certainly have made important contributions in gaining equality and basic human rights. When it comes to reproductive rights, Margaret Sanger was one of those brave souls.

In 1999 the *Ottawa Citizen* paid tribute to Sanger:

> A former nurse who had seen too many impoverished women struggling with unwanted pregnancies, Margaret Sanger (1879–1966) set up the first birth-control clinic in 1916 and the American Birth Control League (later renamed Planned Parenthood) in 1921. Telling women about methods of birth control was still a crime ... But almost every issue of The Birth Control Review featured letters, often anonymous, from mothers looking for information or advice, despite the risk. Sanger herself was jailed and faced numerous legal battles in her pioneering attempts to educate women about their choices.

In 2009, women are still attempting to gain the legal right for women around the world to have access to family planning programs.

Women are still pleading for the patriarchal decision-makers to provide funding for family planning programs and to allow women to make their own decisions regarding their own bodies. In this respect, women still have a long way to go in convincing men to give up this control over women.

In 1999 a fragile deal between the White House and House Republicans to end a fight over abortion and UN dues drew scathing criticism from abortion rights advocates.

"Women's lives have once again been sacrificed for political expediency," said Gloria Feldt, president of Planned Parenthood Federation of America, which uses less than 1 percent of its funds for abortion services.

Ninety-two years after Margaret Sanger opened the first birth control clinic, an abortion advocate was nominated for the top Human Rights post at the United Nations. Another woman had just become a modern-day hero.

> United Nations Secretary-General Ban Ki-moon is expected to name abortion advocate Navanethem "Navi" Pillay of South Africa as the UN's High Commissioner for Human Rights (UNHCR) this week, despite reservations from the United States.

"Abortion Advocate Nominated for Top Human Rights Post at UN,"

OneNewsNow.com, 26 July 2008

> According to the New York Times, the United States has privately raised concerns about Pillay's nomination to the top human rights post because of her strong support for abortion. Pillay is a founding member of the international non-governmental organization Equality Now, a group that has spearheaded campaigns for abortion access in Poland and Nepal. Pillay remains on the board of the organization which receives major funding from

> pro-abortion foundations, including George Soro's Open Society Institute and the Ford Foundation.
>
> Pillay became prominent for her role as presiding judge of the International Criminal Tribunal for Rwanda, a post she occupied from 1995 until her appointment to the International Criminal Court in 2003. Pillay has been a favorite among women's groups and is consistently endorsed by feminist NGOs for top level jobs at the UN, including Secretary General.

Of course, Pillay did go on to fill the human rights post, and on 23 March 2009 she spoke at a conference for the National Human Rights Commission in New Delhi. She said that the absence of women in the National Human rights Commission and the Supreme Court was a kind of "discrimination." Pillay spoke at length about women's empowerment in India and on expanding the role of women in various spheres of the society.

Empowerment of women is an issue that is relevant to women around the world, and we should all be giving more thought to it. Until we regain that momentum we had in the '70s, we will continue to be victims of sexual assault and lack of family planning programs.

A PARADIGM SHIFT —THE MORAL DILEMMA

In Bangladesh, the Green Umbrella is the symbol of a successful health care and voluntary family planning campaign. Bangladesh is a very impoverished country with a high illiteracy rate and many malnourished people. Bangladesh's growing numbers of people have placed increasing demands on agriculture and natural resources in that land. Family planning efforts have helped.

Family planning has the potential to create a success story in every country on this planet if we would allow and promote that mentality.

This will take a paradigm shift, a new awareness of the population crisis, and a willingness to solve it.

GROWING PAINS

As the title of this book suggests, the growing pains being experienced on this planet are causing a great deal of distress. These growing pains can only be eased when the planet stops growing. This needs to happen in several ways:

- The economy must stop growing.
- Our consumption must stop growing.
- The human population must stop growing.

These are all issues that bring up a lot of moral and ethical debate. One's gut reaction when looking at these monumental problems might be to say that they are just far too big to tackle. Not so. Once we wade through the taboos and myths that have been purposely thrown in our path to put us off track, the going gets much easier. Many of these myths have been discussed in Part 2. Next we have to explore the ethical and moral issues. Then we will deal with the options and solutions in Part 4.

ECONOMY MUST STOP GROWING

The nation's leading policy institute dedicated to smart economics, Redefining Progress, develops solutions that create a just society, protect the environment, and shift public policy to achieve a sustainable economy. This is done by using the Genuine Progress Indicator (GPI), a system of accounting that is far more ethical and logical than the Gross Domestic Progress (GDP) that is presently used.

Redefining Progress, a San Francisco-based group, created the Genuine Progress Indicator in 1995 as an alternative to the Gross Domestic Product. The GPI enables policymakers at the national, state, regional, or local level to measure how well their citizens are doing both economically and socially.

Economists, policymakers, reporters, and the public rely on the GDP as a shorthand indicator of progress, but the GDP is merely a sum of national spending with no distinctions between transactions that add to well-being and those that diminish it.

> Think about this: The Exxon Valdez oil spill was a multi-billion-dollar boost to Alaska's economy. Alaska's GDP went up because the costs of cleanup and litigation were included as economic growth. In calculating GDP, pollution is not only counted as a positive but may be counted as a positive three times: when it is produced, when it is cleaned up and through its cost to health.
>
> That's because GDP simply adds up all financial transactions, including useful and harmful activities. Every time a woman is treated for breast cancer the GDP goes up. If you drive to the store instead of walking, the GDP goes up. If you turn on the air conditioner instead of opening a window, the GDP goes up. If you have triple bypass surgery instead of exercising and eating healthier, the GDP goes up.
>
> Barry Marquardson,
> *Calgary Herald*,
> 1 February 1998

Marquardson points out that with the GPI, activities that harm our environment, health, and quality of life are measured as costs. Activities such as volunteer service, eldercare, childcare, and household work are all counted as benefits. Honest national accounting would inject a large dose of accountability to the political process. It would stop politicians and interest groups from hiding the implications of bad policy behind what amounts to a rigged set of books.

So how would using the GPI help control population? Well, the GPI counts resource depletion as a cost, and as the population increases, resource depletion increases. This becomes more evident as the standard of living rises in countries like China and India and as more Third World citizens immigrate to developed countries. Both of these situations increase resource depletion.

Redefining Progress explains that if today's economic activity depletes the physical resource base available for tomorrow, then it is not creating well-being; rather, it is borrowing it from future generations. The GDP counts such borrowing as current income. The GPI, by contrast, counts the depletion or degradation of wetlands, forests, farmland, and nonrenewable minerals (including oil) as a current cost.

Long-term environmental damage arising from the use of fossil fuels, chlorofluorocarbon, and atomic energy are unaccounted for in ordinary economic indicators. On the other hand, the GPI treats environmental damage as a cost to society. Interestingly, while the GDP has been rising for decades, the GPI has actually been falling since the mid-1970s.

Redefining Progress warns that with both individuals and governments around the world borrowing and spending well beyond their means, we are accumulating a huge load of debt on future generations. With each additional person on this planet, both economic and environmental debt increases, causing loss of biodiversity and scarcity of resources.

GROSS PRODUCTION VS. GENUINE PROGRESS, 1950-2004

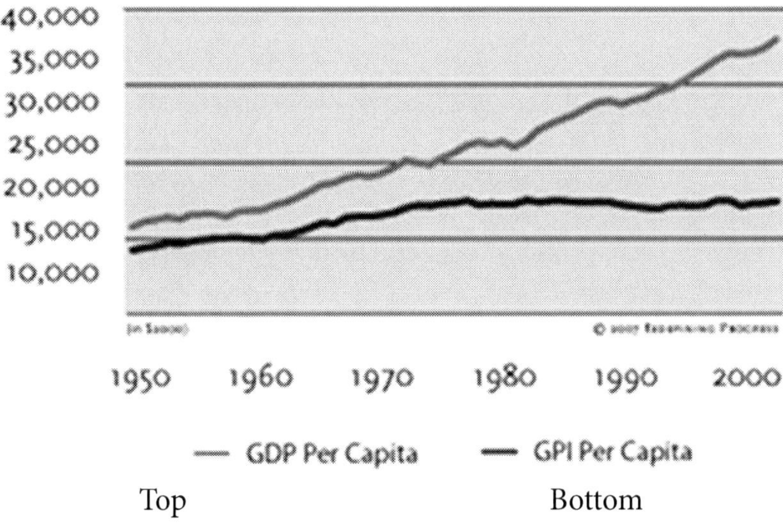

Top Bottom

Graph is courtesy of Redefining Progress

If every country adopted the new Genuine Progress Indicator method of accounting, we would have a better picture of reality and more incentive to improve our well-being. We would also have a more honest indication of the costs of overpopulation. Presently, a huge gap exists between the fraud of economic growth as defined today and what it really is given the depletion of the world's ecosystems / services.

CONSUMPTION MUST STOP GROWING

> We must alert and organize the world's people to pressure world leaders to take specific steps to solve the two root causes of our environmental crises—exploding population growth and wasteful consumption of irreplaceable resources. Overconsumption and overpopulation underlie every environmental problem we face today.
>
> Jacques-Yves Cousteau

It is not consumption *or* population, but both together that are destroying our planet and our well-being. We must deal with both of these issues simultaneously. Yet, while reducing consumption seems to be the buzzword these days, population remains a taboo issue.

There is no doubt that developed countries are consuming far more than their fair share of the earth's resources, especially the 5 percent of the world's wealthiest citizens. We all must do our part to reduce our footprint on the earth and live within our carrying capacity. Everyone from Oprah to Ann Landers is going green these days, and almost every TV ad has joined the movement. Is it enough? Not by far, and it is our children's legacy that we are squandering along with an alarming loss of biodiversity.

It is not that we don't know better, but rather that we lack the willpower to live more sustainably. This issue of consumption is a book in itself, and of course there are plenty on the bookshelves already. We just have to start taking it seriously, set goals, and stop living on credit. Ethically, we have no right to continue stealing from future generations and the other critters on the planet.

But the most important thing to remember here is that this is not a consumption OR population debate, any more than we can ask if we need food OR water. Of course, both are important, and must be dealt with at the same time.

Again, this is a question of ethics. In our evolution of growth we have achieved higher incomes but reduced our respect for the planet and each other. We have multiplied our possessions but reduced our values. When our sense of morality is restored, the planet's well-being will be restored.

POPULATION MUST STOP GROWING

> Which is the greater danger—nuclear warfare or the population explosion? The latter absolutely! To bring about nuclear war, someone has to DO something; someone has to press a button. To bring about destruction by overcrowding, mass starvation, anarchy, the destruction of our most cherished

> values—there is no need to do anything. We need only do nothing except what comes naturally—and breed. And how easy it is to do nothing
>
> Isaac Asimov

Because we have neglected this problem for far too long, there are no easy answers left when it comes to morality and ethics. It has now come down to choosing what is the least inhumane solution. It is like dealing with logging practices that should have been controlled decades ago; we now have few choices left. Should we cut down our precious rainforests or resort to helicopter-logging to get the last few remaining trees on the mountainsides? Likewise, we have to make choices regarding dwindling gas and oil reserves, now that all the easy supplies have been used up. Should we promote expensive and environmentally devastating extraction from the tar sands or extracting from the depths of our oceans?

The dilemma of overpopulation forces us to face similar moral and ethical choices, and we have to ask ourselves which of the often distasteful choices are more acceptable and logical. Ann Landers addresses one of these moral choices:

> I realize that all people, underprivileged included, have the right to be parents, but I also believe that if they can't feed their children, they have no right to bring them into the world. What kind of love is it that can look into the eyes of a starving child, knowing that the child will die of malnutrition?
>
> To those who feel that birth control is a sin, I'd like to ask, is it less of a sin to bring children into the world who are destined to die of starvation? … Unfortunately, funding to help these women has been sharply reduced. How shortsighted can we get?
>
> "Let's tackle the issue of birth control help for women of the Third World," Ann Landers, *Vancouver Sun,* 22 March 1989

Along a similar line, twenty years later on 13 March 2009, Michael Lardelli explores common myths of the population debate with this comment on the myth that **China's one child policy is a violation of the human right to control one's own fecundity:** "We need to decide which human right is more important—the right to unrestricted reproduction or the right not to starve to death. People who reproduce at a rate that increases the population size threaten the survival of their own children and the children of all others."

"Stop! Think! Do You Really Want That Baby?" Afsaneh Knight, *The Times*, 23 May 2009

Ms. Knight asks:

> What is it with women and babies? Why do we feel that to be successful, to be valued, to be simply what we are—feminine—we need to reproduce like Victorians?
>
> I'm not talking about the likes of Nadya Suleman, aka Octomom, the American woman who, with her 14 fatherless children, could be considered badly misguided. Or about rural South Americans, whose instruction on contraception comes from the Pope. I'm talking about the educated, professional middle classes—yoohoo, readers!—who hit a certain age, ignore the rich and varied lives they already have, and decide that what they really need to be doing is having babies, like, now.
>
> We've been to school, we watch the news, we heard David Attenborough loud and clear when, last month, he called the world's ongoing population explosion "frightening." We're told that global numbers are increasing by 80 million a year (that's an entire new Germany), and our resources dwindling. And yet we want babies. Loads of lovely, chubby babies who smell of sugar and powder. And if we don't want babies there must be something wrong with

> us. We must be Susan Boyle, living a life of unkissed spinsterhood. Or we must be barren, geriatric and broken-hearted; the five rounds of IVF (fertilization) must have failed.

Ms. Knight warns that, in 2009, if you want a baby you had better want one badly. Badly enough to be introducing him or her to a world groaning at the seams, with drying resources, melting icecaps and bombs strapped to various parts of some of its inhabitants. And don't forget that in Britain, according to the friendly society Liverpool Victoria, the average cost of raising a child to the age of twenty-one is 193,000 pounds (345,470 dollars Canadian). Knight concludes,

> The only conceivable reason for having a child would be that parenting that child is your vocation. The Optimum Population Trust, with Sir David Attenborough as patron, is campaigning that we have no more than two children. It may be too easy for me to say this now, but we need to start thinking harder about whether we have children at all.

IS CHILDBEARING A RIGHT OR A PRIVILEGE?

Iran has one of the world's more aggressive programs to encourage smaller families: to get a marriage license there, you must take a course in family planning.

"Now instead of thinking about the quantity of Muslims we have to think about the quality; we need healthier, more educated and better informed Muslims," said Ayatollah Makaram-Shirazi. In the late 1980s, Iranian officials pondered their future prospects and made this startling policy reversal.

The idea of having to take a course to prepare for parenthood makes a whole lot of sense to me. It has always puzzled me that parents in most societies make more of an effort preparing to get a driver's license than to have a child. Being allowed to drive a car is a privilege, and you must pass a test and qualify for this privilege. Yet, having a child is considered a right, and no preparation is required.

It is little wonder that many mothers enter parenthood in a state of shock and panic. Is this morally fair to the child?

> The population problem concerns us, but it will concern our children and grandchildren even more. How we respond to the population threat may do more to shape the world in which they will live than anything else we do.
>
> Lester Brown, Worldwatch Institute

> Instead of controlling the environment for the benefit of the population, maybe we should control the population to ensure the survival of our environment.
>
> Sir David Attenborough

Attenborough's premise that overpopulation is making it impossible to protect the environment must also be addressed. Johann Hari brings up a good point in "Are there just too many people in the world?" which appeared in *The Independent/UK* on 15 May 2008:

> How can you be prepared to cut back on your car emissions and your plane emissions but not on your baby emissions? Can you really celebrate the pitter-patter of tiny carbon-footprints?

People who believe that humans do not contribute toward climate change should consider this fact from Zero Population Growth Canada:

> The average human converts about 85% of the oxygen he breathes into CO^2. This results in an output of about 650 liters (1.3kg) per day. Over the course of a year, this amounts to 2.4 trillion kg of CO^2 expired from Earth's 5 billion inhabitants. (almost 7 billion

> now) This is roughly equal to the carbon release from worldwide deforestation.

Since most inhabitants live and breath in developing countries, perhaps they do contribute their fair share of CO^2. When you also consider the deforestation necessary to provide their firewood alone, the destruction of wildlife habitat and carbon sinks is staggering.

FEEDING PEOPLE VERSUS SAVING NATURE?

When we must choose between feeding the hungry and conserving nature, people usually come first. This is the point made by Holmes Rolston III from the book *World Hunger and Morality*, 1996. He points out:

> A bumper sticker reads: Hungry loggers eat spotted owls. That pinpoints an ethical issue, pure and simple, and often one where the humanist protagonist, taking high moral ground, intends to put the environmentalist on the defensive. You wouldn't let the Ethiopians starve to save some butterfly, would you?
>
> Humans win? Nature loses? After analysis, sometimes it turns out that humans are not really winning if they are sacrificing the nature that is their life-support system. Humans win by conserving nature—and these winners include the poor and the hungry.

Rolston makes a good point about our lack of respect for nature. It is not simply a trade-off over hungry people versus nature. It is a matter of finding a win-win situation that will provide for people's needs in the short term without destroying the resource base that is essential to providing for those needs. If the alleviation of human suffering always results in an increase in population, we are simply creating a larger problem—and more human suffering—in the future. This is exactly what we have done every time we have provided food aid in Africa with no effort to stem the rapid population growth. The number of hungry people in each crisis simply gets larger, and the environment becomes more degraded. The protection of nature and human well-being both depend on our acknowledging the population crisis.

No matter how unpleasant the solutions may seem, they are far more appealing than the alternatives. If we continue to destroy our planet and our life-support systems, we will suffer far greater sorrows than limiting our family size. This is no time to be timid—we must attack the population problem with all the foresight and wisdom we can muster.

There are recognized "rights" to clean air, sanitation, water, food, and all the other things that make life possible and worth living, and there are recognized "responsibilities" toward our fellow human beings and the planet and its vast diversity. However, these rights and responsibilities cannot be fulfilled if we do not have a sustainable population level.

A population level of almost 7 billion is not sustainable by any expert's measures. Should we then start a class action law suit against our governments or the United Nations for purposely obstructing our human rights by not controlling our population? What measures will it take to get the attention of our world leaders and global citizens?

> Basically, then, there are only two kinds of solutions to the population problem. One is a "birth rate solution," in which we find ways to lower the birth rate. The other is a "death rate solution," in which ways to raise the death rate—war, famine, pestilence—find us.
>
> Paul Ehrlich, *The Population Bomb*, 1968

Which of these solutions do our world leaders prefer? Well, in Canada our prime minister's choice is clear. A 2008 poll showed that 65 percent of Canadians supported the appointment of Dr. Henry Morgentaler to the prestigious Order of Canada; however, Prime Minister Stephen Harper joined the minority by voicing his opposition.

Eighty-five-year-old Morgentaler is well-known for leading a controversial movement to legalize abortion in Canada, opening his first clinic in Montreal almost four decades ago. Countless feminists and pro-choice activists see his induction as long overdue and believe that he should be recognized for his hard work and dedication to Canadian women's rights. Bestowing the highest honor in the country on Morgentaler showed recognition for an important milestone in women's rights.

Morally, we know that legalizing abortion changed the lives of thousands of women for the better. Back in the '60s even a teenager who was molested by a priest or gang-raped couldn't get an abortion. Surely, these women should not be forced to pay for this injustice. If we want to prevent abortions, then we need to do more to reduce the high incidence of rape and to ensure that all women have access to safe and effective birth control. The "take home message" here is that we **have got to** take more aggressive action when urging our governments to make the interests of sexually abused citizens a priority.

Ultimately, we would all like to eliminate the need for abortion, but until that day comes women should have a choice. Policies that forbid abortion not only demonstrate a shocking lack of compassion, they also directly contradict strong evidence that restricting abortion access does not make abortion less common—it just results in more women dying or being injured by clandestine and unsafe procedures.

Empowerment of women is essential.

> More importantly, international population and family planning assistance is about giving women control, not taking it from them. A woman in the developing world is the center of her environment … In order to effectively manage her life and her environment, every woman must have the right and the means to make informed decisions regarding the number and spacing of her children.

National Audubon Society U.S.,
Guide to Population Assistance, 1993

WHAT IS TRULY THE SELFLESS ACT?

Many who would like to perpetuate population growth say that choosing to be childfree is morally a selfish act. But is it really? At a time when overpopulation is threatening our security, resources, and environment, it is having a large family that should be viewed as an act of betrayal, selfishness, and excess!

The Canadian Center for Policy Alternatives released a study on 15 April 2009 that found that middle-income Canadian families enjoy *public* services worth about $41,000 a year. Our taxes pay for these services even if we don't have children, and childfree couples pay a proportionally larger percent of taxes than those with children. This is due to child credits and tax deductions allowed for each child, school tax, health insurance, welfare, public housing, etc., that discriminate against childfree citizens. A large portion of that $41,000 spent on family costs by society is being paid by childfree taxpayers.

Then there are the non-monetary contributions that childfree citizens make to the children of our society. Valerie Bell makes this point in her book *Nobody's Children* when she points out that loneliness is a tragedy that millions of America's children live with on a day-to-day basis. It sends them off to school in the morning and greets them at the end of the day. For an increasing number of American children, the need for love and attention from the adult world is unmet. Because these kids feel so emotionally detached, on that level they are indeed "nobody's children." Ms. Bell says,

> To whom can children look in the quest for belonging? Who will pick up the emotional slack too often unrecognized by their own parents? … Thank God for public school teachers, day-care workers, Sunday school teachers, and youth workers, who recognize the emotional needs of children and give more than

> their share of love and professional care every day. But this isn't just a job for the "professionals."
>
> It's a job for any sensitized adult who recognizes when a child is asking, "Are you my mother?" It's a job for adults who are "there" with enough time to make a child feel that he belongs. It's a job for perceptive adults who are selfless enough to ask, "What is best for children?" It's a job for anyone whose heart aches knowing a nearby child feels like nobody's child.

Many childfree people take up the slack for parents who don't have adequate time to give their children. I know that I certainly put in a lot of hours helping my sisters out with their children. I enjoyed taking them hiking, teaching them to swim, and often babysitting for a weekend to give the parents a break. I did this gladly, as I am sure many of those who are childfree do in their own way.

I also worked as a tutor for eleven years, work which often included a parental type of communication, since my Japanese students were far from home and their families. Many of these students were feeling like "nobody's children" at the time and were craving attention, guidance, and acceptance. So those who choose not to breed often make great contributions to those who do breed, which I would call a very selfless act indeed!

An overcrowded planet is also making life harder for all of us, and many people are asking if this is fair ethically. Should couples really have the right to have as many children as they wish, when it causes such chaos, pressure, and conflict in the world?

> Every day, we see the consequences of too many Americans: temper-testing traffic; a shortage of affordable housing nationwide; trash at parks and on beaches; pollution in rivers, lakes and bays; and sprawling development that covers the best farmland and diverse wildlife habitat with master-planned suburbs, miles of freeways and acres of parking lots.

> Basically, everything we love about America—from amber waves of grain to purple mountains majesty—is threatened by overcrowding.
>
> *The Population Bomb,*
> *www.peak-oil-news.info/population-bomb,*
> 3 October 2006

> Surprisingly, nobody makes the ethical connection between human predicament and extinction of habitats and species, scarce resources, famine, constant ethnic frictions, and more. Humans hungry for land, which they stole from wild species, reducing likewise the biodiversity to a few useful domesticated ones, destroyed wildlife long ago in Europe. History repeats itself: this time around there's less land to steal and more people to feed. Every new life exercises a right over resources, which affects the right of the already living and future human beings—and other species. We reach the point where and when every place of the Earth is being occupied, exploited and eventually depleted, with dire consequences to Biological Diversity and Sustainable Development.
>
> World Population Awareness, 9 March 2007

Morally, would you want to die and leave your children a huge debt to pay off and a huge mess to clean up? Would your conscience allow you to do this? Well, that is exactly what we are doing to the children of the world when we leave them an overcrowded and vastly diminished planet.

Immigration is another ethical issue that has people screaming "Racist" if any country protests the huge influx of aliens. Yet, others argue that no country has a moral obligation to admit immigrants if it threatens the country's environment, social well-being, democratic rights, or cultural integrity. This is not racist; this is self-preservation.

We often hear the lifeboat scenario used to describe this situation, as the analogy is so fitting. Then the moral question is raised: do we allow unrestricted immigration or protect our own life-support system first, and then help other countries protect theirs? By allowing overpopulated countries to continually export their population problem, the exporting country never gets a true picture of the extent of their problem. The present population levels of many developing countries do not reflect the huge number of emigrants, who have gone forth to greener pastures.

It would be far more realistic and effective for each country to develop a population policy based on carrying capacity and then set a limit for immigration. The billions of dollars being spent to subsidize immigration in the receiving countries could then be channeled into foreign aid programs instead, where the funds could be used for family planning and other programs.

Besides, many feel that it is morally reprehensible for Canada to encourage the most highly skilled and educated in the Third World to immigrate to Canada. These people are much more desperately needed in their homelands than abroad.

It is unfortunate that many of the critics opposed to reducing population levels have purposely misrepresented the many moral and ethical issues involved here. Often the debates surrounding this issue are hysterical and full of unfounded accusations that are ethically unsound and illogical. Neither reason, nor truth, nor justice, nor the greater good of society stands a chance in this atmosphere.

Part of the solution would be to bring this issue out in the open, conduct extensive public consultation and discussion, dispel many of the taboos and myths, and develop population policies for every country. These policies would represent the wishes of the majority of citizens, and we could then move forward to implement sustainable population programs.

This concept is one of the solutions that will be discussed in Part 4.

PART 4:
SOLUTIONS

21.12.12 YOU may want to take note of this date, 12 December 2012. According to the Mayan calendar, this date marks the beginning of a new period in human evolution. Quite amazingly, a great galactic alignment takes place on this date, involving a solar eclipse and other extraordinary phenomenon.

> The Hopi and Mayan elders do not prophesy that everything will come to an end. Rather, this is a time of transition from one World Age into another. The message they give concerns our making a choice of how we enter the future ahead. Our moving through with either resistance or acceptance will determine whether the transition will happen with cataclysmic changes or gradual peace and tranquility. The same theme can be found reflected in the prophecies of many other Native American visionaries from Black Elk to Sun Bear.
>
> Joseph Robert Jochmans,
> "3rd Rare White Buffalo Born on Wisconsin Farm,"
> 23 November 2007
> Mayan End Time Prophecy,
> *www.adishakti.org/mayan_end_times_prophecy_12-21-2012.htm*

We are living today in the cusp of the Mayan end times, the end of a galactic day or time period spanning thousands of years. One galactic day of 25,625 years is divided into five cycles of 5,125 years.

The Mayans had a very precise understanding of our solar system's cycles and believed that these cycles coincided with our spiritual and collective consciousness. The Mayans prophesied that from 1999 we have thirteen years to realize the changes in our conscious attitude to stray from the path of self-destruction and instead move onto a path that opens our consciousness to integrate us with all that exists. (See above website for more info)

It will be up to all people to determine whether this period will be a time to fear or a time to anticipate with excitement and hope. To ensure that this shift in galactic alignment brings positive change, the world's people will need to implement a new earth credo to heal the planet and reduce human suffering, according to the Mayan prophesy.

SETTING GOALS

Whether you take this prediction seriously or not, I suggest that we set 2012 as a target date to set our compass by, and set our population objectives on that course. Although few people have a true understanding of how urgent the population crisis is, there is a new awareness dawning that will bring many global citizens on board in a very short time. We must start setting goals now that we can work toward for 2012. If we don't seize the momentum that is building, and put it to good use, we will miss out on a rare opportunity.

In fact, it is every individual's right and responsibility to help shape our future in a way that will benefit all humankind and protect the myriad other species with which we share this planet. Achieving a sustainable population globally is a goal that is within our means. We already have the knowledge and resources to accomplish this goal.

Never before on this planet have so many inhabitants been so misinformed about something that is so important and urgent as with the population issue. The lack of universal consciousness that exists today is due to the mythology surrounding the population debate that is working as a smokescreen to cloud the issue. In order to restore a sustainable population level on earth, we must remind citizens of how far we have strayed from our basic human rights due to overpopulation.

In 1948, the United Nations developed the UNIVERSAL DECLARATION OF HUMAN RIGHTS. This declaration has served to guide organizations like Zero Population Growth and the Sierra Club to endorse the intent of this historic document with the following resolution:

> Every human being, present and future, has a right to a world with a healthy environment, clean air and water, uncluttered land, adequate food, sufficient open space, natural beauty, wilderness and wildlife in variety and abundance, and an opportunity to gain an appreciation of the natural world and people's place in it through firsthand experience.

How attainable are these human rights in a world so overpopulated that our natural web of life is unraveling and rapidly destroying our life-support systems? Not only will future generations have no chance of appreciating a beautiful world of abundance, but most citizens living today will have no opportunity to appreciate it either. And what of the wildlife and natural beauty declared as a universal right? Who will be our champion to defend this declaration if not the United Nations who created the document? How can we get there from here?

The fourth *Global Environment Outlook report* released by the United Nations Environment Program in October 2007, prepared by about 390 experts, points out that population growth combined with unsustainable consumption has resulted in an increasingly stressed planet. The report makes an *urgent* call for action and says, "Fundamental changes in social and economic structures, including lifestyle changes, are crucial if rapid progress is to be achieved. Our common future depends on our actions today, not tomorrow or some time in the future."

This report points out that humanity's survival will be largely determined by the decisions individuals and society make *now* to reduce population. Time for delaying action has run out if we are to defuse the population time bomb and avoid even more catastrophic consequences than we are already witnessing.

> World population problems have remained the concern of demographers and historians. Even today, when politicians or international organizations deal with such questions, they consider them either as individual and personal, or a specifically internal and national problem, rather than viewing the population issue from a global perspective.

A World Population Policy for the World Population Year by
H. V. Muhsam
Hebrew University,
Jerusalem Australian National University,
Canberra, 1973

The author argues that individual and national population decisions impinge on broader interests—illustrated by the "tragedy of the commons." He urges that world population problems be presented as a dilemma of worldwide scale, soluble only by worldwide action.

> *The problems in the world today are so enormous they cannot be solved with the level of thinking that created them.*
>
> *Einstein*

Of course, each individual plays a role in reducing population, but if we are to aspire to a truly sustainable population level, we need strong leadership and international cooperation. Derrick Jensen's article in *Orion* magazine, posted 13 July 2009 makes this point quite well:

> Would any sane person think dumpster diving would have stopped Hitler, or that composting would have ended slavery or brought about the eight-hour workday, or that chopping wood and carrying water

would have gotten people out of Tsarist prisons, or that dancing naked around a fire would have helped put in place the Voting Rights Act of 1957 or the Civil Rights Act of 1964? Then why now, with all the world at stake, do so many people retreat into these entirely personal "solutions"?

Part of the problem is that we've been victims of a campaign of systematic misdirection. Consumer culture and the capitalist mindset have taught us to substitute acts of personal consumption (or enlightenment) for organized political resistance. An Inconvenient Truth helped raise consciousness about global warming. But did you notice that all of the solutions presented had to do with personal consumption—changing light bulbs, inflating tires, driving half as much—and had nothing to do with shifting power away from corporations, or stopping the growth economy that is destroying the planet?

A LITTLE GOOD NEWS

When thinking about solutions to the population crisis, I can't help but think of Ann Murray's song "A Little Good News." Just think about how nice it would be to turn on the radio and hear these breaking headlines:

- The Red List has just been revised to indicate that every species on the Endangered Species List has now been safely recovered due to increased protection and habitat recovery. As the human population continues to decline, mankind is gradually giving back the land we stole from other living species. We are, therefore, able to restore wildlife habitat and biodiversity at an impressive rate. A new appreciation for nature is now being realized, along with an increased civility toward the animal kingdom.

- The United Nations has announced that every woman worldwide now has access to safe and effective family planning programs. This was accomplished by reallocating one week's budget from global military spending, since peace has now been reached in the Middle East. Public outrage and a dwindling supply of expendable soldiers were also contributing factors to ending these wars.

- The Vatican announced last week that they have heeded the wishes of the majority of Roman Catholics and have decided to support family planning programs to reduce the poverty, misery, and spread of AIDS in developing nations. Due to public protest, the Vatican has also given up their veto power in the United Nations and will no longer be recognized as a participating country, but rather as a religious entity.

- The World Health Organization has confirmed that great strides have been made in reducing the number of women and children being abused through the slave trade, child soldiers, child labor, and various forms of rape. This has greatly reduced the number of unwanted pregnancies and improved the well-being of women and children worldwide.

- The Board of Education has announced that family planning and parenthood classes have been approved in schools around the world. This will better prepare students to make decisions regarding family choices that will greatly affect their futures.

- The Union of Concerned Scientists is pleased to announce that there are positive indications that global citizens have taken their "Warning to Humanity" seriously and are taking measures to reduce the human footprint on this planet. There are now signs of reduced population, consumption, and economic growth on every continent.

- Economists worldwide are now reporting that the Genuine Progress Indicator, developed by Redefining Progress, has now replaced the Gross Domestic Progress as a tool for shifting the economy toward sustainable practices. Besides economic health, the GPI also measures indicators that really matter to people—a sustainable population, health, safety, a clean environment, and the social well-being of a nation.

- The United Nations has announced the creation of the World Population Organization to address the population crisis in the context that it is linked to environmental, economic, health, social, and political issues. This new initiative is expected to radically change the international community's approach to population governance and to be as effective as the World Health Organization and World Trade Organization.

- The Global Media Network has launched a multimedia strategy dedicated to population outreach and partnership building. Over one hundred media strategists have been appointed to market and promote the human aspect of a conscious, intelligent, and creative population vision. They will keep track of important changes in the population landscape and bring new ideas to the world to usher the population movement into the twenty-first century. This program will include press conferences, commercial design, monitoring, and analysis that will contribute to the population report card.

- Both leading traditional and new media outlets will be used to connect with all audiences and encourage citizens to embrace new media tools to tackle the population crisis. Overpopulation will be recognized as a global emergency, and a coordinated world effort will be designed to achieve a sustainable environment for the well-being of all life-forms. The media now recognizes that reducing population will positively impact every aspect of our lives, global biodiversity, and our life-support systems.

- Feminist organizations on every continent have joined forces and have launched a global campaign to eradicate degradation of women and renew their demand for equal rights. This movement is long overdue, and echoes the enthusiasm of the '70s, with peaceful protests and effective media campaigns.

- Doctors for a Sustainable Population in Australia have rallied the medical profession worldwide to address the issue of overpopulation, as it greatly affects the public's health and well-being and diminishes our quality of life. As the population continues to decline, statistics are showing enormous reductions in communicable diseases and stress-related illnesses.

- The United Nations recently confirmed that every country now has a population policy in place to guide the people to sustainable lifestyles. These policies reflect a country's carrying capacity, as well as cumulative and long-term impacts of population levels, and include guidelines for appropriate immigration numbers.

- Governments around the world are developing incentive programs that encourage voluntary population reduction and small families. These include reproductive health worker programs, media campaigns, tax incentives, and various reward programs that have proven very successful.

- The World Wildlife Fund has noted that the numerous "Plant a Tree" projects being implemented in most of our world's great forests are creating new habitat for wildlife and reducing CO^2 emissions. As the declining human population retreats from wilderness areas, we are able to reclaim and replant our lost forests.

- Population groups on every continent are now issuing Population Report Cards that indicate the level of participation each country has reached in achieving a sustainable population. Due to a concerted effort through the United Nations, and involvement of women at all levels, great progress is being made.

- Right to Die groups around the world have reported that government policies to allow death with *dignity* are being implemented for those with terminal illnesses and reduced quality of life. This marks a milestone for citizens petitioning for humane and compassionate treatment of those living in constant misery.

- Oxfam recently reported that they have created the International Women's Panel on Population, consisting of women from every corner of the planet to participate in decision-making at every level of government. This panel has been recognized by the United Nations and will have direct input at UN conferences and meetings. Participants include women representing feminist groups, human rights, the medical field, environment, legal issues, justice and security, seniors groups, science, education, population groups, foreign aid programs, indigenous groups, politics, women in poverty, and youth groups.

- The World Health Organization has announced that all forms of fertility treatment have been banned and are encouraging couples to "consider adoption an option" instead. This strategy has proven to be very helpful in reducing the number of world orphans, especially those whose parents have died of AIDS and other devastating pandemics. It is no surprise that a decrease in racial conflict and more cooperative international communication have occurred as a result of adoption negotiations.

- The Pentagon has just announced that it will be leading a global campaign to withdraw all forces from foreign countries in an effort to reevaluate the "permanent state of war" mentality, which clearly is not working. A new strategy of cooperation, relationship building, and conflict resolution will be designed to end the senseless continuation of war our leaders have become obsessed with. As the population continues to decline, there has also been a substantial decline in conflict over natural resources, bringing peace to many regions.

The "War Machine," strongly promoting and greatly benefiting from perpetual war, will be dismantled as demand for its services wanes and its methods are recognized as unacceptable. Public outrage is demanding major changes, and declining population is facilitating those changes.

- UNESCO has just announced a substantial increase in protected and park land to provide citizens with opportunities to experience uncluttered wild spaces, encounters with wildlife, and places of natural beauty. Studies have shown that these kinds of primal encounters provide a sense of connectedness and well-being that is sadly missing in our modern lives. This has been made possible by reducing our human population so that more land is available for wilderness experiences.

- The media, governments, the medical community, the education establishment, and non-government organizations are making population the buzzword through TV ads, billboards, magazine ads, brochures, and most importantly through dinner discussions. The Internet, which has often been faulted for its unsavory uses, such as promoting pornography, racism, hate crimes, and material wealth, has now become the catalyst for population consciousness and environmental stewardship.

- And the good news just keeps on coming, as a heady mood of competition has taken hold in countries from Iceland to Uganda. There are now reports of acts of civility and global stewardship coming in from every continent. The number of confirmed cases of childfree couples has reached a record high, and children of the world are being treated with a newfound respect. It seems that the "pay it forward" effect (as depicted in the movie *Pay it Forward*), has manifested throughout the land, and a new sense of optimism has been documented, the likes of which has never been seen on this planet before.

Wow! Can you imagine the impact of a truly responsible and honest commitment to the Declaration of Human Rights? But wait a minute—this isn't all just a pipedream. Many countries are already at an enviable level of fertility that would allow a declining population—*if* their immigration levels were reduced. If we truly wanted to, we could stop the growth factor in these countries tomorrow, and allow the healing to begin.

TAKING ACTION

> While politicians, media and government-funded advisory groups like the Economic Council of Canada avoid drawing the link between human overpopulation (whether by immigration or by natural growth) and the lowering of the quality of life, Canadians have already made their decision privately. Individually and collectively, we have decided to have smaller families, suggesting that we want a declining birth rate. Were it not for officially sanctioned immigration, Canada would be in the enviable position of having a declining population. We would have a chance to preserve our ecology from the grim reaper of overpopulation. To begin the process of healing and restoring our damaged and most beautiful earth, we need fewer people, considerably fewer. Population reduction is the highest and most moral of all human goals …
>
> Efforts should be made to improve the quality of life in areas of human concentration, and not on spreading people over parts of the earth that are not yet savagely degraded.
>
> "The Dreaded 'P' Word,"
> by Ted Mosquin, *Borealis 2* (4), 1991

Instead of inviting population refugees to developed countries, we could greatly increase aid to their countries, with family planning incentives a priority. With our declining population rates, we could set a good example for them. And with their low consumption rates, they would set a good example for us. It could be a win-win situation.

> Moreover, slowing population growth by the ethical means outlined above is surprisingly cost-effective. For example, the developed countries' share of the cost to provide reproductive health services for every woman on earth is $20 billion—about what the bankers on Wall Street gave themselves in bonuses last year.
>
> "The Population Debate is Screwed Up"
> by Laurie Mazur,
> AlterNet, posted 28 March 2009

I think Mazur is absolutely right: our priorities certainly are screwed up. Perhaps the paltry sum needed for family planning programs could come from a luxury tax imposed on Wall Street. Or, funding for this foreign aid could be recouped from military budgets if all countries put war on hold for just *one day.*

> We taxpayers give the military about one billion a day ($355 billion/yr). A war is ready to start against Iraq which the President estimates will cost another $200 billion. Recently the President vetoed $34 million going to UN Family Planning. The Director of UNFPA, Thoraya Ahmed Obaid, said the $34 million U.S. contribution would have helped prevent 2 million unwanted pregnancies, 800,000 induced abortions, 4,700 maternal deaths, and 77,000 infant and child deaths. We need to stop and re-evaluate where we are putting our tax dollars.

Elder Bill Denneen,
"War & Family Planning: Priorities"
WOA Population News Monthly, 14 November 2002

Not only is our constant state of war depleting our economies, but it is also a losing battle that is unjustified. Chris Hedges makes this point in his article "There Is No Reason for Us to Be in Afghanistan—Everyone Knows It, and It Spells Defeat," posted on the website Truthdig on 21 July 2009:

> Al-Qaida could not care less what we do in Afghanistan. We can bomb Afghan villages, hunt the Taliban in Helmand province, build a 100,000-strong client Afghan army, stand by passively as Afghan warlords execute hundreds, maybe thousands, of Taliban prisoners, build huge, elaborate military bases and send drones to drop bombs on Pakistan. It will make no difference. The war will not halt the attacks of Islamic radicals. Terrorist and insurgent groups are not conventional forces. They do not play by the rules of warfare our commanders have drilled into them in war colleges and service academies. And these underground groups are protean, changing shape and color as they drift from one failed state to the next, plan a terrorist attack and then fade back into the shadows. We are fighting with the wrong tools. We are fighting the wrong people. We are on the wrong side of history. And we will be defeated in Afghanistan as we will be in Iraq …
>
> The only way to defeat terrorist groups is to isolate them within their own societies. This requires wooing the population away from radicals. It is a political, economic and cultural war. The terrible algebra of military occupation and violence is always counterproductive to this kind of battle.

We are often told that the US war in Afghanistan is being waged to help secure the rights of Afghan women. However, this couldn't be further from the truth:

> While I fully agree with the FM (Feminist Majority) that the US must stop supporting warlords, and pour resources into development and aid I disagree that dropping bombs, fighting ground offensives, imprisoning Afghans, and all the byproducts of war are somehow making women safer …
>
> But even cursory examination of the actual situation on the ground reveals that aside from theoretical changes embodied in the constitution, women's rights have actually deteriorated as a direct consequence of deliberate US policy. This policy has included empowering anti-woman warlords who have committed rape and thrown out female members of parliament, appointing a fundamentalist judiciary that has imprisoned women for adultery and being victims of rape, etc. Additionally, the US war has fueled a misogynist insurgency that has only gotten stronger and worsened anti-women sentiment …
>
> The Feminist Majority, Howard Dean and other American liberals in support of this war need to re-analyze the situation in Afghanistan and examine the real consequences of the US war over the past 8 years that have done more harm than good to women's rights.
>
> "Afghan Presidential Candidate:
> The U.S Occupation Must End"
> by Sonali Kolhatkar
> Posted on AlterNet, 23 July 2009

It is not that world governments are unaware of the urgency of the population crisis. It is just that most of them have their own agendas, which do not include reducing population as a priority. For decades now, warnings about overpopulation have been issued from various governments, scientists, and progressive thinkers, but these warnings have been systematically ignored. For example, the US House-Senate Concurrent Resolution 17 was submitted to the House of Representatives on 19 January 1999 by Rep. Tom Sawyer for himself and Rep. Constance Morella. It read:

> Resolved by the House of Representatives (the Senate concurring), that it is the sense of the Congress that the United States should develop, promote, and implement, at the earliest possible time and by voluntary means consistent with human rights and individual conscience, the policies necessary to slow the population growth of the United States, and thereby promote the future well-being of the people of this Nation and of the world.
>
> Global Population Concerns,
> Ottawa, newsletter, 12 September 2000

One could argue that the UN population programs need to step up their performance in regard to solving the population crisis. But are they rich and powerful enough to reverse the trend? We must remember that they depend on participating countries to follow through on their commitments, and this is often lacking. The UN is often underfunded, understaffed, and facing great opposition from the Vatican and others who shape the world in which they operate. The UN is often manipulated by institutions like the World Trade Organization, which are not held accountable and which cannot always deliver what they promise:

> Now it [UN] finds itself up against the policies of the International Monetary Fund and the World Bank. What it can do will always be bitty and piecemeal, all its projects swimming against a hostile tide. UNEP, the UN Development Programme, the children's fund UNICEF, all suffer as well from the way in which rich countries, the US in particular, use their purse strings to manipulate the UN.

Andrew Simms,
of the New Economic Foundation report
"It's Democracy, Stupid"
BBC Report by Alex Kirby, September 2000

Of course, many governments want large populations to enhance their prestige, military strength, and negotiating power. On the international level, many governments feel more secure with a large population so that they can hold their own against domineering neighbors or the vast populations of countries like India or China.

> After 200 years of continuous rapid population growth, there is little that inspires as much panic from political leaders, big business and right-wing populists as the prospect of population decline—which is imminent, according to the UN, in more than 60 countries.
>
> Population decline drums up visions of collapsing markets, permanent recessions, devastated communities, bankrupt pension funds and decrepit wrinklies with no young to replenish and support them. All this might indeed come to pass if population decline were rapid. A gradual population decline would be a different matter. The environmental benefits are obvious—fewer cars, fewer houses, more wilderness. But population decline could also empower workers, raise the status of the socially marginalized, reduce inequalities and eradicate poverty. It will not make Britain poorer, as the politicians fear, but wealthier. From British universities to Japanese think-tanks, the benefits of slow population decline are being increasingly studied and promoted. But this new thinking has yet to reach the echelons of elected politicians.

Pop the Pill and Think of England,
by Anthony Browne,

environment editor of the *Times*
4 November 2002

Browne points out that population decline also leaves fewer children to support, train, and educate for the first twenty economically unproductive years of their lives. So, the dependency ratio of workers to non-workers is virtually unaffected. In most instances, the only adjustment that is needed is a shift from caring for children to caring for the elderly.

A shift in our thinking is also required. Perhaps the world's most creative sales pitch is in order here, for the world's most urgent challenge. If we could find within ourselves the same passion we conjured up for buying the Cabbage Patch doll, dancing the Macarena, and promoting the green revolution, we would be off to a good start indeed! It would launch us into a millennium of hope, which is rather rare today, with population pressures causing a growing state of discontent.

The public needs to appreciate that the longer we neglect the population problem, the more difficult it will be to resolve. The public also needs to appreciate that when "pro-lifers" talk about protecting life—they mean human life only. They don't really give a care for the gorillas, grizzly bears, or elephants sentenced to death by our frenzy of human procreation. When they talk about "pro-life," they are talking about quantity of life, not quality. They don't care in the least that often these children will be delivered into a hostile world, unwanted and unloved. Nor do they lose sleep over the billions of children born into poverty, AIDS, rat-infested slums, abusive homes, the slave trade, drug-addicted families, the sex trade, or many of the other hopeless situations that exist today. As long as they get their way and are able to stop abortions or birth control programs (even if they have to kill a doctor or two to do it), they feel that they have succeeded in accomplishing their goal.

Could there possibly be a more self-centered and inhumane ethic of conduct?

> In 1968, when Paul Ehrlich wrote *The Population Bomb,* there were about one billion people enjoying a decent standard of living and 2.5 billion living in misery. We now have 1.2 billion people living decent lives, and 4.1 billion in poverty. Eight hundred million people are worse off than they were ten years ago. Eighty-six of the 90 armed conflicts in the world between 1989 and 1994 took place inside the territory of states, only four occurred between states. Competition for diminishing resources drives many of the territorial, ethnic and religious conflicts now wracking much of the developing world. The number of refugees has increased 10-fold in the past two decades: 80% are women and children. Landmines kill or maim at least 850 women and children each month.
>
> The refusal to recognize the reality of the population factor by many activists in the women's movement is indeed a betrayal of those they claim to speak for, because poor women and children are the most adversely affected by the deterioration of the planet. It is a shame that sensible feminists are reluctant or afraid to challenge the false feminist orthodoxy that addressing the population issue violates the rights of women.
>
> Madeline Weld,
> Personal communication,
> August 1995

At this specific time in history, we find ourselves *at a crossroads.* In preparation for 2012, or just because the population crisis demands an urgent response, we must decide now what direction we are heading. But first, we need to Stop, Look, and Listen, before we cross that road.

AT A CROSSROADS

STOP

1. Stop at two, or better yet, choose to be childfree or adopt.

   Some of the same race, class, and gender-sensitive Americans who enthusiastically voted Obama into office are among those doing the finger-pointing. After eight years of an environmentally tone-deaf president and a runaway big business culture that has our country's finances in ruin, they now see an opportunity for change. But this new frugality isn't just directed at Wall Street minions or banks, but is being projected onto the bodies of individual women—those who have more than one child … they are looked upon by some as not all that different from overpaid executives looking to use taxpayers' stimulus money for a joyride on a private jet, embodiments of a bloated age of conspicuous consumption we would rather forget.

   Dispatch,
   "The New Eugenics,"
   by Kara Jesella, June 2009

2. Stop promoting the mythology that is hampering efforts toward population reduction. All the arguments against gradual population decline are based on unfounded fear, outdated traditions, false assumption, or greed.

3. Stop allowing the media and politicians to keep this a taboo issue. We can use the Internet to get the word out and hold our leaders and media accountable.

4. Stop allowing the Vatican to have veto power in the UN, as this power is hampering family planning programs.

5. Stop allowing unaccountable institutions to manipulate UN decisions and spending.

6. Stop using an economic indicator (GDP) that does not account for population and environmental impacts. The Genuine Progress Indicator is a far more useful and effective tool.

7. Stop the degradation and abuse of women and children. We must call on the UN, the International Monetary Fund, the World Bank, and the World Trade Organization to take the issue of women's rights to a healthy life, free of oppression, poverty, and violence, as their responsibility to a just society.

8. Stop the deception and delusions—*our present actions are not working*:

- Our many years of effort to reduce worldwide poverty *are not working*. Despite the fact that developed countries have poured billions of dollars into foreign aid programs to fight poverty, there are more people starving today than ever before. According to a United Nations news report on 19 June 2009, one in six people on this planet is now hungry—that equals over one billion people. Our focus for foreign aid should be family planning programs first, as they have received comparatively little funding and would be far more effective at reducing poverty in the long-term.

  This situation should concern everyone, not just those in Third World countries. The fact of the matter is that many of the hungry will end up on our doorsteps if we do not help them in their native land. If we plan ahead, we can create a stable world. If we do not plan ahead, these populations will become destructive to themselves, the environment, and others.

  In 1996, Professor Homer-Dixon, a University of Toronto political scientist, was in Washington, where he presented a briefing on his case studies on environmental scarcity and violent conflict to the State Department. He pointed out that traditional military intervention does not work. We must deal with issues like family planning and the environment.

Prof. Homer-Dixon said, "All I want people to understand is what we have empirically discovered in the research: that there are linkages, sometimes powerful linkages, between environmental and demographic factors and violence. Internal violence, for the most part, diffuse and chronic."

He concluded that scarce resources lead elites to seize control of them and drive the less powerful to the margins. As a result, scarcity divides and polarizes societies rather than impoverishing them as a whole. This causes conflict between peasants and local elites.

In a dire situation such as this, we must choose survival of the planet and our life-support systems over individual needs and military intervention, no matter how callous this may appear at the present time. Once safe and effective birth control is available to all women who are now being denied it, and rampant sexual abuse often resulting in pregnancy is being dealt with effectively, military action will be uncalled for. We can then focus our attention on other urgent issues like poverty, education, and medical aid. Or better yet, perhaps the billionaires' club could help out so that we could address both population and poverty simultaneously.

- Our effort to separate population growth and environmental destruction *is not working*. Despite the monumental effort millions of people have put into protecting our environment, it has never been in a sadder state. Governments and environment groups must recognize the missing link here and commit to making population a priority. Humanity cannot afford to gamble with our life-support system.

I came to the realization that reducing population is the key factor in protecting our environment after working with environment groups for over twenty-five years. When I realized that the growing population had undermined any progress I thought we were making, I felt compelled to shift my focus to population issues and writing this book. I can honestly think of no better way to help the planet than to devote my life to the population crisis facing humanity.

- Our constant state of war to alleviate terrorism and violence *is not working.* According to the Women's Global Network for Reproductive Rights, the rise in military expenditure by governments also has consequences for other sections of public spending:

> Military spending undermines the security of human life and affects the well-being of women and children around the world by using up precious resources that could be spent on meeting basic human needs. For the fiscal year 1995, the USA spent 257 billion dollars on military expenditure whereas education, housing, environmental protection, job training and economic development added up to only 71.4 billion dollars. The Clinton government has recently recommended a huge increase to the military budget for the year 1999, while cutting budgets for welfare programs which have a direct effect on the lives of women and the poor. The ecologically-destructive practices of military and corporate institutions must also be addressed. The U.S. Pentagon generates one ton of toxic waste per minute through the production of weapons.

The Audubon Society is in complete agreement with this sentiment and adds:

> We are not asking for an increase in foreign assistance. We are asking that the existing amount be allocated differently. According to a study just released by Bread for the World Institute on Hunger and Development, of the $14.7 billion to be spent on foreign assistance in 1993, only $4

billion, or 27 percent, will support humanitarian and sustainable development activities. The U.S. should reprogram scarce foreign assistance funds into programs focusing on poverty alleviation, population, health care, increasing opportunities for women, sustainable agriculture, and energy and natural resource conservation and away from areas such as foreign military financing and base rights payments.

- Our obsession with the "American Dream" *is not working*. The illusion that we can continue to have big families, big houses, and big bank accounts is destroying our economies and environment. We must replace this fallacy with a realistic and sustainable lifestyle while implementing luxury taxes and other incentives to encourage people to live within their means. We must formulate a population policy with strong measures to reduce our population.

- Our tendency to allow our medical system to make our reproductive choices for us *is not working*. The number of medical professionals refusing or complicating procedures regarding women's reproductive health is disturbing. We need universal health care programs that provide a full range of family planning options, without bias or hostility. The days of backroom abortions and refusing a tubal ligation to a woman choosing to be childfree must end.

It was heartening, therefore, to read that the *British Medical Journal* published an editorial in its 25 July 2008 issue telling British parents to have fewer children to save the planet. The editorial, by John Guillebaud, emeritus professor of family planning and reproductive health at University College in London, and Pip Hayes, a general practitioner in Exeter, promote bringing the fertility rate in the UK down to 1.7 from the current 1.9, which would lead to a halving of the population within six generations.

These doctors suggest that general practitioners are to encourage the view that bigger families are as environmentally dubious as owning a patio heater or driving a gas-guzzler.

- Our present system of economics, based on the Gross Domestic Product, *is not working*. We must replace this with a system like the Genuine Progress Indicator that will result in sustainable economics and support a sustainable population.

  In 1972, following two years of research and public hearings, the final report of the President's Commission on Population Growth and the American Future was released. What was its major conclusion?

  > We have looked for, and have not found, any convincing economic argument for continued national population growth. The health of our economy does not depend on it. The vitality of business does not depend on it. The welfare of the average person certainly does not depend on it.

  In fact, it was found that the US economy could actually benefit from a move toward a stable population. For example, per capita income would rise, the dependency ratio would decrease, quality of life would improve, and pressure on the labor force would be eased.

- Our present immigration system *is not working*. Every country needs to adopt a population policy with goals for overall population size and annual limits on legal immigration.

  According to Vivian Pharis with the Alberta Wilderness Association, in the *SusPop News*, January 1995 issue, Canada has the highest intake rate in the world—more than double that of the United States or Australia. She noted the recent successes in the polls of Australia's single-issue party, Australians Against Further Immigration, which advocated a non-discriminatory immigration level of 30,000 a year, just offsetting emigration.

The October 1990 *Globe and Mail*–CBC News Poll indicated that 46 percent of Canadians wanted to see current immigration levels reduced and only 16 percent who wanted them increased. There was clearly no mandate for the government to expand Canada's population and even less to maintain current immigration levels (200,000 per year). Yet, since that time immigration levels have increased even more. (ZPG Canada, 1991)

- Our present tax system, which encourages large families through child tax credits, child care benefits, child fitness credits, refundable medical expenses, income tax deductions for all children, welfare, public school tax, and other incentives, *is not working*. It should be replaced with a system where parents are responsible for costs for all children after the first two. This new system would not discriminate against childfree citizens, punishing them with a higher tax load for not producing offspring, as the present system does. It would also encourage parents to plan and prepare for having a family, which is often not the case today.

Penalizing small and childfree families through our tax system is not the answer. To the contrary, we must reward those individuals who consider the environmental and social impacts of their childbearing decisions, both morally and financially. In fact, some countries have already proposed policies that would reward those with small families:

> In an effort to check the country's population boom, India plans to bar couples who marry too young from state jobs. A new national population policy would ban men married before 21 and women who married before 18 from government jobs … The draft of the new policy also recommends that only couples with no more than two children should be eligible for tax benefits and for promotion in government jobs. There will be laws banning those who do

> not adopt the small-family norm from entering politics.
>
> "No State Jobs for Couples Who Marry Too Young,"
> by Rahul Bedi,
> *The Daily Telegraph,* January 1997

- The attitude of the media, growth lobby, non-government groups, and education system toward the population issue *is not working.* As a society, we are failing to recognize the consequences of our actions. We are putting personal wishes before consideration for the common good, with devastating results. We need to adopt a new mindset that puts the environment, our life-support systems, social well-being, and the common good first. Self-centered attitudes are a luxury that we can no longer afford to support, since they interfere with the well-being and survival of the planet.

> Ask not what your country can do for you, ask what you can do for your country.
>
> John Kennedy

- The present feminist movement *is not working.* Almost at a standstill, the feminist movement is making little headway in empowering women worldwide to achieve increased freedom, equality, and choice regarding reproductive health. Women in every corner of the planet must step up efforts and join forces to overcome oppression and injustice and to protect the defenseless children of the world.

  Female empowerment is essential, since it embraces access to health and family planning resources, access to education, an opportunity to earn an independent income, and the opportunity for women to make meaningful decisions about their own lives. They could then better avoid situations of sexual abuse resulting in pregnancy and make their own choices regarding reproductive health.

International population and family planning assistance is about giving women control, not taking it from them. A woman in the world today is often the primary resource manager and food provider, and she knows the needs of her family. In order to effectively care for her family, she must have the right and the means to make informed decisions regarding the number and spacing of her children.

According to Zero Population Growth (now Population Connection), in 1994 women earned only 10 percent of the world's income and owned 1 percent of the world's property. However, they performed 66 percent of the world's work. This is unacceptable, and the situation has changed little since that time.

The twenty-first century must be a feminists' century. We desperately need to evolve to a gentler, more nurturing behavior toward our planet and fellow beings if we are to have a world that is tolerable for all inhabitants. Women must get the feminine adrenaline flowing when they strive for respect and equality, and they must insist that they be included in all decision-making at all levels of government. Women must have a stronger voice in the dialogue taking place about population issues.

We need to focus the attention of politicians and the media on the essential role women must play in the population movement if we are to make any meaningful progress toward true empowerment.

- Abstinence-only education (as promoted by the Vatican and the Bush administration) and coerced parenthood *are not working*. It is little wonder that by 2009 most states in the United States had rejected financial bribes to teach an abstinence-only curriculum in favor of a more comprehensive curriculum. Research has shown that abstinence-only education is ineffective and puts teenagers at risk.

We must ensure that other countries where abstinence-only birth control is being promoted are given this same opportunity to choose a more effective and humane alternative. All women should be allowed to choose what form of reproductive health care they prefer.

Coerced parenthood takes many forms, as outlined in Part 3, from the pressures of grandparents who want more grandchildren to the pressures of religious representatives who place unfounded and outdated expectations on their congregations. Women are all too often bullied into having children or are chastised for being childfree or having small families. Being denied birth control options and being the victim of rape are even more abhorrent forms of coerced parenthood, giving the woman no choice but to have another unwanted and unplanned child.

- The male population's promotion of, or indifference to, the present appalling global situation *is not working*. Men also need to be involved in promoting gender equality and ensuring women's reproductive health, especially since they make many of the decisions affecting women's rights and often shape public opinion. Fathers and partners often play a key role in reproductive decisions affecting women, so it is imperative that they step up and protect women from oppression and sexual abuse. We must achieve a sense of cooperation between genders to solve this problem.

  What ever happened to male chivalry? We need to revive the notion of chivalry, and find a King Arthur to champion the cause of women's rights once again. Don't you suppose that there is at least one knight in shining armor out there who feels that this is a worthwhile cause?

- The present operation of the United Nations, which gives the Vatican veto power on population-related issues, *is not working*. We must revoke this undeserved privilege, so that greater progress can be made toward formulating sustainable population goals and initiatives in the UN. This issue was discussed in great detail in Part 2.

- Our present political system does not truly reflect the wishes of the majority of citizens regarding population issues, so it *is not working*. All politicians should be required to make population and immigration issues part of their election campaign and debates and a focus of their sustainable lifestyles platform. Elections should include a referendum on population choices, allowing every individual a voice on this urgent matter.

> The only thing that will enable the world's governments to build a more just and sustainable international system is aroused and informed public opinion.
>
> Jane Taylor, *www.earthaction.org.uk*

The task before our leaders is to recognize the consequences if they continue to ignore their responsibility regarding overpopulation and to take effective and timely measures to achieve a sustainable population to benefit the common good.

The task before our citizens is to recognize that we can no longer sit back and allow big power governments, big corporations, and international institutions to determine our global destiny. We must no longer allow global decision-making to be controlled by a handful of tyrants with a questionable agenda. We must take the initiative to make global decision-making more accountable to the public, especially when it comes to reproductive health care.

> When we get piled upon one another in large cities, as in Europe, we shall become as corrupt as Europe.
>
> Thomas Jefferson

Comic used with permission from Mike Keefe

LOOK

1. Look at the devastation being caused by overpopulation.

   An unprecedented population summit of the world's scientific academies, meeting in New Delhi in October 1993 issued a statement containing the following:

   > The magnitude of the threat to the ecosystem is linked to human population size and resource use per person … As human numbers further increase, the potential for irreversible changes of far reaching magnitude also increases. Indicators of severe environmental stress include the growing loss of biodiversity, increasing greenhouse gas emissions, increasing deforestation worldwide, stratospheric ozone depletion, acid rain, loss of topsoil, and shortages of water, food and fuel-wood in many parts of the world … In our judgment, humanity's ability to deal successfully with its social, economic and environmental problems will require the achievement of zero

> population growth within the lifetime of our children …
>
> Sustainable Population Society, 1994

2. Look at reports from many universities, think tanks, population groups, and other distinguished thinkers that indicate that a sustainable population level would be between 1 and 3 billion, rather than our present level of almost 7 billion.

    > We must provide a compelling vision of the many benefits resulting from a much lower global human population of, for example, one billion, which was approximately the population of the Earth in 1850 … The quality of life of all people would soar. We would have all the advantages of modern technology but little, if any, environmental deterioration.
    >
    > *www.populationinstitute.ca*, 23 November 2003

3. Look at the population community's proposals for population policies for each country, based on carrying capacity and sustainable well-being.

4. Look at who has to gain from increasing population levels, at which lobbies, institutions, and other entities are standing in the way of reaching a sustainable population level. We must not allow the growth lobby and those with ulterior motives to undermine efforts to reduce population.

LISTEN

1. Listen to the millions of women around the world who are pleading for safe and effective family planning programs. We could use Bangladesh's symbol of a successful family planning

campaign, the Green Umbrella, to inspire a movement that would satisfy this urgent need.

> AND … MOST IMPORTANTLY …*ACCESS TO SAFE AND AFFORDABLE CONTRACEPTION*! Because the simple truth is … if women could choose the number of children they wanted, when they wanted, our population growth problem would be solved!
>
> Zero Population Growth
> (now Population Connection), 1998

2. Listen to the untold number of women and children who are being sexually abused, and often impregnated, due to the horrific sex trade industry and unjust male dominance. This situation is a real travesty and is unacceptable and preventable by means we already possess.

   > Let all babies be wanted and loved.
   >
   > Dr. Henry Morgentaler

3. Listen to the reports of habitat loss, biodiversity loss, and animal trafficking, which are all increasing as the human population increases. In 1995 a "Petition for the Rights of Future Generations" was being circulated by the Cousteau Society. This petition called on all of humanity to be responsible stewards of the planet as a fundamental duty of each generation to those of the future. It asked all leaders of states to exercise their influence to have the petition taken into account by the General Assembly of the United Nations. This is the kind of initiative we need to promote, but on a much grander scale and on every continent.

4. Listen to the silence of the media on the most alarming problem on the planet—population. This is truly a tragedy,

> especially for future generations who will live in a world greatly diminished.

Once we have stopped to reconsider the wisdom of our growth ethic; once we have looked at the evidence and taken inventory; once we have listened to the voices of those in misery, those speaking for wildlife, those who desperately want to be heard—how can we not make population a priority for the twenty-first century?

The prospect of adding several more billion people to our planet over the next fifty years is nightmarish. This will have a devastating effect on ecosystems already reeling under current human demands. The Population Institute of Canada advises:

> The international community needs to come to an unequivocal agreement that a significant reduction of human population is a desirable goal. All steps should be taken by individual nations to make it happen quickly and humanely. The Cairo conference on population in 1994 was a tentative but totally inadequate step in that direction. In this time of crisis, governments will need to show real leadership by designing institutions that help humanity shrink its way to sustainable prosperity. Countries that are in the lead in reducing their populations should not give in to the advocates of growth by allowing massive immigration. This rewards those who multiply irresponsibly. The various peoples of the Earth will need to assume responsibility to restore their respective regions of origin into lands of hope. In an overcrowded world, mass migration is no longer a reasonable option to address overpopulation. The problems must be resolved in situ.

A POPULATION REPORT CARD

Now that we are aware of the actions necessary to achieve a sustainable population, we need to monitor and report on our progress toward that goal. And the best way to do that would be for population groups around the world to produce a yearly "report card" to update global citizens on positive actions taking place to achieve that goal. This report card would evaluate every country on activities such as:

- Each country should develop a population policy that would also determine immigration levels.
- A full range of family planning programs should be made available.
- A country must support efforts to revoke the Vatican's veto power in the UN.
- Every country must make efforts to substantially reduce child slavery and sexual abuse, along with the resulting pregnancies.
- Each country is responsible for establishing regular media reports on a wide range of population issues.
- All countries should ban fertility treatments and promote adoption as an option.
- Each country is responsible for legalizing right to die programs in a compassionate and humane way.
- The implementation of meaningful economic indicator methods, such as the Genuine Progress Indicator, should be initiated.
- Efforts should be made to empower women to make their own choices regarding birth control methods and to attain equality and freedom from abuse.

- Reducing the incidence of women and children being abused as sex slaves or child soldiers must be a priority for all governments and citizens.
- The Vatican's proposal to implement abstinence-only sex education should be rejected by all countries.
- Every country must ensure that population, parenting, and family planning courses are included in school programs.
- Each country should participate in engaging doctors and medical staff in programs to encourage family planning options and working with research facilities in further development of birth control methods.
- Every country should make it a priority to organize media campaigns to remove the taboo stigma from the population issue and resolve the many myths that have clouded this topic. This campaign could include billboards, magazine and TV ads, slogan or poetry competitions in schools, etc. A few slogans that I like and use are:

Stop at one—even better, have none

Choose to be—Childfree

Consider adoption an option!

People could create their own slogans, bumper stickers, posters, T-shirts, etc. The Population Connection in the United States (formerly Zero Population Growth) already has many population promotional items available. But most of all, we just need to start talking about the dreaded "P" word—get informed and make it personal. We need to introduce comprehensive, medically accurate sexuality and parenthood education into schools worldwide.

Those who are innovative and creative could make population a focus topic at Toastmasters, a class presentation in school, a discussion topic during their lunch break at work or school. Just imagine what students in art class could come up with! Teachers could make population an essay assignment and adopt a population curriculum similar to that used by the Yale New Haven Teachers Institute, which can be found on their website as "The Population Explosion: Causes and Consequences," written by Carolyn Kinder: *www.yale.edu/ynhti/curriculum/units/1998/7/98.07.02.x.html.*

Government representatives could conduct surveys that included an array of population-related questions. Religious organizations might want to become an agent of change by addressing the need for population reduction in their prayers and sermons.

Why not make this a referendum issue during elections? Taxpayers could vote on issues such as how quickly they want population growth to decline, at what rate immigration should be reduced, what priorities should be for foreign aid, etc. Politicians could make population report card goals part of their platform and promote this program as part of a sustainable lifestyle.

The findings of this report card would be announced on the radio and TV annually on World Population Day, 11 July, as well as appearing in newspapers and magazines. The population report card would be the focus of United Nations conferences, where comprehensive policies would make it a priority. There would be both economic and trade incentives to encourage countries to make every attempt to meet population goals. Immigration to developed countries would be conditional to a commitment to the receiving country's population policy.

THE CONUNDRUM—WHY THE APATHY? WHERE IS THE OUTRAGE?

With the high incidence of overpopulation, poverty, suffering, loss of biodiversity, injustice, corruption, and child cruelty, where is the outrage? Are we really so preoccupied and indifferent that we have no time to protest against the greatest tragedy on earth? We need a new earth credo that will empower citizens to stop the insanity of overpopulation. Solving the population crisis is an idea whose time has come.

> Nothing is as powerful as an idea whose time has come.
>
> Victor Hugo

We will be seeing more population awareness programs in the near future as people who care refuse to remain unheard. By targeting school-aged children we will be setting the tone for the next generation. Our children will grow up with the knowledge, the awareness, and best of all, the answers. Population awareness will become as much a part of their lives as growth, poverty, waste, and denial have become a part of ours. But first we, the adults they depend on for a safe and prosperous future, must face the reality!

> This is a column I don't want to write. Its subject is ugly; it makes me instinctively recoil. I have chastised people who bring it up at environmentalist meetings. The people who talk about it obsessively have often been callous about human life … and yet … there is a grain of insight in what they say.
>
> The subject is overpopulation. Is our planet over-stuffed with human beings? Are we breeding to excess? These questions are increasingly poking into public debate, and from odd directions. Phillip Mountbatten—husband of the British monarch Elizabeth Windsor—said in a documentary screened this week: "The food prices are going up, and everyone thinks it's to do with not enough food, but it's really (that there are) too many people. It's a little embarrassing for everybody, nobody knows how to handle it." He is not alone. A strange range of people have voiced the same sentiments over the past few months, from the Dalai Lama to Hu Jintao, from Conservative mayor Boris Johnson to Democratic Governor Bill Richardson.
>
> But if this is a problem, is there a solution that isn't abhorrent? … There is a far better way—and it is something we should be pursuing anyway. It is called feminism. Where women have control over their own bodies—through contraception, abortion and general independence—they choose not to be perpetually pregnant. The UN Fund for Population

> Activities has calculated that 350 million women in the poorest countries didn't want their last child, but didn't have the means to prevent it. We should be helping them by building a global anti-Vatican, distributing the pill and the words of Mary Wollstonecraft.

"Are There Just Too Many People in the World?" By Johann Hari, 15 May 2008, *The Independent/UK* article printed from *www. CommonDreams.org*

There may be help on the way from other high places as well:

> Some of the richest men and women in the world met secretly recently in New York to conspire on using their vast wealth to bring the world's population growth under control.
>
> The meeting included some of the biggest names in the "billionaires club," according to the *London Times*—Bill Gates, David Rockefeller, Ted Turner, Oprah Winfrey, Warren Buffet, George Soros and Michael Bloomberg.
>
> The meeting at the home of Sir Paul Nurse, a British Nobel Prize-winning biochemist and president of Rockefeller University, was the inspiration of Gates and took place three weeks ago.
>
> "Secret Billionaire Club Seeks Population Control," WorldNetDaily, posted 24 May 2009

Everyone in the group agreed that the population crisis is something so nightmarish that it needs big-brain answers. They felt that the group needed to be independent of government agencies, which seem unable to head off the disaster we all see looming.

John Harlow reported in the *Sunday Times* on 24 May 2009, "the philanthropists who attended a summit convened on the initiative of Bill Gates, the Microsoft co-founder, discussed joining forces to overcome political and religious obstacles to change."

One would expect to hear concern for the growing numbers from groups who tend to care about disappearing wildlife habitat, loss of biodiversity, and environmental degradation—but, except for a rare few, environment groups are sadly silent. Instead, support for population control is coming from some of the most unlikely sources:

> Listen, man, if you want to do something, don't buy yourself a hydrogen-fuel-cell car or an electric car or even a bus pass and think you're saving anything. If you really want to make a difference, the only thing you can do—the only thing—is to dedicate the rest of your life to population control as if the earth depended on it. Population control is ultimately the one thing that's going to save us, our kids and our kid's kids. But that's the long-range view. For now, enjoy yourself.
>
> "Just Relax and Enjoy It"
> by Mark Vaughn,
> *Auto Week Magazine*, June 2009

QUIZ QUESTION

Of the following individual actions, which one do you think will have the greatest long-term environmental impact?

----- owning a car ----- having a child

----- buying plastic items ----- throwing out trash

According to Zero Population Growth, who created the quiz that included this question, the answer is—you guessed it—**having a child.**

> I think we will work our way toward a position that says that having more than two children is irresponsible. It is the ghost at the table. We have all these big issues that everybody is looking at and then you don't really hear anyone say the "p" word.
>
> Many organizations think it is not part of their business. My mission with the Friends of the Earth and the Greenpeaces of this world is to say: "You are betraying the interests of your members by refusing to address population issues and you are doing it for the wrong reasons because you think it is too controversial."

Jonathon Porritt, chair of Britain's Sustainable Development Commission, February 2009 *Sunday Times*, "Two Children Should Be Limit"

SUCCESS STORIES

The good news is that the task before us is not as complicated or expensive as many people would like you to believe. We don't have to reinvent the wheel here, for there are many success stories to guide and motivate us from both developed and developing countries.

> "What Bangladesh has done is a remarkable achievement," said Jagmohan Kang, a population specialist with the World Bank in Dhaka. "In the past 20 years, the fertility rate has been cut by half through a voluntary program, which has not happened in any other large developing country to date."
>
> "A Rare Family Planning Success"
> by John Stackhouse,
> *Globe and Mail*, 22 July 1996

Stackhouse points out that the villages in the Matlab region of Bangladesh are approaching the population problem differently. In 1971, when Bangladesh was part of Pakistan, the contraception rate in both nations was about 4 percent. In 1996, Pakistan's rate was 15 percent, Bangladesh's was 45 percent. In Matlab, the rate was close to 70 percent. Bangladesh's improvement on Pakistan's performance means 1.8 million fewer births every year. So, how did they do it?

> "It is a total package," said Aparajita Chakroborty, a village health worker in Matlab since 1985. "There is a trust. Because I have helped people's children, I have their confidence."

Bangladesh employs 23,000 women like Ms. Chakroborty, who, for a salary of about one hundred dollars a month, ensures that 200 couples around her village have access to modern birth control as well as maternal and child health care.

Stackhouse notes that unlike the governments of many countries that believe the poor want large families, the Matlab program assumed couples everywhere wanted birth control, especially when it came as part of a bigger health package.

The link is as simple as a village health worker, a local woman with no more than a high-school education who not only sells the idea of contraception but provides doorstep health service. This concept could easily be replicated in every city, town, and village around the world and in many cases be included in existing programs so that additional costs would be minimal.

"We succeeded with service," said Mohammed Yunus, coordinator of the Centre for Health and Population Research in Matlab, which runs the local family planning program for 210,000 couples. "In a lot of countries, emphasis was placed on family planning, but not on quality."

This program was not only voluntary but gladly welcomed by those receiving the long-awaited birth control services. One recipient was Monowara Manufa, a field laborer.

She said, "We can provide a better living and more education for our children this way. And my health is better."

A pilot project conducted by India's health officials has also proven to be successful. Reporter Gethin Chamberlain explains,

> Thousands of couples in India who agreed to put off having babies for at least two years after their wedding will collect cash payments this month as health officials attempt to curb the country's rapidly growing population.
>
> While neighboring China shows the first signs of relaxing its strict policy of one child per couple in the face of an ageing population, India is searching for a way of restricting the size of families as the battle over scarce resources grows.
>
> "India Pays Couples to Put Off Having Children,"
> *The Observer*,
> 2 August 2009

Chamberlain adds that the country's population now stands at 1.2 billion and is expected to reach 1.53 billion by 2050, overtaking China to become the world's most populous nation. But increasing pressure on resources means that there is barely enough water and food to go round even now.

Satara, funded by the National Rural Health Mission, is offering couples a reward of 5,000 rupees if they delay having a child for two years (seventy rupees a day is a good wage in rural areas). If they wait another year, they receive a further 2,500 rupees. The project initially attracted 977 couples, but that figure has risen to 2,366 in 2009. Couples who take part are also eligible for family planning advice and free condoms.

In the September 1992 *Zero Population Growth Reporter* appeared "A Recipe for Success: Ingredients for a Successful Family Planning Program." I will outline a few of the examples given in that article.

Jennifer Merrill with ZPG tells us that once a country has accepted the need for a variety of contraceptive options, getting birth control into the hands of childbearing-age couples presents the next challenge. The most significant factors hampering effective distribution are rural, isolated populations and cultural attitudes. But several countries are trying innovative approaches to those roadblocks, with notable success.

Indonesia, for instance, has established "floating clinics"—located on boats navigating Indonesia's many waterways—which are better able to provide general and reproductive health services to rural populations not accessible by road. Thanks largely to the clinics, and increased availability of hormonal injections and Norplant, Indonesia now boasts a contraceptive prevalence rate of 53 percent, higher than all but a few developing nations.

On an international scale, the Japanese Organization for International Cooperation in Family Planning (JOICFP) recently began shipping bicycles to developing countries to better help family planning clinics located in towns and villages with poor roads or transportation systems. JOICFP officials say the very presence of clinic staff on bicycles enhances their status as peers in the community, and consequently, the program has seen greater success.

Many developing counties also support contraceptive social marketing (CSM) programs, which use already existing distribution networks, such as local shopkeepers and market stallholders, and offer contraceptives at government-subsidized prices. CSM programs acknowledge that many people are willing to pay for contraceptives when they are conveniently located at a nearby pharmacy or shop.

In Zaire, CSM programs saw a more than doubling of condom sales between 1989 and 1990. And in Egypt, the only country with a CSM program selling IUDs, IUD use jumped from 11 percent in 1975 to 42 percent in 1988. Egypt's CSM program operates primarily in urban areas, where there are many private physicians able to insert the IUD. In 1992 there were more than twenty countries maintaining CSM programs.

Many countries have further increased contraceptive prevalence rates through multimedia promotion—radio, television, video, films, newspapers, magazines, and billboard and poster advertising. Dr. Phyllis Piotrow of John Hopkins' Center for Communication Services stresses that a successful multimedia campaign is carefully researched and targeted; it "does not try to change an audience's mind. It tries to build on what the audience already thinks and wants most."

And the success stories are numerous. In three Brazilian cities, a recent multimedia vasectomy campaign resulted in an 80 percent increase in the average number of vasectomies performed monthly at the Pro-Pater male health clinics. In Turkey, a multimedia campaign is estimated to have encouraged approximately 240,000 women to start using or to switch to modern contraceptive methods. And in Ibadan, Nigeria, nearly one-quarter of all new clients at family planning clinics cite television as their source of referral.

But for many countries where the status of women is low and high fertility rates are valued, family planning providers face the challenge of convincing potential clients of the many benefits of using contraceptives.

In Zimbabwe, the Family Planning Council is reaching out to men—educating them about birth control and the advantages of smaller families. "We know they make the decisions," says Dr. Alex Zinanga, executive director of the Council. "We want them to make the decisions on facts, not on misconceptions." Zimbabwe now reports one of the highest uses of modern contraceptive methods anywhere in Africa.

Merrill points out that the Center for Development and Population Activities (CEDPA) takes a different approach. CEDPA recruits women leaders from Asia and Africa and trains them to implement family planning services, often within the context of already established health or other social services. One of their striking success stories is in Ahmedabad, India. There CEDPA works with the Gujarat State Crime Prevention Trust, an all-woman social welfare organization operating primarily in the city's poor communities.

Together they helped increase from 12 percent to 61 percent the contraceptive prevalence rate in impoverished neighborhoods.

Perhaps most crucial to a successful family planning program is government support. Indeed, the kinds of incentives and investments governments make toward lowering fertility rates can have dramatic effects.

For example, Thailand has received almost universal praise for its family planning program. In just seventeen years, between 1970 and 1987, the contraceptive prevalence rate rose from 10 percent to 68 percent, and the total fertility rate fell from 6.2 to 2.2. The program's success rests on the commitment of, and cooperation between, public and private sectors.

From multimedia campaigns to programs within Boy and Girl Scouts, the Thai public is surrounded with family planning information and services. These include "family life education," a wide variety of contraceptives easily available free of charge or at highly subsidized prices both from physicians and non-physicians, and the deployment of mobile and stationary family planning clinics reaching urban and rural areas with women trained to work with women.

Merrill notes that whether the family planning providers are found on floating clinics, in neighborhood shops, or door-to-door, high motivation of the workers, combined with their respect for the community's own values, is viewed as essential to successful family planning programs.

Closer to home, professors at a US university have come up with an incentive program that has proven to be extremely successful:

> A pregnancy prevention program based at the University of North Carolina at Greensboro that pays 12 to 18 year old girls one dollar for every day they are not pregnant has spurred conversation and raised eyebrows as it has made its way through the blogosphere. *College Bound Sisters* was founded in its most infant stages almost 20 years ago by Hazel

> Brown, professor of nursing, and Rebecca Saunders, associate dean of the graduate school. But the program made headlines after a Fox News story brought to light its incentive-based system.
>
> Brown emphasized that College Bound Sisters is more than just a monetary transaction. The money—which gets deposited into a college savings account—is given to the participants only after they achieve all three goals of the program: not getting pregnant, graduating from high school and enrolling in college. The girls also receive $5 per week for transportation to the program's classes in sexual health and preparation for college. Some students who have stuck with it have received over $2,000 toward a college degree.
>
> Ben Eisen.
> "A Dollar A Day Not to Get Pregnant,"
> 9 July 2009

There is no reason in the world that we could not use these successful methods to create effective homegrown programs that would work anywhere on this planet. In fact, both developed and developing counties could learn a great deal from many of these success stories as far as building cooperation and developing comprehensive strategies that are effective. All we need now is the allocation of funds and political will to see this through.

To a great degree, funding could come from the billions of dollars that would be saved when we reduce immigration levels in developed countries to a rate that would just offset emigration. At present, taxpayers in countries like Canada are spending billions of dollars to accommodate immigrants, money that would be better spent as foreign aid to assist them in their homeland.

> Our politicians justify their desire for more immigrants by raising the spectre of an aging population and telling us immigration is the only

answer to this dilemma, and yet there is not a shred of truth to this argument. Immigration does not provide the answer to population aging and there is a multiplicity of studies done in Canada and elsewhere that proves this. Moreover, there is no evidence that a larger labour force necessarily leads to economic progress. Many countries whose labour force is shrinking are still enjoying economic buoyancy. Finland, Switzerland and Japan are only a few examples of countries that do not rely on massive immigration to succeed. Productivity is the answer to economic success not a larger population.

Most Canadians assume that our immigrants are selected because they have skills, training and education that will enable them to enhance our labour force but only about 18 to 20 per cent of our immigrants are selected for economic factors. By far the bulk of the immigrants we receive come here because they are sponsored by relatives or because of so-called humanitarian reasons and none of these have to meet the "points system" of selection. This is why over 50 per cent of recent immigrants are living below the poverty line and why they are not earning nearly the wages paid to equivalent Canadian workers.

It also explains why a study published this year by professor Herbert Grubel of Simon Fraser University revealed that the 2.5 million immigrants who came to Canada between 1990 and 2002 received $18.3 billion more in government services and benefits in 2002 than they paid in taxes. As Prof. Grubel points out, this amount is more than the federal government spent on health care and twice what was spent on defense in the fiscal year 2000/2001. Isn't it time our party leaders were made aware of this study?

"Canada: The Truth About Immigration Is That Costs Exceed Benefits," by James Bissett, a former executive director of the Canadian Immigration Service, 30 September 2008, Immigration Watch International

WHAT ARE WE WAITING FOR?

Is it possible that all of the people who have been quoted in this book are wrong? Do you really think at this point that we can continue on the path of growth that today's decision makers are promoting? If so, I would like to hear how this would be possible. I would like to leave you with a couple of challenges—opportunities to prove the population reduction proponents wrong.

1. The first challenge was issued by Carrying Capacity Network in 1994:

> On the local, state, national, and global level, every problem of the environment such as pollution, loss of biodiversity, etc.; every problem of social justice, such as racism, sexism, unequal distribution of wealth, etc.; every economic problem such as unemployment, inflation, etc.; every problem related to resource scarcity and conflict, such as war, famine, etc.; is made worse by increases in population. Conversely, all these problems would be easier to solve if populations were not growing or were smaller.

Carrying Capacity Network (CCN) points out that this statement is widely believed to be true. They challenge anyone to submit exceptions, substantive rebuttals, or contradictions to this statement. For example, they challenge people to cite specific cases where a cause-and-effect relation can be demonstrated in which a population increase can be shown to result in the solution of any of these (or any other) problems rather than making them all worse.

A director of CCN, Dr. David Pimentel, gives this warning:

> Even the most diligent conservation efforts will be effective only if they are accompanied by stopping population growth. If returned to a self-sustaining renewable energy system, the earth will be able to support a population of approximately two billion people living in relative prosperity.

Dr Pimentel recognizes that "a drastic demographic adjustment to two billion humans will cause serious social, economic and political problems," but insists that "continued rapid population growth will result in even more severe social, economic and political conflicts—plus catastrophic public health and environmental problems."

In order to prevent the disastrous worldwide poverty and privation that a continued population increase would produce, he recommends profound revisions in our relationship to the environment and an end to population growth.

His report concludes with both a warning and promise.

> Decision-making tends to be based on crisis; decisions are not made until catastrophe strikes. Thus, decisions are ad hoc, designed to protect or promote a particular aspect of human well-being instead of examining the problem in a holistic manner. Based on past experience, we expect that leaders will continue to postpone decisions concerning human carrying capacity of the world (Fornos, 1987), maintenance of a standard of living, conservation of resources, and the preservation of the environment until the situation becomes intolerable, or worse still, irreversible.
>
> Starting to deal with the imbalance of the population-resource equation before it reaches crisis level is the only way to avert a real tragedy for our children's children. With equitable population control that respects basic individual rights, sound resource management policies, support of science

> and technology to enhance energy supplies and the environment, and with all people working together, an optimum population can be achieved. With such cooperation efforts we would fulfill fundamental obligations to generations that follow—to ensure that individuals will be free from poverty and starvation in an environment that will sustain human life with dignity.

2. The second challenge comes from Professor Albert A. Bartlett. Although I used this challenge earlier in the book, I feel it is worth repeating now that you have been given all the pertinent information:

> Can you think of any problem in any area of human endeavor on any scale, from microscopic to global, whose long-term solution is in any demonstrable way aided, assisted, or advanced by further increases in population locally, nationally, or globally?
>
> Dr. Bartlett,
> Emeritus Professor of Physics,
> University of Colorado

In our modern world, we can forget how linked we are to our wild spaces and how these places protect the very things we hold dear. We may not realize that the birds singing in our backyards migrate every year to the disappearing rainforests. We may not understand that the rivers that provide our drinking water are being threatened by contamination and over-use on their way from our boreal forests.

It would be easy, in our busy lives, to say that we don't have time to worry about our population or our life-support systems. Let someone else worry about it—after all, that's what our governments are paid to do, right? Well, that kind of passive approach may have been acceptable at one time, but it isn't good enough today in our current situation. We all need to take action to protect our special places, as well as our future security, as they may not exist forever.

While you have this book in your hands, please make a commitment to do your part to ensure a sustainable population and a healthy and safe future for yourself and future generations. I will end with a passage from the "World Scientists' Warning To Humanity," composed by 1,670 of the world's top scientists, members of the Union of Concerned Scientists, in April, 1993:

> A new ethic is required—a new attitude towards discharging our responsibility for caring for ourselves and for the earth. We must recognize the earth's limited capacity to provide for us. We must recognize its fragility. We must no longer allow it to be ravaged. This ethic must motivate a great movement, convincing reluctant leaders and reluctant governments and reluctant peoples themselves to effect the needed changes.

~

> The only thing necessary for the triumph of evil is for good men to do nothing.
>
> Edmund Burke

BIBLIOGRAPHY

Introduction and Part 1

Abernethy, Virginia."Attitudes." *The Pherologist* 2, no. 3 (August 1999).

Bartlett, Al. "Al Bartlett: Professor Emeritus, Physics." http://*www.albartlett.org.* 8 January 1996

Bartlett, Albert. "Why Have Scientists Succumbed to Political Correctness?" *Teachers Clearinghouse for Science and Society Education Newsletter* 27, no. 2 (Spring 2008).

Black, Richard. "Birth Rate Harms Poverty Goals." www.bbc.co.uk/science/nature/62199 8 January 2007.

Brown, Lester. "As Dow Jones Goes Up, Earth's Health Goes Down." *Ottawa Citizen* (17 January 2000).

Bukwa, Bonnie. "Presentation at Sustainable Population Workshop." College of the Rockies, Cranbrook, B.C., 13 March 1993.

Chesworth, Ward, Michael Moss, and Vernon Thomas. *Malthus and The Third Millennium*, 2000 ser., University of Guelph, 2001.

Chivian, Eric. "Science, Religion and the Environment." *http://www.oprah.com.*

College of Agriculture and Life Sciences at Cornell University. "Will Limits of the Earth's Resources Control Human Numbers?." Cornell University, 25 February 1999.

Delaney, David. "Overshoot in a Nutshell (Malthus was an Optimist)." *www.geocities.com*

Doyle, Alister. "Humans Living Far Beyond Planet's Means." *Living Planet Report*. World Wildlife Fund, October 2006.

East Kootenay Environmental Society (now known as Wildsight)

EKES. "Economic Sustainability: The Problem." EKES Factsheet #5, 1995

Ehrlich, Paul. *The Population Bomb*. Ballantine Books: New York, May 1968.

Ferguson, Andrew. *Assessing the Millennium Assessment.* Millennium Ecosystem Assessment (MA) Synthesis Report, Optimum Population Trust Journal Vol. 5, No.1 April 2005

Ferguson, Niall. "The Population Bubble." *Los Angeles Times* (30 July 2007).

Gardner, Gary. "The Challenge for Johannesburg: Creating a More Secure World." *State of the World, 2002*. Norton: New York, 2002.

Grant, James. "Opportunity Knocks." *State of the World's Children Report 1994.*

Grant, Lindsey. "In Support of a Revolution." *www.npg.org/forum_series/support_revolution.htm.*

Grant, Lindsey. "Optimum Population." *www.secularhumanism.org.*

Gunter, Lorne. "We Should Laugh after 'Bomb' Exploded in Ehrlich's Face." *Edmonton Journal* (15 November 1995).

Hardin Garrett. "Nobody Ever Dies of Overpopulation." *Science Magazine* 171, no. 3971, (12 February 1971).

Helliwell, Tanis. "A Symbol of Transformation." *Synchronicity: The Magazine* (February/March 2001)

Hoff, Brishen. "How Badly Overpopulated Will We Be In 40 Years?" *www.ecologicalcrash.blogspot.com/2009/01/how-badly-overpopulated-will-we-be-in.html January 2009*

Hume, Mark. "Like Too Many Rats." *Vancouver Sun* (19 February 1994).

Macpherson, Andrew. "Stopping Population Growth Essential to Saving the Environment." *Environment Network News* (September/October 1992).

Mitchell, Alanna. "Earth Faces Supply Crisis, Study Finds." *Globe and Mail* (25 June 2002)

Mosquin, Ted and Stan Rowe. "A Manifesto for Earth." *Ecospheric Ethics* (June 2006).

National Academy of Science and Royal Society of London. *World Scientists' Warning to Humanity*. 1993

Negative Population Growth. *NPG Internet Forum*. The Physics Teacher Vol. 44 Pgs. 623–624, December 2006

Pharis, Vivian. "The AWA Supports a Position Paper on Population." *Wild Lands Advocate* 2, no. 4 (1994)

Pimentel, David. "Life on Earth is Killing Us." *BioScience Journal* (October 1998).

Pimentel, David. " *Optimum Population Trust Journal* 6, no. 2, (October 2006).

King, Rev. Martin Luther, Jr. "Family Planning—A Special and Urgent Concern." *www.plannedparenthood.org* (accessed 13 October 2009).

Population Institute of Canada. *Famous Quotes.* Captain Paul Watson Quote, Website *www.populationinstituteofcanada.ca* accessed 2009

Population Institute of Canada. "Population, Sustainable Development and Security." www.populationinstituteofcnada. ca (accessed 12 November 2003).

Population Reference Bureau. "Family Planning Saves Millions of Women and Children's Lives." *Women's International Network News*. (5 February 1997).

Potts, Malcolm. "Sex and the Birth Rate." *Population and Development Review 23*, no.1 (March 1997).

Rapley, Chris. "This Planet Ain't Big Enough for the 6,500,000,000." *The Independent.* (27 June 2007).

Rolston, Holmes. "Feeding People Versus Saving Nature?" *World Hunger and Morality*, 2nd ed. Prentice-Hall: Englewood Cliffs, NJ, 1996. 248-267.

Sustainable Population Society. "Know the Facts!" *Sustainable Population Society* Fact Sheet, February 1997.

Templeton, Sarah-Kate. "Big Family an 'Environmental Misdemeanour': Report." *Ottawa Citizen* (6 May 2007).

UN Wire. "Mexico: Fertility Rates Falling." www.unfoundation.org.

Weinstein, David & Davis, Donald. "Americans Lose $68 Billion a Year from Immigration." *www.columbia.edu/~drd28/Migration.pdf*

Weld, Madeline and Whitman Wright. "Confronting the Population Crisis." *Responses to the Twenty-One Most Commonly Used Arguments to Confound the Issue.* Canadian Population Action. October 1996.

Weyler, Rex. "The Tyee: Biophysical Economics." *The Tyee.* (2 January 2009).

Zachary, Pascal. "An Unconventional Academic Sounds the Population Alarm." *Wall Street Journal*, (31 July 1998).

Zero Population Growth. "The Heirs of Our Ways." *The ZPG Reporter* 25, no. 2/3. (May 1993).

Zero Population Growth (Renamed Population Connection). *Population Policy Campaign.* 23 November 1993

Zero Population Growth (Population Connection). "Beyond the Green Revolution: Singin' the Population Blues." *The ZPG Reporter* 24, no. 4 (September 1992).

Zero Population Growth. "For Children's Sake." ZPG Reporter (May 1993)

PART 2

African Wildlife Foundation. "About AWF." www.awf.org/section/about (accessed 26 March 2009).

Alberta Wilderness Association. "Environmental Impacts of Motorized Recreation." Alberta Wilderness Association Position Statement, April 2002.

Aronson, Ronald. "Personal God Going the Way of the Dodo?—40Million Nonbelievers in America? The Secret is Almost Out." www.alternet.org/story/139788/.

Asimov, Isaac. "Interview by Bill Moyers on a World of Ideas." *www.en.wikiquote.org/wiki/Isaac_Asimov* (accessed 26 August 2009).

Beaujot, Roderic. "Johns Hopkins Report on Family Planning." *SusPop News,* 1995.

Bentley, Fred. "Perspective." *Sustainable Population Society News,* July 1994.

Berle, Peter. "Why Do Environmentalists Need to Worry About Population?" *Why Population Matters Handbook.* National Audubon Society, 1991.

Bernstein, Carl and Marco Politi. "The Angry Pope." *Conscience xvii,* no. 4, (Winter 1996/1997): 14-17.

BBC. "Global Dimming." Science & Nature - Horizon TV Documentary, 15 January 2005. www.globalissues.org/print/article/529.

Brown, Lester. "Population Growth Sentencing Millions to Hydrological Poverty." *Worldwatch Institute Issue Alert.* 21 June 2000.

Brown, Lester. "Ecological Deficits Taking Economic Toll." *Earth Policy Institute News Release*, 3 October 2002.

Canadian Population Action Network. "The Religious Consultation on Population, Reproductive Health and Ethics." *SusPop News*, June 1994,

Canadian Population Action Network. "International Conference on Population and Development." *SusPop News*, June 1994.

Canadian Population Action Network. "Population and Biodiversity." *SusPop News*, no. 10 (September 1994).

Canadian Population Action Network. "Limits to Growth (Club of Rome)." *SusPop News*, no. 12 (June 1995).

Can Do Better. "Martin Luther King "Family Planning – A Special and Urgent Concern." *www.candobetter.org/node/988* (accessed on 17 January 2009).

Catholics for a Free Choice. "The 'See Change' Campaign." *www.seechange.org*, 1995

Centre for Research on Population and Security. *Petition to Withdraw UN Observer Status from the Holy See*. 1995

Childfree by Choice. "The Childfree Life – Happily Childfree." *www.childfreebychoice.com* (accessed 26 March 2009)

Climate Camp. "Fifteenth UN Climate Conference Copenhagen 30th of November, 2009." *www.climatecamp.org.uk/node/475* (accessed 25 April 2009).

Clinton, Hillary. "Obama Reverses 'Global Gag Rule' for Family Planning Funds." Agence France-Presse, 23 January 2009.

Coyne, Jerry and Hopi Hoekstra. "The Greatest Dying-A Fate Worse Than Global Warming." *The New Republic* (24 September 2007).

Crossette, Barbara. "Rethinking Population at a Global Milestone." found in *New York Times – Week in Review. New York Times (19 September 1999).*

Cuker, Prof. "A Plea for Population Control to Save the Earth." *www.dailypress.com* (29 December 2007)

De Souza, Mike. "Oil Giant funds Climate-Change Skeptics, Greenpeace Claims." *Ottawa Citizen* (19 May 2007).

Doctors for a Sustainable Population. "Oil Depletion and Health." www.doctorsandpopulation.org (accessed 20 April 2009).

Dunn, Seth & Christopher Flavin. "Moving the Climate Change Agenda Forward." *Worldwatch Institute's State of the World 2002*. Norton: New York & London, 2002: p. 3.

Economist. "The Path to Ruin." *www.economist.com*. 10 August 2006.

Eilperin, Juliet. "Dust Storms Escalate." *Washington Post. www.washingtonpost.com* (23 April 2009).

Engelman, Robert, Brian Haliweil and Aanielle Nierenberg. "Rethinking Population, Improving Lives." *Worldwatch Institute's State of the World 2002*. Norton & Company: New York and London, 2002. p. 141.

Environmental News Service. *"Scientists Predict Future of Weather Extremes." Environmental News* (29 October 2006).

Ferguson, Niall. "The Population Bubble." *Los Angeles Times* (30 July 2007).

Freston, Kathy. "13 Breathtaking Effects of Cutting Back on Meat."www.alternet.org/story/137737/.

Ganeva, Tana. "Most American Catholics Far More Liberal Than Church Leadership." www.alternet.org/134608/.

Grant, Lindsey. "The Economists' Myths." *Optimum Population Trust Journal* 7, no. 2. October 2007.

Grant, Richard. "Drowning in Plastic: The Great Pacific Garbage Patch." UK Telegraph, *www.telegraph.co.uk/earth/environment/5208645/*.

Hartman, Edward. *The Population Fix*. Think Population Press: Moraga, CA, 2006. p. 154.

Harris, Gillian. "Off-Road Drivers Blamed for Increased Dust Storms." *Ottawa Citizen* (20 August 2004).

Hedges, Chris. "Are We Breeding Ourselves to Extinction?" *www.alternet.org/story/130843/*

Holmes, John. "Disasters—The New Normal." United Nations Climate Change Conference in Copenhagen, 4 September 2009. *www.en.cop15dk/blogs/view+blog?blogid=1018*

Indo Asian News Service. "Mosques in Pakistan to Preach Family Planning." *Indo-Asian News*, 18 December 2006.

Jaimet, Kate. "Animal Extinctions Termed Situation of 'Crisis Proportions.'" *Ottawa Citizen* (29 September 2000).

Kunstler, James. *The Long Emergency*. Grove Press: New York, 2005. p. 241.

Kuper, Alan. "From Sentience to Silence." The Court of Wisdom-Free Inquiry. *www.secularhumanism.org*.

Lorenz, Andreas. "The Chinese Miracle Will End Soon." Associated Press, 7 March 2005.

McKee, Jeffrey. "Anthropologist Predicts Major Threat to Species Within 50 Years." *EurekAlert!*. 9 June 2003.

Meaney, Ken. "Humans Eating Frogs into Extinction: Study." *Ottawa Citizen* (27 January 2009).

McMullen. Alia. "Forget Oil, the New Global Crisis Is Food." National Post. www.fi nancialpost.com/story (accessed 15 April 2009).

Monbiot, George. "Bring on the Recession." www.alternet.org/story/66629/.

Mosquin, Ted. *Personal Communication.* Ted Mosquin. 13 November 1992.

Nicholson-Lord, David. "Whatever Happened to the Teeming Millions?" *Green Futures Magazine* (Nov/Dec. 2005).

Noble, Justin. "Indigenous Communities Unite Against Climate Change." *www.nunatsiaq.com/news/climate/90417_2084.html.*

Optimum Population Trust. "Attenborough Is New OPT Patron—Greens Urged to Spell out Population Dangers." *OPT News* (April 2009).

Optimum Population Trust. "Contraception is 'Greenest' Technology." Optimum Population Trust News Release, 9 September 2009.

Paddock, William. "Our Last Chance to Win the War on Hunger." *Carrying Capacity Network Focus* 4, no. 1, (1994). p. 52.

President's Commission on Population Growth and the American Future. "Population and the American Future." *Cairo 94 Bulletin 1*, no. 4, (May 1994).

Rachman, Tom. "Population in India Passes 1B, UN Says." *Ottawa Citizen*, 16 August 1999.

Rapley, Chris. "This Planet Ain't Big Enough for the 6,500,000,000." *The Independent*, 27 June 2007.

Sheppard, Robert. "Rice Riots and Empty Silos: Is the World Running Out of Food?" *CBC News: In Depth*, 30 April 2008.

Sinnamon, James. "How the Growth Lobby Threatens Australia's Future." *OnLine Opinion www.onlineopinion.com.*

Spears, Tom. "Global Water Plan Far From Developed." *Ottawa Citizen*, 14 April 1999.

Surette, Louise. "World Water Crisis Looms, Expert Warns." *Ottawa Citizen*, 1 April 1999.

Trowbridge, Erin. "South-South Initiative." *Earth Times News Service*, no. 7 (8 July 1999).

Union of Concerned Scientists. *World Scientists' Warning to Humanity.* April, 1993.

Vanden Driessche, Jacqueline. "Association Anti-Pollution 2000 (Dalai Lama Visit)." *The Phenologist* 2, no. 3 (August 1999): 2-3.

Ward, Chip. "Our Worst Enemies Aren't Terrorists: Rethinking National Security on a Sinking Planet." www.alternet.org/story/129660

Weld, Madeline. *Speaking Notes for Address to the Humanist Association of Canada.* Population Institute of Canada, 23 June 1995.

Wikipedia. "Famine." Wikipedia. www.en.wikipedia.org/wiki/Famine (accessed 15 April 2009).

Women's International Network. *"Peru: Catholic Church Resists Family Planning."* New York Times, 12 August 1995.

Worldwatch Institute. *State of the World 2002.* Norton & Company: New York and London, 2002: p. 141.

Zero Population Growth. "Wildlife sends S.O.S.: 'Save Our Species.'" *ZPG Fact Sheet*, February 1990.

Zyp, Hank. "Listening to the Excluded." *Alberta Council for Global Cooperation Newsletter* (Spring 2002): p. 4–5.

PART 3

Anti-Slavery Society. “The Modern West Africa Slave Trade.” Anti-Slavery Society. www.anti-slaverysociety.addr.com/slavetrade.htm.

Bambrick, Kati. *An Evaluation of Post-War Rape*. Campaign for Good Governance, November 2004.

BBC News. “Asia’s Sex Trade is ‘Slavery.’” Asia -Pacific BBC News. news.bbc.co.uk/2/hi/asia-pacifi c/2783655.stm.

BBC News. “Liberia’s child rape victims.” http://newsvote.bbc.co.uk.

BBC News. “Human Smuggling Eclipses Drugs Trade. http://news.bbc.co.uk/2/low/in_depth/2056662.stm.

Bell, Valerie. *Nobody’s Children*. Word Publishing: United States, 1989.

Boyes, Roger. “Death for Hire—Suicide Machine Lets You Push Final Button.” *The Times*, 29 March 2008.

Bukwa, Bonnie. *Letter of Comment on “Growing Pains.”* Personal Communication, 2009.

Butts, Charlie. “Chinese Policies at Root of Gender Imbalance.” OneNewsNow.com, www.onenewsnow.com.

Canadian Center for Policy Alternatives. “Public Services a Bargain for Canadians: Study.” www.policyalternatives.ca/news/2009/04/ pressrelease2190/.

Carrying Capacity Network. “Hot Topics: Welfare Reform.” *CCN Clearinghouse Bulletin*. June 1994, p. 3.

P. 3

CBC Radio. “Interview with Debra Hamilton.” CBC Radio, 7 February 2008.

CBC TV. “The Final Legal Word,” CBC Television Archives, Broadcast 20 May 1993.

Divine, Caroline. "My Uterus, Husband and I All Agree—No Children" *www.alternet.org/story/133473.*

Edwards, David and Webster, Stephen. "Afghan Law Legalizing Marital Rape Put on Hold After Firestorm." rawstory.com.

Freedman, Alix. "Americans Export Sterilization to the Third World, *Asian Wall St. Journal*, 19–20 June 1988. panindigan.tripod.com/quinacrine.html.

Frogameni, Bill. "The Vatican's Perverted Sense of Justice." www.alternet.org/story/136012/.

Hari, Johann. "Are there just too many people in the world?" *The Independent/UK*, 15 May 2008.

Hein Sohn, Gunnar. "Ending the West's Proxy War Against Israel." *Wall Street Journal Europe,* 12 January 2009.

Hundredth Monkey. "Hundredth Monkey." www.hundredthmonkey.net.

Hedges, Chris. "The Disease of Permanent War." www.alternet.org/story/140106

Huffington Post. "Desmond Hatchett: 29 Year Old with 21 Kids." *www.huff ngtonpost.com.*

Human Rights Watch. "Saudi Arabia: Rape Victim Punished for Speaking Out." *www.hrw.org/en/news/2007/11/15*

Jesella, Kara. "Dispatch: The New Eugenics." http://babble.com/content/printerfriendly.aspx?ciid=10893.

Knight, Afsaneh. "Stop! Think! Do You Really Want That Baby?." The Times. women.timesonline.co.uk/tol/life_and_style/women/families/article6342116.

Lunau, Kate. "Tying The Knot." Macleans. www.macleans.ca/science/health/article.

Landers, Ann. *"Let's Tackle the Issue of Birth Control Help for Women of the Third World." Vancouver Sun* (22 March1989).

Lippes, J. "Quinacrine: Permanent Female Contraception." www.quinacrine.com.

Loyola. "Date Rape." www.loyola.edu/campuslife/healthservices/counselingcenter/daterate.html.

Marquardson, Barry. "Using GPI Instead of GDP Makes Economic Sense." *Calgary Herald* (1 February 1998).

Martin, Courtney. "The End of the Women's Movement." www.alternet.org/story/135334/.

Missy. "A Week Late and Very Scared, What To Do?." www.standupgirl.com.

Mitchell, Lois. "An Act to Amend the Criminal Code (Right to Die with Dignity)." *Canadian Baptist Ministries Information Bulletin and Discussion Paper* (November 2005).

Myers, PZ. "Grim Tales of Abuse Emerge from the Irish Catholic Church." *www.alternet.org.*

National Audubon Society *U.S. Guide to Population Assistance.* National Audubon Society.1993.

Newman, Amie. "Court Rules on Emergency Contraception: Is Long Reign of Un-Science, Un-Reason Over?" www.alternet.org/story/133174/.

OneNewsNow. "Abortion Advocate Nominated for Top Human rights Post at UN." www.OneNewsNow.com.

Ottawa Citizen. "1922: August—A Mother of Two to Margaret Sanger (letter)", *Ottawa Citizen* (19 December 1999).

Peak Oil News. "The Population Bomb." Augusta Free Press. *www.peak-oil-news.info/population-bomb.*

Pregnant Teen Help. "Teen Pregnancy Statistics, Prevention and Facts." *www.pregnantteenhelp.org.*

RAINN. "Who Are the Victims?." RAINN—Rape, Abuse & Incest National Network. *www.rainn.org/print/286.*

Redefining Progress. "Redefining Progress-the Nature of Economics." *www.rprogress.org.*

Reynolds, Paul. "Clinton Backs Clampdown on Child Slavery." BBC News Online. news.bbc.co.uk/2/low/370743.stm.

Rolston, Holmes. "Feeding People Versus Saving Nature?." *World Hunger and Morality*. Prentice-Hall: Englewood Cliffs, NJ, 1996. 248-267.

Robinson, Sara. "Private RU-486 Confounds Anti-Abortionists: Who Can We Harass Now?" Group News Blog. www.alternet.org/story/75201.

Schmitt, Eric. "Deal on U.N. Dues Breaks an Impasse and Draws Critics." *The New York Times* (16 November 1999).

Sherk, Kirstin. "The Youngest Victims: Child Rape Survivors Must Have Right to Abortion." www.ipas.org.

Sloan, Louise. "Pills, Rings, Patches, Shots: What's New in Hormonal Birth Control?." www.health.com/health/condition-article/print/0,,20188900,00.html.

Sokol, Ronald. "The Right to Die." *The New York Times* (21 March 2007).

Stewart, Fiona. "Curtailing Our Right to Know about the Right to Die with Dignity." onlineopinion.com.au/print.asp?article=3472.

Tibbetts, Janice. "Most Canadians Support Morgentaler's Prize: Poll." *Canwest News Service*, 8 July 2008.

TimesOnLine. "Why Patricia Hewitt is Fighting for the Right to Die with Dignity."www.timesonline.co.uk/tol/news/uk/article5947262.

Tubeza, Philip. *"Condom Protest." Philippine Daily Inquirer* (27 September 2002).

Union of Concerned Scientists. *World Scientists' Warning to Humanity*. April 1993.

Center for Ethics, Philosophy and Public Affairs, Department of Moral Philosophy, *The Body as Unwarranted Life Support: A New Perspective on Euthanasia*. University of St. Andrews: Edgecliffe UK, September 2007..

Valdez-Rodrigues, Alisa. "Is Porn That Depicts the Subjugation of Hispanic Women Tied to the Rise of Hate Crimes Against Latinos?" *alternet.org/module/printversion/139926*.

Wade, Maggie. "Statutory Rape Victim Speaks Out." www.wlbt.com/global/story.asp?s=8293688&ClientType=Printable.

Wikipedia. "*War Rape*." www.wikipedia.org/wiki/War_rape.

Wither, Emily. "British Teenager Wins Right to Die with Dignity." ABC News. abcnews.go.com/print?id=6229156.

Wolf, Naomi. "Why the Pentagon is Probably Lying About its Suppressed Sodomy and Rape Photos." Independent Media Institute. www.alternet.org/story/140357/.

World Federation of Right to Die Societies. "Ensuring Choices for a Dignified Death." www.worldrtd.org.

World Population Awareness. "Green Umbrella Walk."www.green-umbrella.net/pressRelease.html.

World Population Awareness. "Comments on the Conference on Global Ethics in a Humane World." World Population Awareness. www.population-awareness.net.

Zero Population Growth Canada. "Population Myths and Solutions We Know and Love." *Zero Population Growth Fact Sheet*, 1991.

PART 4

Bedi, Rahul. "No State Jobs for Couples Who Marry too Young." *The Daily Telegraph*, January 1997.

Bissett, James. "Canada: Th e Truth About Immigration is That Costs Exceed Benefits." Immigration Watch International. jonjayray.wordpress.com/2008/09/30.

Browne, Anthony. "Pop the Pill and Think of England." *The Times* (4 November 2002).

Carrying Capacity Network. "Living Within Our Environmental Means: Natural Resources and an Optimum Human Population." *Carrying Capacity Network Clearinghouse Bulletin 4.* no. 6 (June 1994).

Chamberlain, Gethin. "India Pays Couples to Put Off Having Children." *The Observer* (2 August 2009).

Cousteau, Jacques. "Petition for the Rights of Future Generations."Cousteau Society. www.cousteau.org, 1995.

Denneen, Bill. "War & Family Planning: Priorities." *WOA Population News Monthly* (14 November 2002).

Eisen, Ben. "A Dollar a Day Not to Get Pregnant." *Inside Higher Ed*, 9 July 2009.

Global Population Concerns. "U.S House-Senate Concurrent Resolution 17." *Global Population Concerns Newsletter*, 12 September 2000.

Guillebaud, John and Hayes, Pip. British Medical Journal published an editorial in its 25 July 2008 issue

Hari, Johann. "Are There Just Too Many People in the World?" *The Independent/UK. www.CommonDreams.Org.*

Harlow, John. "Billionaire Club In Bid To Curb Overpopulation." *The Sunday Times*, 24 May 2009.

Hedges, Chris. "There Is No Reason for Us to Be in Afghanistan—Everyone Knows It, and It Spells Defeat." *www.alternet.org/story/141478/*.

Jensen, Derrick. "Taking Shorter Showers Doesn't Cut It: Why Personal Change Does Not Equal Political Change." *Orion magazine*, July 2009.

Jochmans, Joseph Robert. "Mayan End Time Prophecy." www.adishakti.org/mayan_end_times_prophecy_12-21-2012.htm.

Jesella, Kara. "Dispatch: The New Eugenics." babble.com/content/printerfriendly.aspx?ciid=10893.

Kinder, Carolyn. "The Population Explosion: Causes and Consequences." Yale New Haven Teachers Institute. *www.yale.edu/ynhti/curriculum/units/1998/7/98.07.02.x.html* (accessed September 2009).

Kolhatkar, Sonali. "Afghan Presidential Candidate: The U.S Occupation Must End." www.alternet.org/story/141504/.

Mazur, Laurie. "The Population Debate is Screwed Up." www.alternet.org/story/133039/.

Merrill, Jennifer. "A Recipe for Success: Ingredients for a Successful Family Planning Program." *Zero Population Growth Reporter*, September 1992.

Mosquin, Ted. "The Dreaded 'P' Word." *Borealis* 2 (4), 1991.

Muhsam, H. V. "A World Population Policy for the World Population Year." *Journal of Peace Research* 10(1-2), 1973.

National Audubon Society. *Guide to Population Assistance*. Summer 1993

Pharis, Vivian. "News From the Societies—Alberta Wilderness Association." *SusPop News* 11, January 1995.

Population Institute of Canada. "Population, Sustainable Development and Security." www.populationinstitute.ca.

Sierra Club Canada. "Population Policies of the Sierra Club." Asia Pacifi c Alliance. www.asiapacifi calliance.org.

Simms, Andrew. "It's Democracy, Stupid." *New Economic Foundation Report,* Sept. 2000.

Stackhouse, John. "A Rare Family Planning Success." *Globe and Mail,* 22 July 1996.

Sustainable Population Society. "Population—A Critical Environmental and Resource Issue." *Sustainable Population Society Pamphlet,* 1994.

Templeton, Sarah-Kate. "Two Children Should Be Limit. Says Green Guru." *Sunday Times*, 1 February 2009.

Union of Concerned Scientists. *World Scientists' Warning To Humanity*. April 1993.

U.S. Network for Cairo '94. "Population and the American Future." *Cairo '94 Media Bulletin* 1 (4), May 1994.

Vaughn, Mark. "Just Relax and Enjoy It." *Auto Week Magazine*, June 2009.

Weld, Madeline. Personal Communication 29 August 1995.

Women's Global Network for Reproductive Rights. "Position Paper on Women, Population and Development." 1998.

WorldNetDaily. "Secret Billionaire Club Seeks Population Control." WorldNetDaily.com.

Zero Population Growth (now Population Connection). "*Non-Trivial Earth Day Quiz.*" '*94 ZPG Reporter*, February 1994.

Zero Population Growth Canada. "*What Do Canadians Think?*" *ZPG Fact Sheet*. Gallop Polls, 1991.

INDEX

E

G

H

I

O

P

Q

R

U

Y

Z